Katherine's world

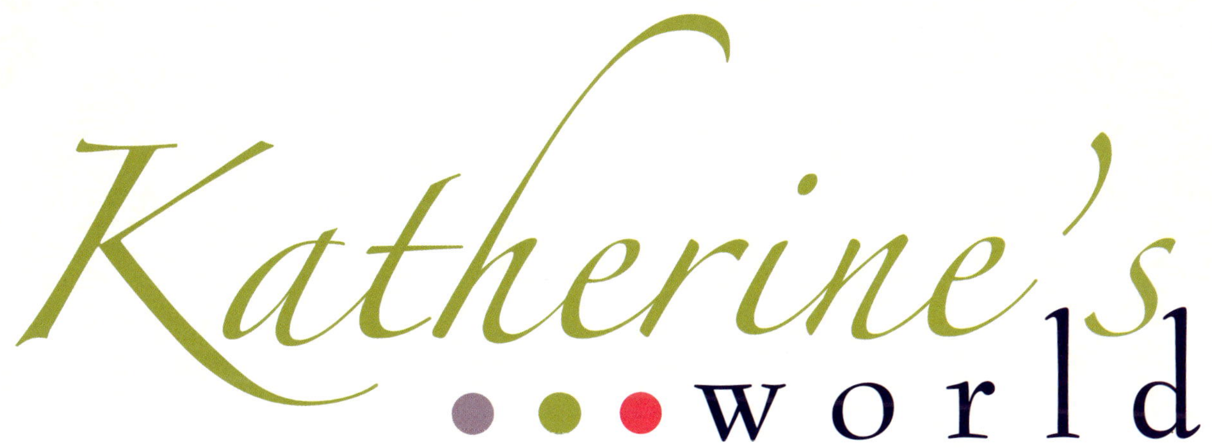

Katherine's world

by Katherine Lollar Rowland

ORANGE FRAZER PRESS
Wilmington, Ohio

ISBN 978-1933197-630

Copyright © 2009 by Katherine Lollar Rowland
All Rights Reserved

Additional copies of *Katherine's World* may be ordered from:

Katherine Lollar Rowland   or   Orange Frazer Press
4502 Daybreak Drive   P.O. Box 214
Lebanon, Ohio 45036   Wilmington, OH 45177
513.932.4975   937-382-3196
kathworld@aol.com   www.orangefrazer.com

Cover Painting "Scotland" by Bruce McGrew
Book Design by Chad DeBoard

Cataloging-in-Publication Data
Rowland, Katherine Lollar.
Katherine's world / by Katherine Lollar Rowland.
p. cm.
ISBN 978-1-933197-63-0
1. Rowland, Katherine Lollar. 2. Painters' spouses--United
States--Biography. 3. Rowland, Elden. I. Title.
ND237.R727R69 2009
759.13--dc22
[B]

        2009002674

Printed in China

Dedication

To Elden—
And all the others
Who enriched my world

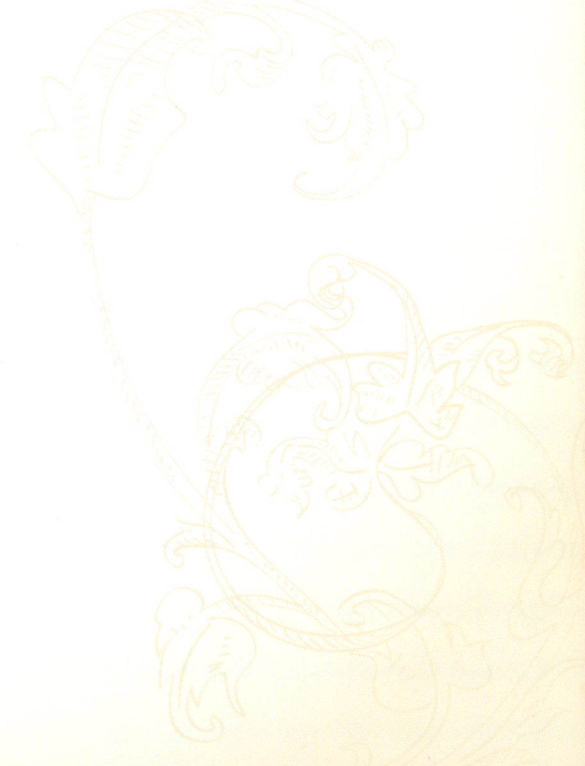

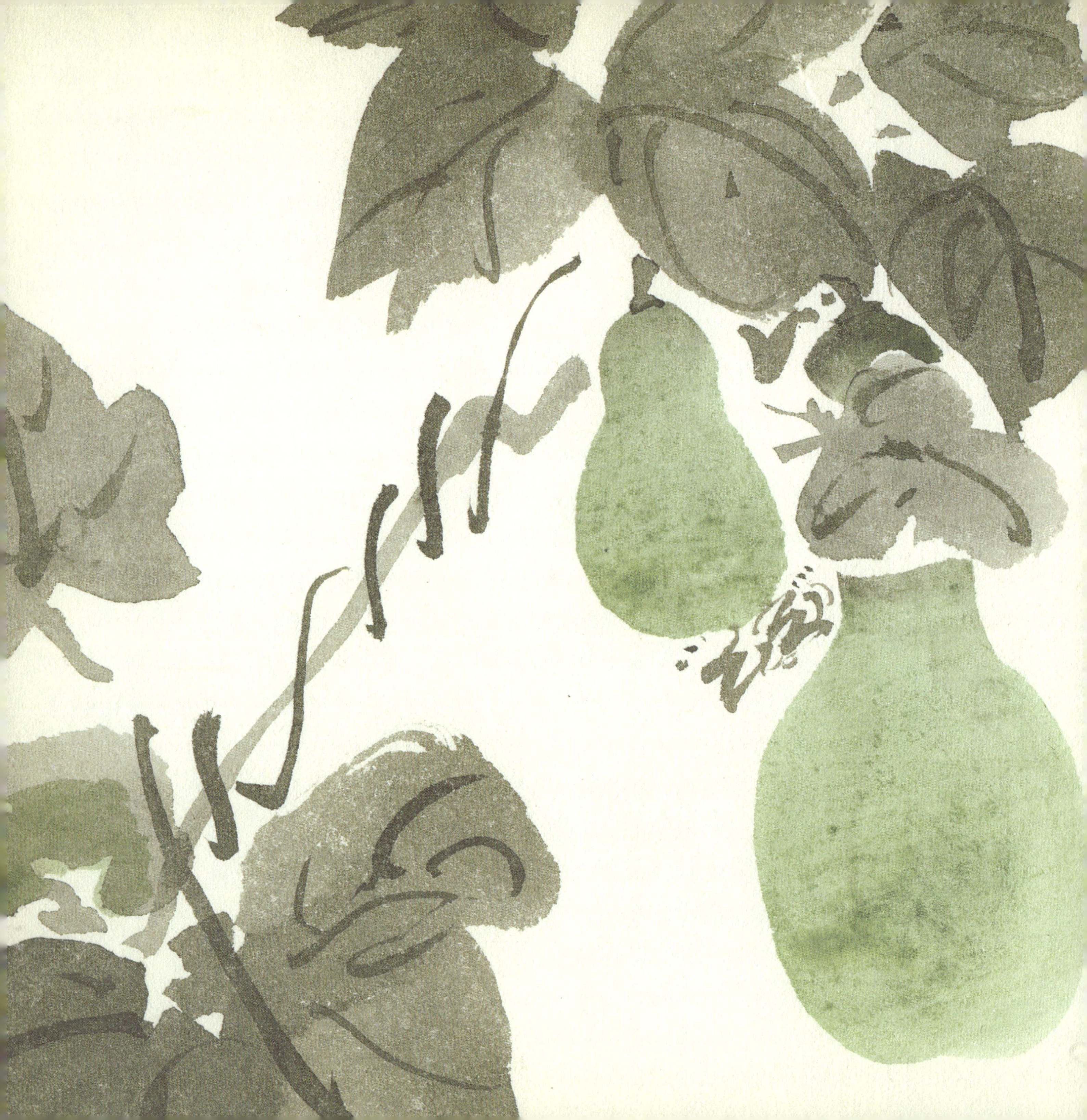

Table of Contents

Preface

When my husband, Elden, passed on in 1982 in Sarasota, Florida, he left quite a different Katherine than the one he had married many years before in Lebanon, Ohio. Forty-two years of being involved in an artist's world had wrought changes and growth in intellect and personality to the twenty-year-old I was when we married in 1939. He left me, at age 63, in a fulfilling job in the world of art in which I could continue to work, and in a beloved small home on Siesta Key in which I could continue to live. These, together with his paintings, his studio, and an inkling into his philosophy of art and living, were his unique legacy to me.

In the ensuing years, that legacy has been the foundation for my life and it has been enriched by contact with countless other people whose paths have crossed mine along the way: family, friends, art instructors and students, fellow enthusiasts about nature, travel, love of country, and delving into family history and Shaker research. This story, in words and pictures, is a token of appreciation, a celebration of their lives, and mine.

Among those in the art world to whom I felt close that are no longer living are: Jerry Farnsworth, Eleanor Hodgins, Eric Hodgins, Emily Holmes, Dorothy Leech, Hilton Leech, Bruce McGrew, Margarette Mead, Marc Moon, Nicholas Reale, Elden Rowland, Helen Sawyer, Robert Sisson, Valfred Thelin, and Suzanne Wilson. Among those still living are: Beth Arthur, Judi Betts, Helen Burkett, Ray Campeau, Pete Carmichael, Alice DeCaprio, Shirley Hummel, Maxine Masterfield, Fox McGrew, Barbara Nechis, Sally Von Conta, and Frank Webb.

Important family influences in my early years were members of the Miller/Evans line and of the Lollar/Jameson line, in particular my mother and father Ruby Miller and Harry Lollar, my brother Robert Miller Lollar, and my grandmother Kittie Jameson Lollar. Outstanding in my adult years, in addition to my husband, was my best friend, Doris Campbell Rooney, who introduced me to her joyous way of life. Now in my ninetieth year, among all of my valued family and friends, five names stand out: Kathy Lollar Divens, Patty Hodgins, Jayre Leech, Nancy Miller Myerholtz, and Ruth Stevens. And as I look to the future, I think of my great grandnephew, one-year-old Alexander Liu Schwarz. Child of my grandnephew, Kevin Robert Schwarz, and his wife Hongfei Liu, little Alex is first in the next generation in the Lollar line, which began when the first David Lollar bought land in Warren County, Ohio, over two hundred years ago!

To all of the above, I am grateful!

—Katherine Lollar Rowland
Lebanon, Ohio
September 2008

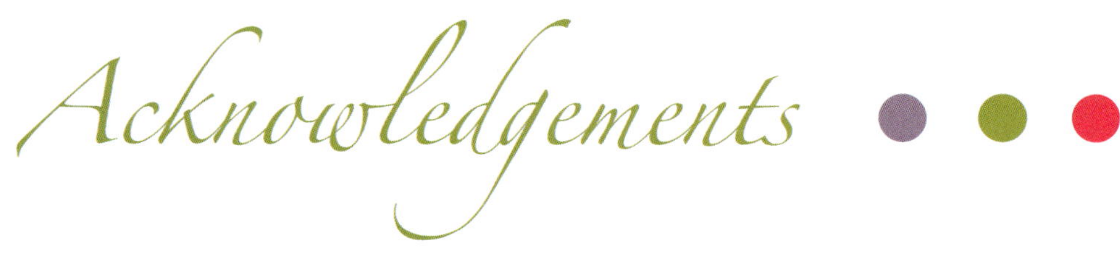

Acknowledgements

Most of the images were provided by the artists, or by the author. In addition, special recognition is given to the following for work reproduced:

SHIRLEY HUMMEL for numerous beautiful images from her files

ANDREA STUPKA BURKS for "Puerto de Fruitas" by her mother, Suzanne Stupka Wilson

MARCIA CORBINO for use of images from her book, *Helen Sawyer, Memories of a Morning Star*

HIGHLAND HOUSE MUSEUM, TRURO, CAPE COD, for material relating to Jerry Farnsworth and Helen Sawyer

PATTY HODGINS for "Green Mansions" by her mother Eleanor Treacy Hodgins

MIKE LAGERMAN, collector, for "Ruby Ridge" by Hilton Leech

JAYRE LEECH for "Montana" by Eleanor Fair, and "Christmas Morning" by her mother, Dorothy Sherman Leech

AMITY MEAD for material relating to her mother, Margarette Mead

RICHMOND ART MUSEUM (Indiana) for "Thunderstorm" by Hilton Leech

EVA THELIN SAWTELLE for "Loon Tunes" by her father, Valfred Thelin

JERRY, JOYCE & ROBYN SCHMIDT, collectors, for "Duck Hunter" by Valfred Thelin

DAVE SCHWARZ for photo of "Sanskrit Palm Leaf Manuscript"

© TRAVERSE, NORTHERN MICHIGAN'S MAGAZINE/BRIAN CONFER for "Suzanne Wilson at Work"

LOU ANN ZIMMERMAN for "Taboret" and "Picket Parade" by her father, Marc Moon

Katherine's world

The *Home* Place ● ● ●

In the early fall of 1918, when the United States was still involved in the "War to End All Wars," a baby girl was born on an ancestral farm three miles south of Lebanon, Ohio. Her parents, Ruby Miller and Harry David Lollar, named her Katherine Lucile, after her paternal grandmother, Kittie Jameson Lollar, and her maternal grandmother, Lucy Evans Miller. Ruby and Harry Lollar already had one child, a little boy, Robert Miller, not quite three years and a half old on that September 24, 1918, when baby Katherine was born.

The joy at the birth of baby Katherine was surely tempered by the knowledge that twelve days prior to her arrival, Harry, her father, had been required by law to register for the draft and was faced with the prospect of going to fight in World War I. However, just two weeks after that, on October 11, 1918, news came of the signing of The Armistice, ending the war in Europe, returning peace to the world, and life on the Lollar farm to a steady unfolding as it had since the first acreage of the land had come into the family in 1838.

Ruby and Harry and the two children lived in the big old white frame house for the next four years and three months. There, little Katherine grew, as babies do, engrossed in her own small activities, not remembering much that went on around her. But gradually, she was acquiring subconscious memories, the basis for the person, Katherine, by whom this story is written. Now, many decades later, I do not remember my graduations from Cradle Roll to Primary Department in the Sunday School of the Cumberland Presbyterian Church in Lebanon which my family attended religiously. Nor do I remember the fine big Willys Overland touring car, one of the first automobiles in the neighborhood.

But I do remember the interior of the big house and even of the barns, with their fragrant haylofts, and the corn sheds conveniently located next to the hog pen where I would stand more than a half century later, as half owner of the farm, and Ooh and Aah over fat little piglets squealing for a place near their massive mothers. And I remember the circle drive with its great maple trees, and the gate at the top of the hill that led down to a creek, and the small extension of the big weathered barn that had been the carriage house before

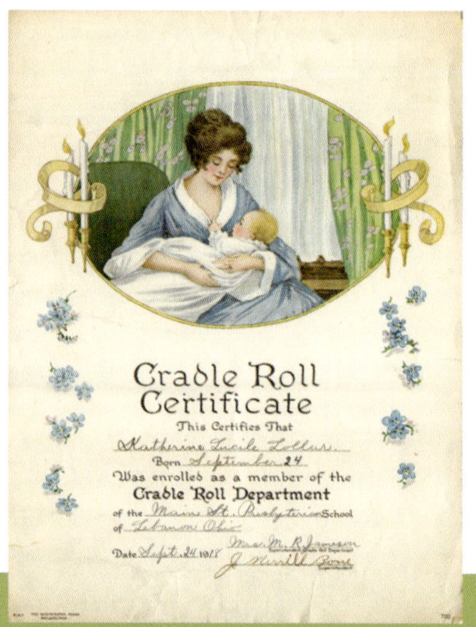

Cradle roll

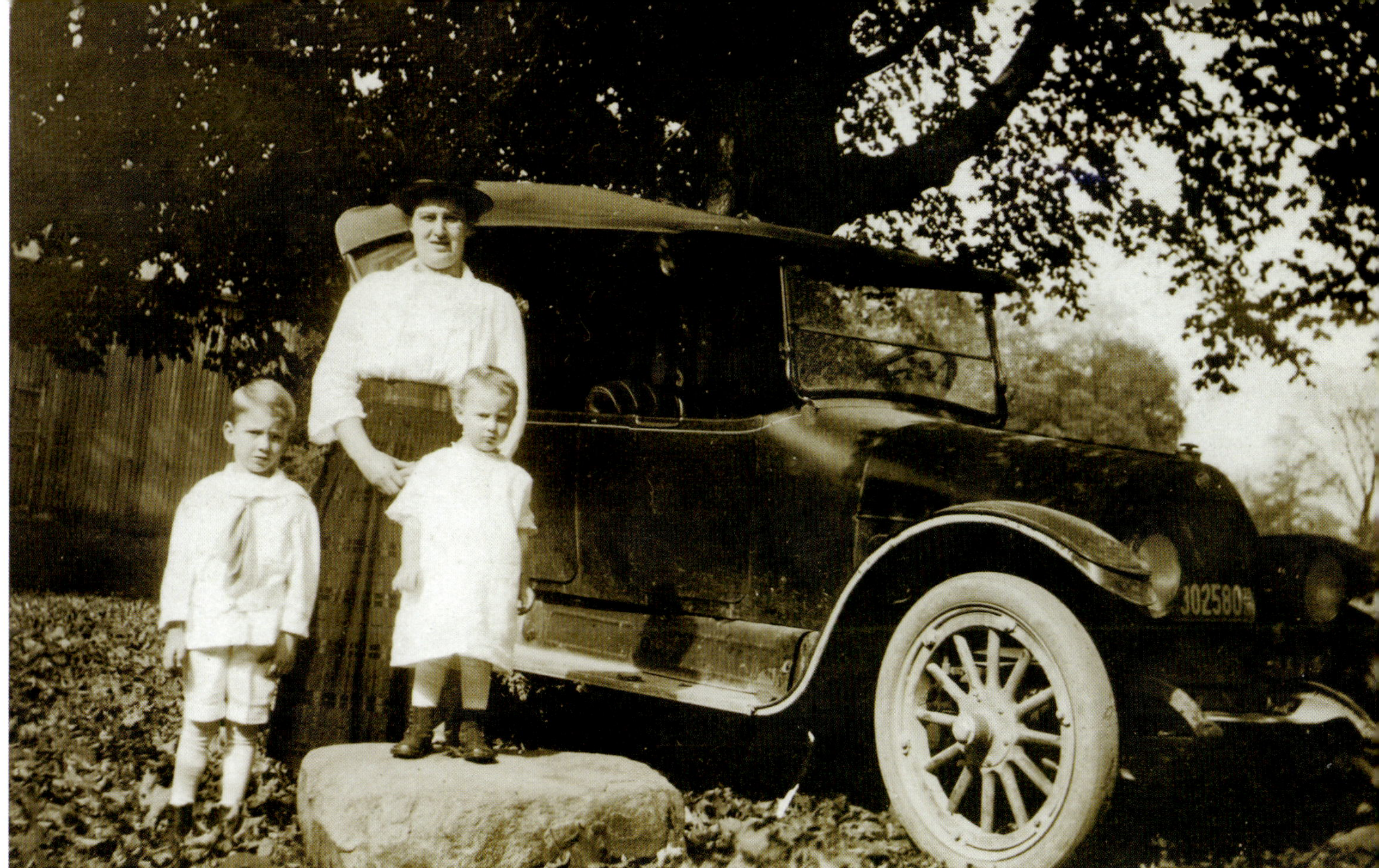

it became the garage into which the Willys Overland snugly fit.

I remember the HUGE blocks of granite that were the high step and entrance into the rarely-used front door of the house. I remember the front hallway with the wide stairway to the second floor and the smooth wide banister, perfect for sliding down by Big Brother Robert, but definitely a forbidden delight for me. I remember the high-ceilinged rooms with sliding doors between them, the kitchen with a narrow, twisting back stair leading to the hired man's room, and a summer kitchen just behind that. And then—the woodshed, with a very scary dark doorway leading into it from the back porch, where the water came reluctantly from a hand-operated pump, even though there was a noisy generator in the smoke house nearby which supplied electricity to the house.

The New House ● ● ●

As Christmas approached in 1922, there was great excitement in the old Lollar Home Place three miles south of Lebanon, Ohio. Harry and Ruby and their children, Robert and Katherine, were moving to a New House! Albeit the New House was less than a quarter of a mile north on the South Lebanon Road from the Home Place, still, complicated plans were involved.

And so it happened that my first memory, at four years and three months old, was of a dream of being worried about how my doll furniture would get from the old house to the new one. There was the tiny doll bed, and the table, and china cupboard carefully constructed by Uncle Earl Banta and the tiny quilt and comforters and pillows made by Aunt Nell. (Now, so many years later, the sturdy little table still serves well as a plant stand.) No memory remains of concern about the little sets of dishes, one of china and one of tin, nor even a doll, around which this all centered. Perhaps it was because I was so fond of this aunt and uncle (Aunt Nell was my mother's older sister) that my concern centered on the things they had made. Or perhaps it was that, even then, I liked hand-crafted things.

On moving day, December 18, 1922, when I arrived at the New House I found my Grandmother Kittie Lollar already there, waiting in the big cozy kitchen, to take care of me during that busy time. Grandma Kittie quickly took off my coat and mittens and had me stand on the metal grating in the floor from which rose warm air! Marvel of marvels, heat that came out of the floor instead of from a fireplace or a wood-burning stove!

The family soon became accustomed to the modern conveniences in the New House, most notably, a bathroom. The tub was so big I felt I could swim in it, although the supply of warm water that came from the furnace in the basement was quite inadequate for that. In the corner of the kitchen as part of the floor-to-ceiling built-in cabinets was a dumbwaiter. This was a contraption of small round shelves bound together by cables so, by turning a crank, food could be lowered into the cool basement. If the crank was not handled carefully and steadily the whole thing could land on the concrete floor below in one grand mishmash of fresh buttermilk and apple sauce and fried chicken. Such a clear memory of that can only come from one's own personal experience!

All four levels of the New House, along with the garage and barns and chicken houses, had electric lights, the power for which was provided by a generator in the woodshed attached to the house. This noisy, smelly, monster had to be watched carefully to keep the charge up in the big square glass batteries, so one of my childhood duties was to go into the woodshed to check whether the white float on the first one was showing, and, if not, indicate to my parents just how far "down" it was.

Prior to the move, my father had spent the entire year on the project of getting the New House built. He carefully typed out all the details and costs to the last penny. The previous summer he had the hired man, Doc McKinney, tear down the house that had been there, presumably since my grandfather Robert Bruce Lollar bought land adjoining the Home Place in November of 1878, a year before he and Grandma Kittie were married. Big old beams and timbers from the original house were carefully kept to be used in the New House. The natural boulders that had supported the original house were ground up to be used in concrete for the new foundation. The big old silver-sided barn was left intact and a shed for the milk cows added to one side.

One December evening, I was urgently sent out to tell my father, busy at his chore of milking the cows, that by fiddling with the "cat's whiskers," my Brother Robert had managed to get a signal from England on the crystal radio. Big Ben was striking the hour telling the world that Christmas Eve had arrived in London! My father quickly put away his three-legged stool to hurry into the house, but not before he delighted me by shooting streams of milk directly from the cows' udders into the waiting mouths of several barn cats. And if he happened to miss their mouths, the cats loved that, too, because then they could spend Christmas Eve licking and cleaning each other's fur.

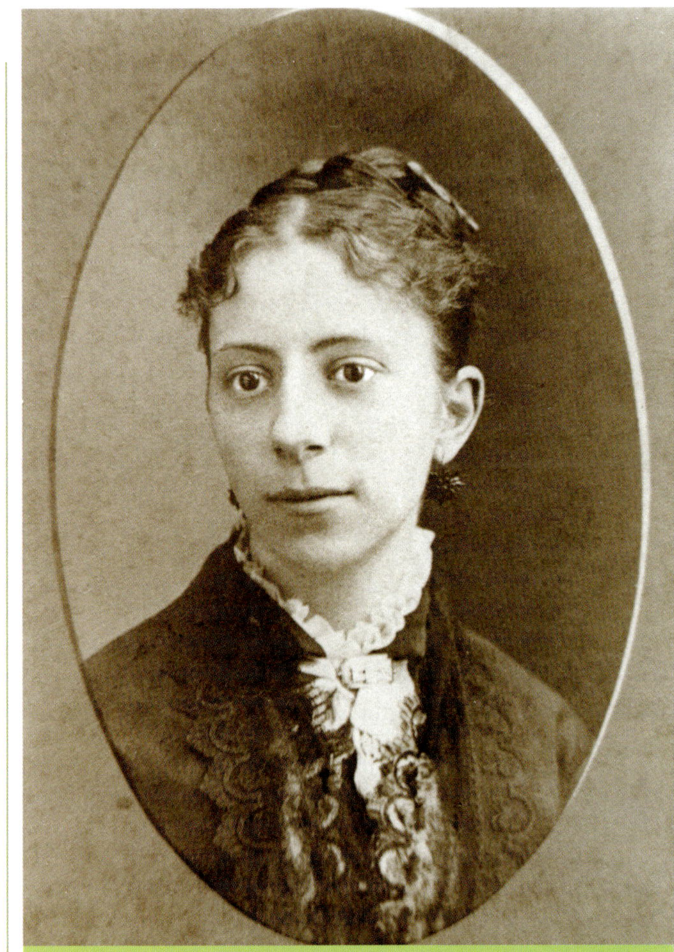

Grandma Kittie Jameson Lollar

The Ridge School

Up the road, around the first bend, less than a quarter of a mile away from the Lollar family's New House, stood the Ridge School. This small white brick one-room schoolhouse was to be central to my life for the next seven years.

From the day that I entered first grade at Ridge School a few weeks short of my sixth birthday, lessons in living in the "real world" began. From being Little Sister at a quiet farm home with no other playmates than my big brother Robert, I now found myself surrounded by a swarm of multi-aged boys and girls with whom I had no idea of how to react. I responded by withdrawing into myself and trying to gain approval in my new world by being a good student.

There were no other children of my age in the Ridge School so I was in a class by myself for all of the years I was there. I sat at my desk toward the back of the room and listened, and absorbed, as all of the other grades went to the big recitation bench near the teacher's desk and were taught their levels of reading and history and arithmetic. And I loved them all—laying the foundations for interests which have continued through my whole life. For the joy in learning which was given to me by the teacher, Mrs. Mamie Retallick, I am forever grateful. Without her enthusiastic commitment to her work—and without my parents' expectation that my brother and I would do well in school—my life would not have been the same.

Actually, perhaps it was my brother Robert who was the greatest incentive to my doing well in school. Wherever I went, he had been there three years before, achieving top grades—how could I do less?

In those early years, there were other lessons to be learned, at which I did not do so well. I was *tall*, with a build that could only be described as *skinny*. When we went to the Cumberland Presbyterian Church for Sunday School, as we always did, well-meaning ladies of my mother's Philathea Class, trying to establish some rapport with this gangling young creature, would say, "Aren't you ever going to stop growing"? I interpreted being different, even while looking down from my superior height, as being inferior. This, combined with a natural tendency to be shy and timid, resulted in the other students at The Ridge School teasing me as being "too dignified."

Nonetheless, at the end of my seventh year at the Ridge School I was "graduated" and sent on to enter Lebanon High School in the fall of 1931, a few weeks before I became 13 years old. At that time, it often happened that students who had achieved a proper level of learning in a one-room school would be promoted to high school at the end of their seventh year. At The Ridge, my brother had been, and also in his class, our second cousin Rebecca Dunham (now Kartalia) and his best friend, Kenneth Revenaugh.

My thirteenth year was also memorable in that I started to wear glasses. I began to get a hint that I could not see well when other students could communicate across the school room by reading lips, but I could not see to do that. So, an appointment was made, and when a prescription was filled for me, the glasses were a *delight*, although fitted into my brother's outgrown round frames. They opened up a whole new world! With my nearsightnedness and astigmatism corrected, for the first time in my life I could see that there were separate leaves on trees and individual blades of grass making up the world of green around me. To say nothing of having a chance to be the first to confirm that it was, indeed, an airplane passing over, as we had hoped when we excitedly reported to the teacher that we thought we heard a motor and she gave us permission to go out into the big schoolyard and search the sky.

Books became an important part of my life, at first *The Bobbsey Twins* series and other children's books, approved by the librarian on our visits to the Carnegie Library in Lebanon. But most of all I loved Gene Stratton-Porter's book about her beloved wild swamplands and forests of Indiana. I somehow discovered *A Girl of the Limberlost, Freckles,* and *Laddie, A True Blue Story,* hidden away in the bottom of the corner cupboard in my parents' big bedroom upstairs. I would creep in and get one to take it away and read in secret places. I did not then, nor do I to this day, understand why they were not considered proper reading for me.

Romances written in the early nineteen hundreds, they were apparently purchased by my father when he left the farm to go to business school and then to Jersey City to work before he and my mother were married. I was fascinated by the gentle love stories, but most of all by the descriptions of the mysteries and beauties of the towering trees of the first-growth forests and of the deep, dark wetlands in which they grew. I mourned with Gene Stratton-Porter that those primeval scenes were disappearing in the rush of the lumber industry to fill the needs of a growing nation. I've kept those three original books and reread them periodically, along with most of the others which Gene Stratton-Porter wrote, as I collected them and shared them over the years. It's been heartwarming recently to learn that the state of Indiana is making a great effort to re-establish the forests and wetlands of the Limberlost.

My childhood was further enriched by my father's penchant for buying books. He had the 1911 "Handy Volume Issue" of *The Encyclopedia Britannica,* all twenty-nine illustrated volumes, reportedly one of the finest years in scholarship and literary content of all of the *Britannicas.* In a letter tucked in the front of one of them, in his fine Spenserian handwriting he apologized to his mother and father for buying them and a set of Stoddard's Lectures on an installment plan. In spite of tissue-thin paper and small type face, the encyclopedia has satisfied my curiosity about countless questions over the years. The ten volumes by Yale theologian and world traveler John L. Stoddard, heavily illustrated by early photographs, stirred a long-standing interest in places and cultures far removed from my origins in southwest Ohio.

During my last years at The Ridge School I began to get a peek into the world of art whenever my father had a load of lambs or pigs to take to the Cincinnati Stockyards. In those years of the Great Depression, my father had transformed the Willys Overland touring car into a truck. Taking off the four-door side panels with their isinglass curtains, he had substituted a flatbed and slatted sidings, leaving the front seat intact as a cab suitable for the driver and a single passenger. My brother and I got to take turns at being the passenger on my father's trips to the city, and after his business was completed he would take us sightseeing (all of us in our bib overalls) up the Incline Railway to Mt. Adams to the Rookwood Pottery or the Cincinnati Art Museum in Eden Park. Little did I dream that some fifteen years later I would be going to that same beautiful big art museum to see a picture painted by my husband hanging in an exhibition of work by Cincinnati artists.

Nor did I realize that in those upcoming years, the Incline Railway, which gave me such a thrilling ride, would go out of existence. One of five such cable platforms which had carried whole street cars in steady elegance up the sides of Cincinnati's many hills for more than fifty years, it was soon to disappear, a part of changes brought about by increase in automobile traffic.

Rookwood Pottery, too, was nearing, at least a hiatus, in its operation. Founded in 1880 by Maria Longworth Nichols, the Pottery had grown into a hugely successful institution, famed world-wide for its architectural and artistic designs. The Great Depression, among other factors, caused it to close, but the pieces themselves went on to become collectors' items highly regarded for their artistic shapes and unique glazes. Although Rookwood did close the doors of the big plant on Mount Adams in 1941, all the moulds and secret chemical formulas were kept intact by a collector and a firm using the same name is now in operation at a different location. A restaurant in the original factory offers the thrilling experience of dining within one of the huge original brick-lined kilns in which so many beautiful pieces were fired. My father, always a conscientious, practical man would have thought it extravagant to purchase a piece of the pottery. Had he used some of the proceeds from the sale of his lambs or pigs to choose a favorite piece, his investment would undoubtedly have increased a thousand-fold by this year of 2008.

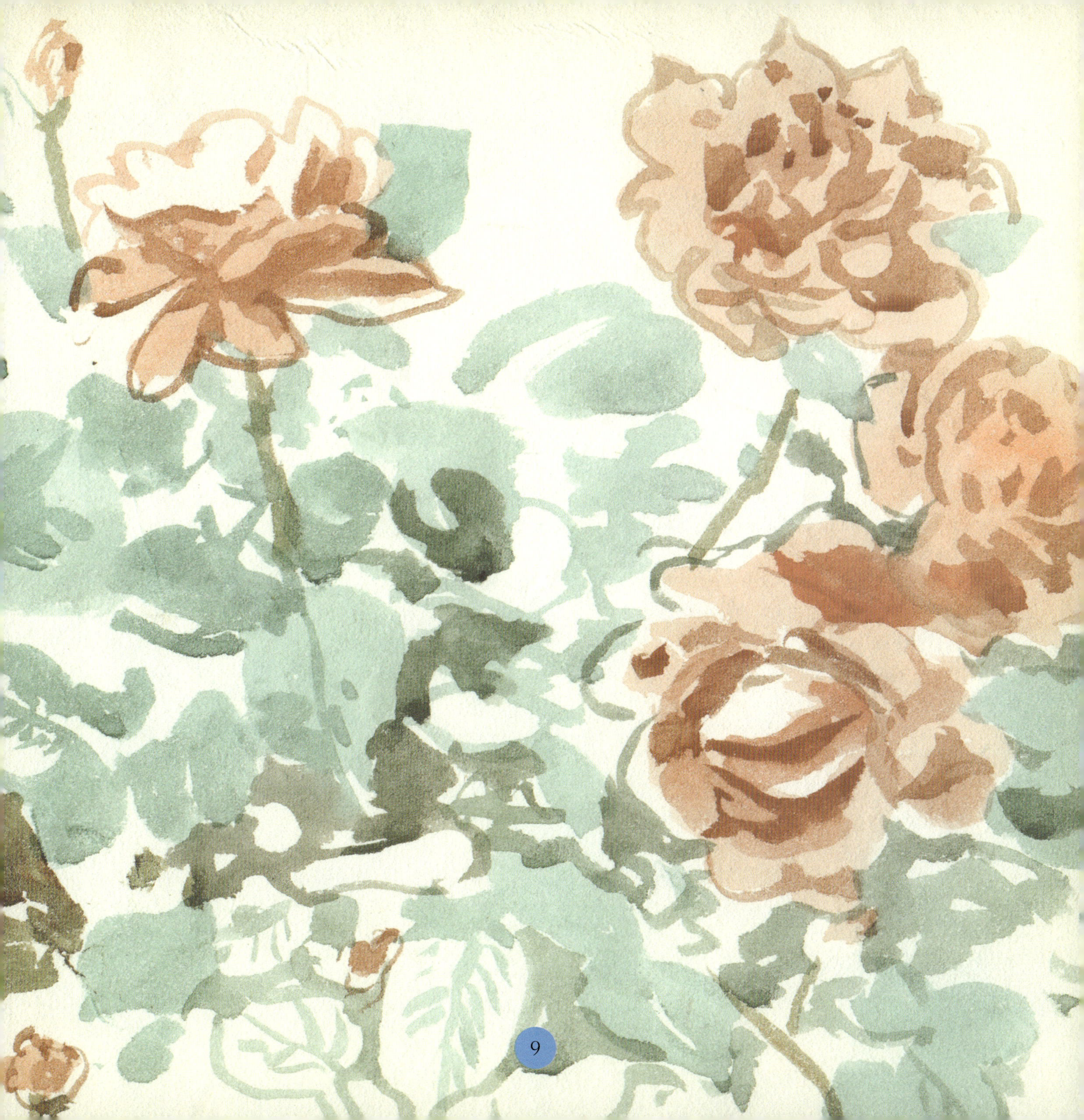

9

Lebanon High •••

When I arrived at the new Lebanon High School as a freshman, my brother Bob was already there as a senior. Following in his footsteps, I enrolled in the College Preparatory Course and started on History, Algebra, English, and Latin in a routine way. However, the routine was soon interrupted by my grandmother Kittie being hit by an automobile. She was walking home from the Lebanon Presbyterian Church early one evening and, as she crossed the dangerous five points at Mound and Main Streets, was struck by a fellow worshipper leaving the same church service in his Model T car.

After Grandma Kittie's accident she needed home care for a couple of months. My mother turned the big front parlor in our New House into a "hospital" room and cared for her there. When my parents built the New House in 1922 they had followed the plan used by so many earlier homes of dividing the front of the house into two big rooms connected by high sliding doors. The front parlor room, which wasn't used much anyway, made a fine place for Grandma Kittie to convalesce, until she recovered and returned to her house in town.

However, the parlor did not at once return to its original purpose because my mother soon needed bed rest to clear up phlebitis in her leg. During that period a much-beloved neighbor, Mrs. Queen Totten McCurdy, came to help with cooking and other household chores. After my mother recovered enough to go on with her usual summer canning, Grandma Kittie came out often to help. I would sit with her for hours on end pitting cherries, peeling apples or peaches, picked from the high, spreading trees planted so long before by the original owner of the land.

I went on with my studies at Lebanon High. Ours was a class of about seventy students, which remained pretty much the same over the four years. Within that group there were eight or ten of us who regularly made the monthly honor roll. Three of us, Martha Wood, Edward Ullum and I seemed to cluster at the top of the class. Until—it came to our senior year when Martha and I slipped and got a B in Physics, spoiling our record of straight A's. Edward passed us with an A in Physics, as well. I was president of the Honor Club and on the Literary Section of the 1935 annual, *The Trilobite*, named for the prized fossil that occurred in the sedimentary rocks so prevalent in our area between the Miami Rivers. My only athletic activity was in running. Being tall, my long legs could flash by others of my age group so easily there was no fun in winning.

Margaret Miller

The congregations of the Cumberland and First Presbyterian Churches decided to combine into one, to be called the Lebanon Presbyterian Church. So members, such as we, left the familiar building at Main and East Streets and became a part of a larger congregation at Warren and East. It did not happen easily. There was much resistance and bitterness in both congregations, very disconcerting to a young person like me, who felt that a church, of all places, should be free of such unhappiness.

Nonetheless, it was reassuring that Grandma Kittie's niece, Nettie Jameson Hatfield, continued as the guiding light in the children's department of the Sunday School of the combined congregation. As it happened, Cousin Nettie's home was directly across the street from the new location. She lived with her father, John A. Jameson, Grandma Kittie's brother, an impressive white-bearded gentleman, and Civil War veteran, who seemed to be the patriarch of the extensive Jameson clan. As he sat in his rocking chair, on the porch in the summer, or in the corner near the stove in the winter, he was an imposing figure. That, and the fact their house was in the same block with the Warren County Courthouse seemed to make a statement that, in spite of the Great Depression, and President Roosevelt's innovative New Deal, all was well with my world.

The Jameson extended family on my father's side, and the Miller extended family on my mother's side, were both an important part of that world. Grandma

Kittie had three brothers and four sisters, all of them living in Warren County, except the youngest girl, Aunt Ella Arthur, who was married to a lawyer and lived in Logansport, Indiana. Large family gatherings were held regularly. At one such Sunday dinner forty Jameson relatives were all seated at one long table in the double front rooms of the New House on The Ridge. I had

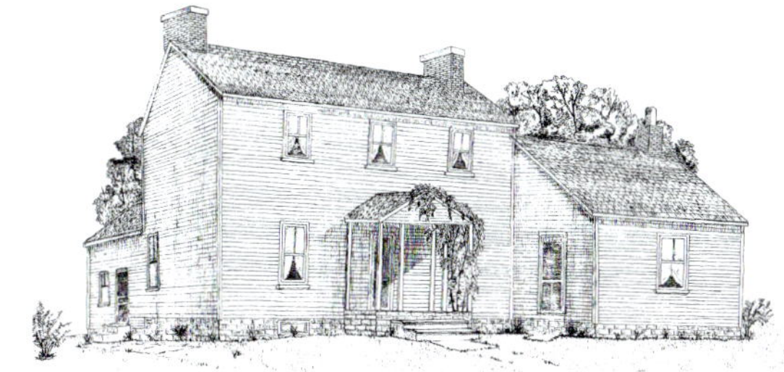

Miller home place

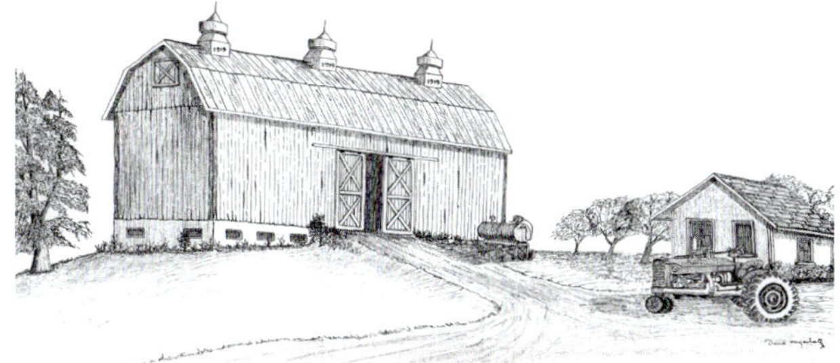

Miller barn

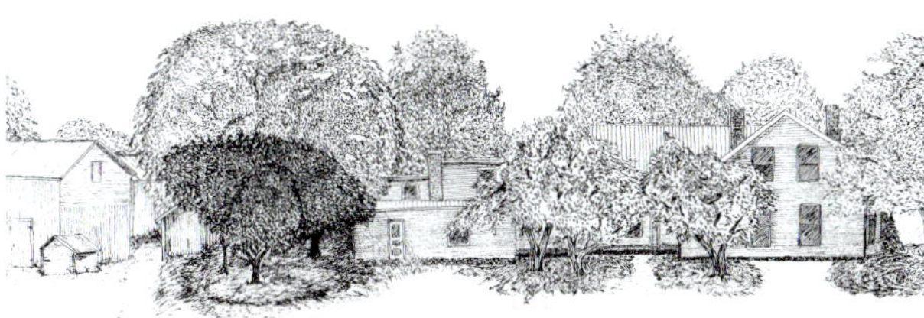

Lollar home place

many Jameson second cousins, but my father was an only child so there were no first cousins.

Members of the Miller extended family were younger in age. None of my grandparents on that side were living when I was born. Because of that, the feeling of family seemed even closer. My mother's sister, Nell Banta, had no children; her brother Roy Miller had a daughter Margaret; her brother Will had a boy, Edwin and a girl, Ellen. With my brother, Bob, and me, that made a unit of Five First Cousins. The family often gathered at the Miller Home Place, the farm north of Lebanon, on what is now known as Miller Road. Another favorite spot was Aunt Nell and Uncle Earl Banta's place in the country on Oregonia Road.

Both the Lollar and Miller ancestral residences are still being lived in and are lovingly cared for by their present owners. However, there is an interesting bit of history connected with the big Miller bank barn. When there came a time that my cousin Edwin Lee Miller had to have the barn torn down, Ed's daughter,

Nancy Miller Myerholtz, and her husband, Dave, were able to save one of the three distinctive cupolas. After keeping it safe for many years, in this year of 2008 a craftsman, who specializes in such things, restored it and its weathervane and the cupola is now installed atop Nancy and Dave's own barn at their home in Waterville, Ohio.

There was a sense of family, too, about The Ridge, where the Lollar farm was located.

This three-mile long community of prosperous places, as the name indicated, was, at 800 feet, one of the highest points in Warren County. There was history, there, too. Numerous branches of the Jameson line had their homes within a two-mile radius, starting with my great grandparents Joseph and Sarah Ann Brown Jameson. They had bought the farm where Grandma Kittie grew up when he left his position as director of the Warren County Infirmary, whose imposing buildings are still standing at the south edge of Lebanon.

In 1933, year of the World's Fair, my mother and brother and I went to Chicago to see the Century of Progress extravaganzas, and stayed with Mary Arthur, daughter of Ella Jameson Arthur, Grandma Kittie's sister. Mary lived in a Southside apartment so close to the University of Chicago that we heard the sound of the carillon bells floating across the campus. She took us to an outdoor concert in Grant Park and we rose, with the rest of the huge audience, in awe at the close of Handel's Messiah. We learned that one does not clap at the close of sacred music (a taboo long since abandoned). We visited her at the downtown office of the Pullman Company, where she was a lawyer, and went across Michigan Boulevard to the Art Institute. There we saw Grant Wood's "American Gothic," the first real oil painting with which I had a love affair, displacing "The Horse Fair" by Rosa Bonheur, a print of which hung on our wall at home.

In my High School years, when my father was working as the bookkeeper at the Lebanon Farmers' Cooperative, it was his Sunday afternoon practice to walk the fields and woodlands which made up the four or five hundred acres of the Lollar farm. Tenants who lived in the buildings at the Home Place and what was called The Roosa Place did the actual farming on a share basis. But my father took a vital interest in the crops and animals, and saw to the repairs needed to fences and buildings. Before my brother left for the University of Cincinnati in my sophomore year at Lebanon High, he and I enjoyed going with my father on his walks. After that, it was I, alone. Although I did not realize it at the time, my father had a deeper reason than enjoying our company in wanting us to go with him on his walks surveying the farms. For he knew that, by the terms of Great Grandmother Eliza Lollar Tingle's 1903 will, the land would eventually come to my brother and me.

In the meantime, I learned to love the land, with its streams and rolling hills, its plots of old forest and young thickets, its tilled fields and night cow pastures.

I loved learning about the rotation of the crops, the wildflowers, and the plants and trees (including the dreaded poison ivy and exasperating thorn locust trees that had to be burned out) but my father never said much about birds. I've often wondered if he, too, was afflicted with nearsightedness to the point that he could not catch the identifying marks as the birds flew in and out of the lush foliage.

And so it was that when it came time in the fall of 1935 for me to go to the Littleford-Nelson Business School in Cincinnati, the years on The Ridge had shaped baby Katherine into a person with strengths and preferences that would last a lifetime, although ready to continue learning and growing. These pages are written in gratitude to all of those who instilled in me the love of learning, the good Presbyterian work ethic, the desire to excel, to be a good person, the enjoyment of nature, the satisfaction of reading, the interest in family history and the history of the world, the fascination of other peoples and cultures, and an endless curiosity about what's around the next corner. I celebrate all of these things but there was more I needed to learn as I left the shelter of Lebanon High: Among them, I needed more social graces; surrounded by role models of rugged individualism, I needed to learn to be a competitor; and I needed to learn how to come out of myself and be a team player.

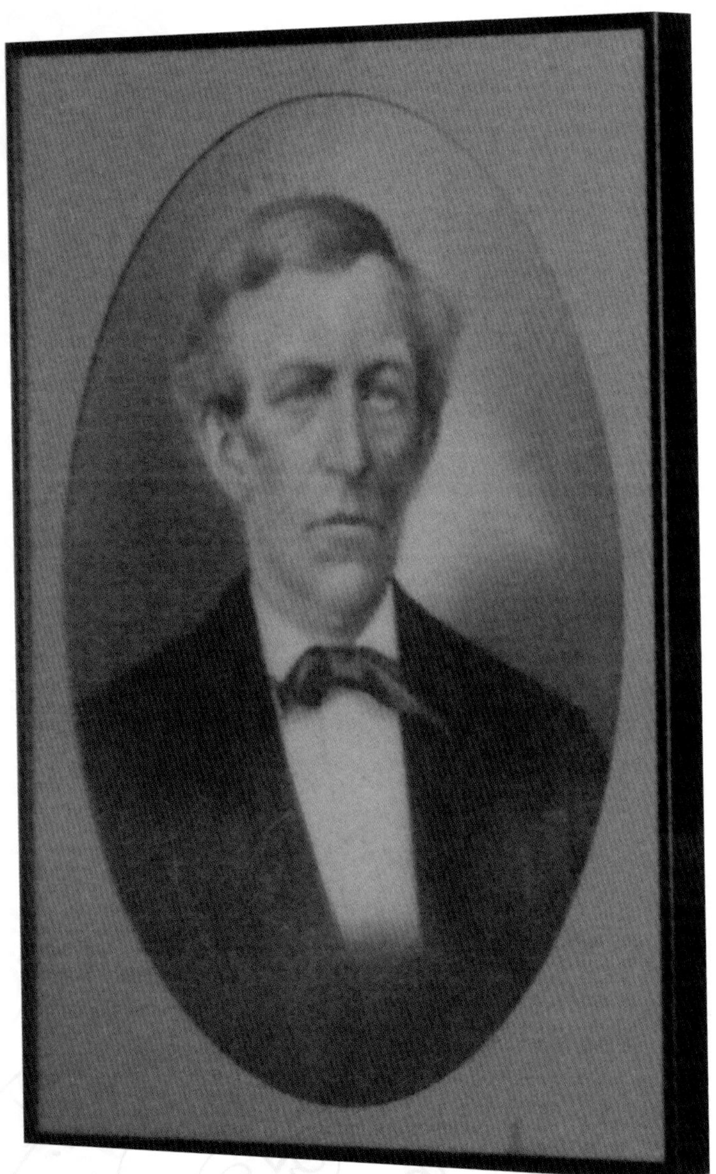
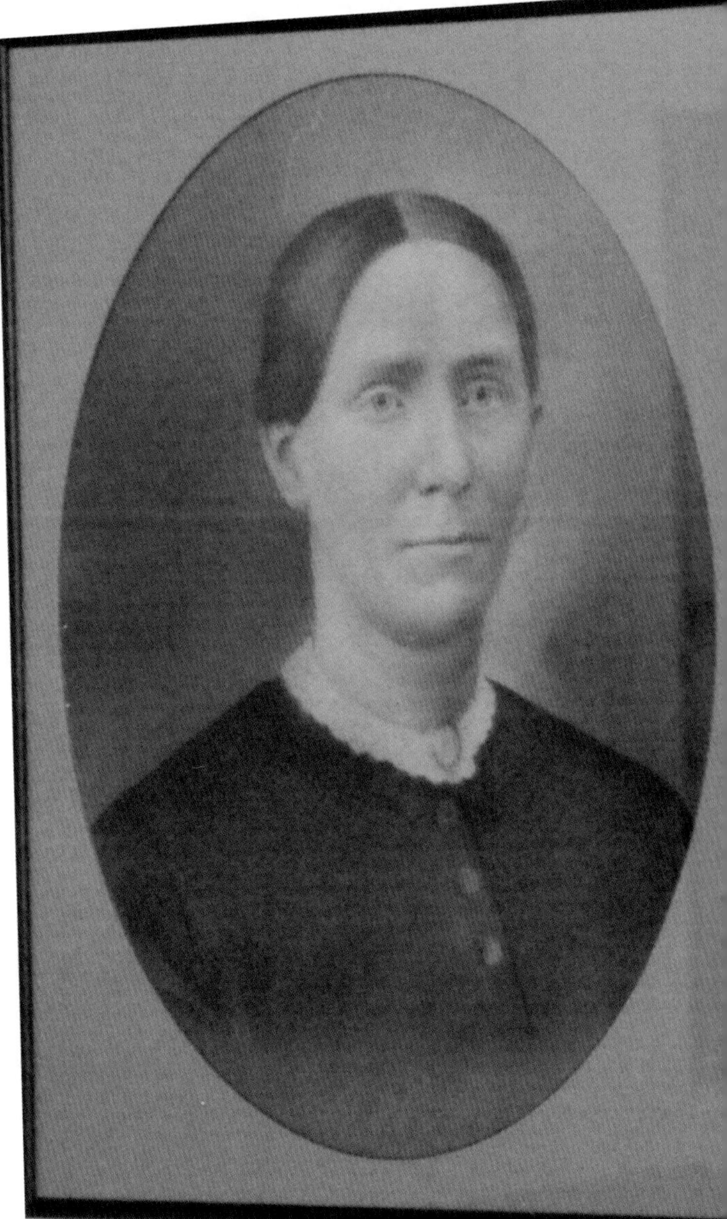

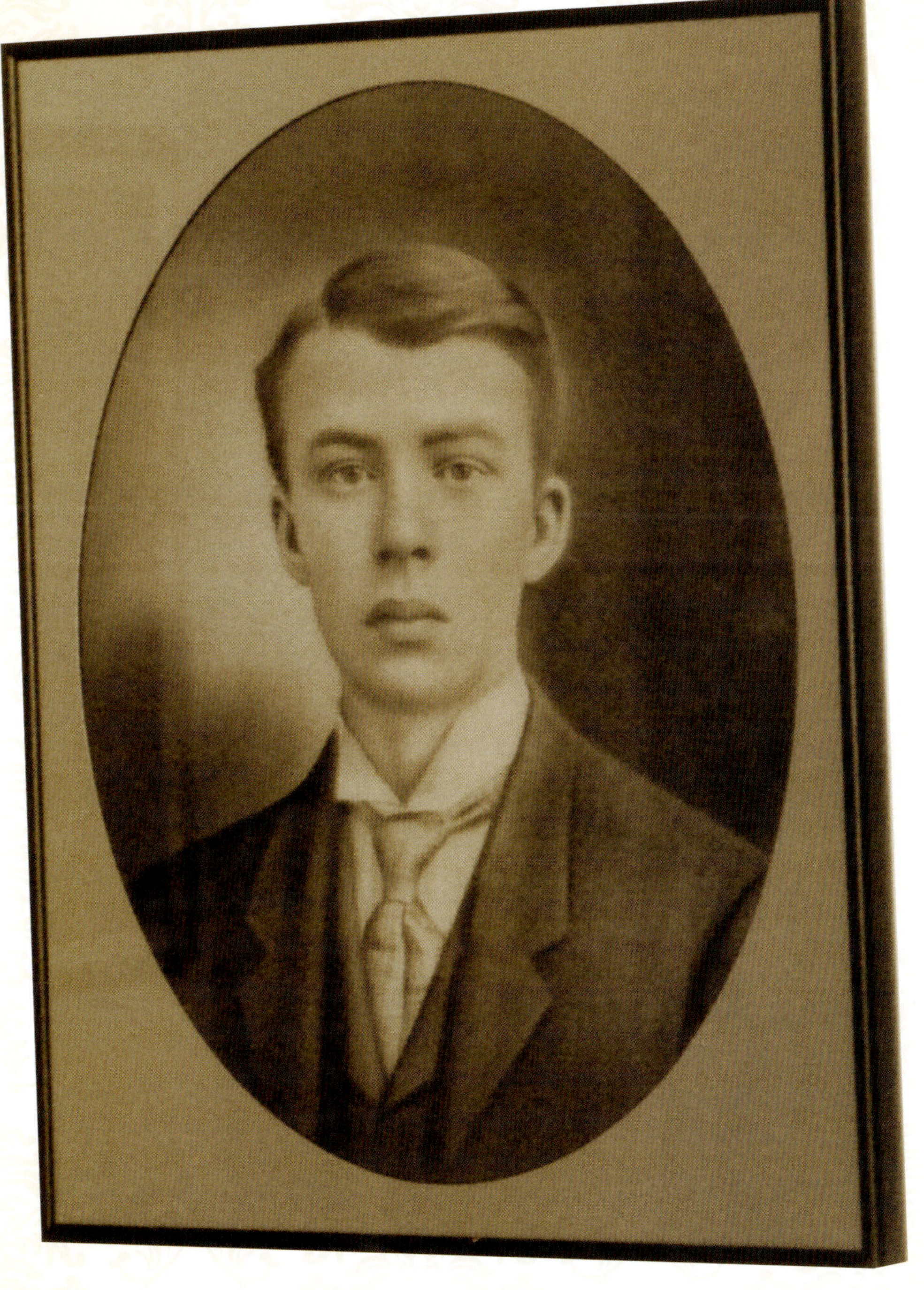

Great Grandparents
Joseph & Sarah Ann
Jameson & father
Harry Lollar

The Big City ● ● ●

When I entered business school I already knew how to type. Although I had not taken any business courses at Lebanon High, my parents had purchased a portable typewriter for me and I learned how to touch type from the instructions booklet that came with it. I was disappointed not to be going to college but the constraints of the Great Depression, and my inability to say just what career I wanted to pursue, made business school the logical alternative. It turned out to be one of the greatest blessings of my life.

I lived at the YWCA on Walnut Street in downtown Cincinnati, not a long walk from the school, on a budget of $9 a week given to me by my parents. The Y had a dining room and I was secure there until the Great 1937 Ohio River Flood came. The whole city was without electricity and the lower six floors of the Y which were intended to be used only as offices were filled with refugees from flooded areas. As I trudged up and down what seemed interminable flights of steps to my room on the eleventh floor I had to pick my way through people and their belongings overflowing into the stairwells.

Eventually the flood waters subsided. I progressed quickly to top speeds in Gregg shorthand and touch typing and completed the required courses in bookkeeping and business ethics in the designated year (with a few months out for an eye infection). The school placed me in a job in the general insurance office of W. S. Hukill, Jr., as a stenographer and policy writer. The offices on the fourth floor of the First National Bank Building had been in continuous use for fifty years with no changes. The bare wooden floors, the high bookkeeping desks, the spittoons, and the hanging green-shaded light fixtures were all dear to Mr. Hukill. And, in addition, there was the letter copying system, an instrument of torture if there ever was one. No matter how perfectly a letter was typed in the required purple ink (I was grateful for office boys who changed typewriter ribbons), it was subject to being destroyed in copying into a book of thin tissue sheets. If the sheets were not moistened with exactly the right amount of water the ink would run into nasty blots of purple, requiring the letter to be retyped, and another try made at copying.

Mr. Hukill, of man of very small stature, often dictated letters, a very difficult task for him. He would sit, running his hand back and forth over his completely bald head, chewing on his small cigars to give him inspiration in finding the precise words, while I fought to stay awake. His son-in-law Hal Balyeat, married to one of Mr. Hukill's twin daughters, was not above mildly flirting with a young office worker.

Mr. Hukill insisted that his office staff be called in the old-fashioned way. There was Miss Kathy, the experienced office manager; and Miss Mary, the bookkeeper who sat at her high desk making flawless

entries in long rows of figures by dipping her steel
pens into small bottles of black ink; and then there
was Miss Marjory, and me—Miss Kay (to avoid
confusion with the office manager), at the bottom of
the scale. I was paid $15 a week.

Something far more precious than any paycheck
was to result from my job at the Hukill Insurance
Office. Miss Marjory (we did have last names, hers
was Rowland) had an older brother, Elden. Marjory
decided her big brother and Miss Kay should get
together and invited me to supper one night at their
home in the Cincinnati suburb of Norwood so we
could meet. And Marjory was right—we did get
together.

Three years older than I was, Elden was working
as ad and layout man at the Reuben H. Donnelly
Corp. publishing the yellow pages of the telephone
book. We started dating in May of 1938. From
his office a few blocks from mine in downtown
Cincinnati, he would meet me for lunch, or rambles
exploring the city, and dinner after work. I was
impressed by his knowledge of Oriental art and
cultures, and fascinated that he could speak strange
Japanese words and also write them in beautiful
calligraphic strokes of a pointed brush, more art than
penmanship.

When Elden was spending a vacation week with
his family at Lake St. Marys that summer I took
a bus up to join them for the weekend. The family
consisted of Martha, his mother; Marjory, his sister,

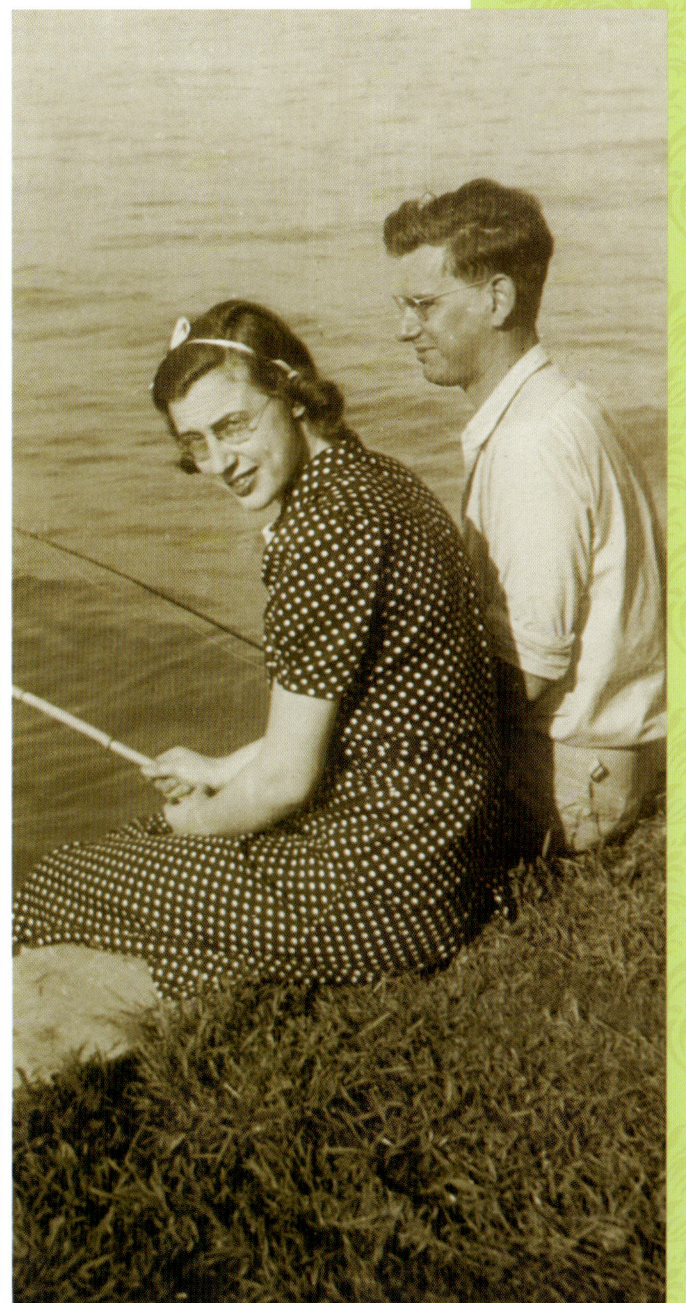

who brought us together; and Glenn, a younger brother. His father, a house painter, died of lead poisoning when Elden was 16.

That weekend at the cottage at the lake, Elden and I became formally engaged. A year after we had met, Katherine Lucile Lollar and Elden Heart Rowland were married on a beautiful spring day —May 13, 1939— in the Lebanon Presbyterian Church, followed by a reception at the New House on The Ridge. My parents loaned us their big Plymouth sedan for a honeymoon trip.

Our two week honeymoon trip broadened horizons for both Elden and me. We saw our first mountains— the gentle, worn Appalachians, as we drove across West Virginia and Pennsylvania to Washington D.C. At Washington, for the first time we experienced the beauties of a big well-planned non-commercial city. We learned how interesting our country's history could be when we visited Williamsburg, Virginia, then in its early years of restoration. We saw the Atlantic Ocean and had our first walk on a beach and our first swim in salt water. And—we heard a mockingbird's song, a gift to us, by our gentle hostess at a Tourist Home on a quiet waterfront at Myrtle Beach, before turning north to return home through the craggy, awesome Smoky Mountains of Tennessee.

Upon reaching home we were saddened to learn that my Grandma Kittie had died three days after our wedding. But the thought that she had been able to attend the wedding and that she had gone so peacefully was comforting. My parents had a question for me because they had not been able to find the big cameo ring Grandma Kittie treasured as part of her engagement gift from her husband Bruce. Did I know where it could be? And I did, indeed, know the answer. When I was a little girl and Grandma Kittie let me snuggle with her in her big bed in her house on Main Street, she would point out to me that she kept that ring hidden way up at the top behind her big dresser with its expansive mirror and marble top. The ring was retrieved and, after being a part of my inheritance for many years, now belongs to another Kittie, Katherine Punteney, Grandma Kittie's great, great granddaughter.

Elden and I moved into a place near the University of Cincinnati I had been sharing with my friend Helen Oyler whom I had known at the YWCA, but soon moved into a larger apartment on Kinney Avenue in Walnut Hills. One of four cut out of a big old mansion, the Walnut Hills apartment was surrounded by trees and had floor-to-ceiling north-facing windows in the living room, a perfect spot to set up Elden's table to practice drawing and whittle small Chinese junks out of Balsa wood. As World War II approached he and Ed and Rosemary Clapper, friends from work, went on short watercolor sketching trips into the hills over the state line in Indiana.

After leaving the insurance office, I worked as the secretary for the Service Department Manager at Bimel and Company, an air conditioning and heating firm. As enlistments in the military cut down on the

number of service men available, the Service Manager
went out into the field and I took over as the sole office
person managing phones and keeping records. Elden
left Reuben H. Donnelly and went off one morning to
Kentucky to enlist in the army. However, he was not
accepted, and came home that same night and soon
received his classification of 4F. War industries were
looking for men with deferments and he was soon
able to start at Cincinnati Milling Machine working
on a big lathe making parts for tanks, he was told, for
the Russians. Although the house we bought in a new
subdivision in Deer Park on the north side of the city
was modest, it was our pride and joy, and we settled in
to work until the war ended. We had bicycles to take
us on trips to the grocery, saving the little Chevrolet
sedan we had acquired so Elden could car-pool to
work, many times on all-night shifts. I walked a mile to
the end of the bus line to go down town to Bimel and
Company, grateful that the frequent tumbles I took on
icy sidewalks never ended in serious injury.

When the end of the war with Japan came on
August 15, 1935, we were ready to join the rest of the
country in enjoying new-found freedoms and making
plans to follow long-delayed dreams.

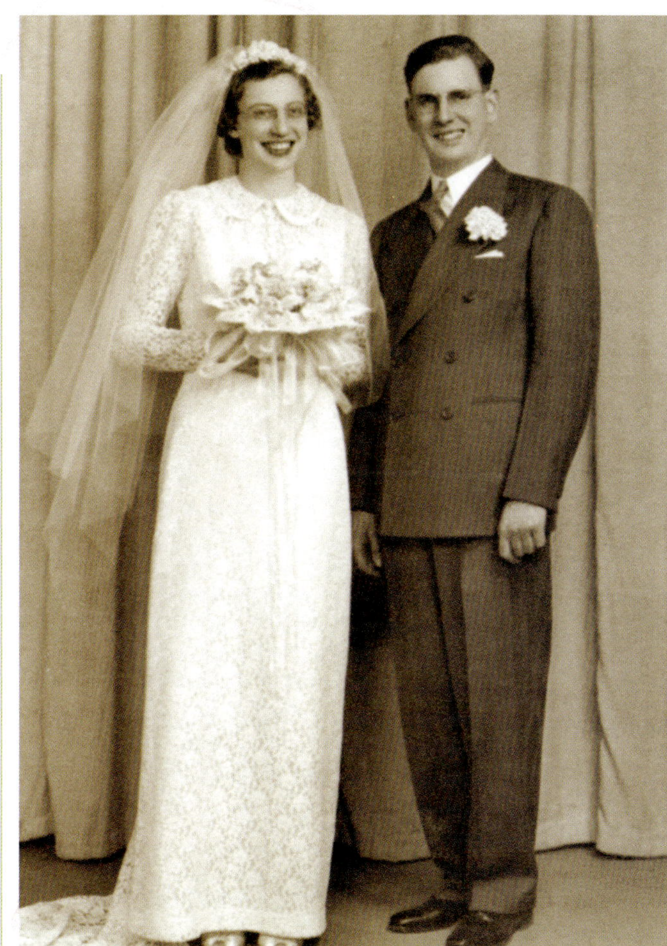

Katherine and Elden wedding picture

Trailer Traveling ● ● ●

In a little over a month after VJ Day 1945, Elden and I started out to follow our dream: to spend three years trailer traveling so he could learn to paint. The first winter after we started out with our 16-foot house trailer hitched to our Chevrolet sedan, we made frequent stops on our trip South. Elden would find oil portraits to paint in the families of service men waiting to be discharged or do watercolors of the landscape which we found so different from Ohio, and I would get temporary office work.

New Orleans was a highlight that year, and in other years to follow. As he sketched the picturesque streets of the French Quarters, Elden met the renowned artist, Alberta Kinsey, who took us to her heart when she discovered I was from Lebanon, Ohio, where she had taught art at the University. One of the most memorable of all my jobs while trailer traveling was at New Orleans. The hypertensive gentleman in charge of a fund raising firm commissioned to gather money for the Eye, Ear, Nose and Throat Hospital was so keyed up in trying to meet deadlines for releases to the *Times-Picayune* that he was prone to pulling paper from a typist's typewriter in mid-sentence, causing several workers to leave just as unceremoniously. But I stayed the full course and at the end felt I had graduated "cum laude" when he told me I was the only one among more than a dozen employees to live up to "his standards."

We made friends; people were receptive to a young couple starting out to follow a dream. We went to movies; we took walks; we baked chocolate chip cookies. We wrote daily letters to our families to share our enthusiasms. In the spring we pulled the trailer North and were graciously allowed by our friends Harold and Magnolia Werner, who were renting our house in Deer Park, to park the trailer in the driveway. I went back to work, temporarily, at Bimel Air Conditioning and Heating.

During the winter Elden had been studying art books and looking at paintings in art museums wherever possible. On a trip to the Cincinnati Art Museum that spring he saw a painting, a sensitive head of a young girl, by Jerry Farnsworth and knew that he had found the teacher he needed. When Elden applied to study at the Farnsworth School in North Truro on Cape Cod he was accepted, although he wasn't on the GI bill as so many applicants were, because we had our own housing—the trailer.

Elden and I were filled with excitement as we pulled the trailer east through Pennsylvania, avoiding cities by using the less-traveled roads. We crossed the Hudson River on the George Washington Bridge north of New York City and enjoyed our introduction to New England as we crossed Connecticut and western Massachusetts. At last, there was one more bridge to cross—the Sagamore Bridge over the Cape Cod Canal. We had reached THE CAPE! It was with a sense of

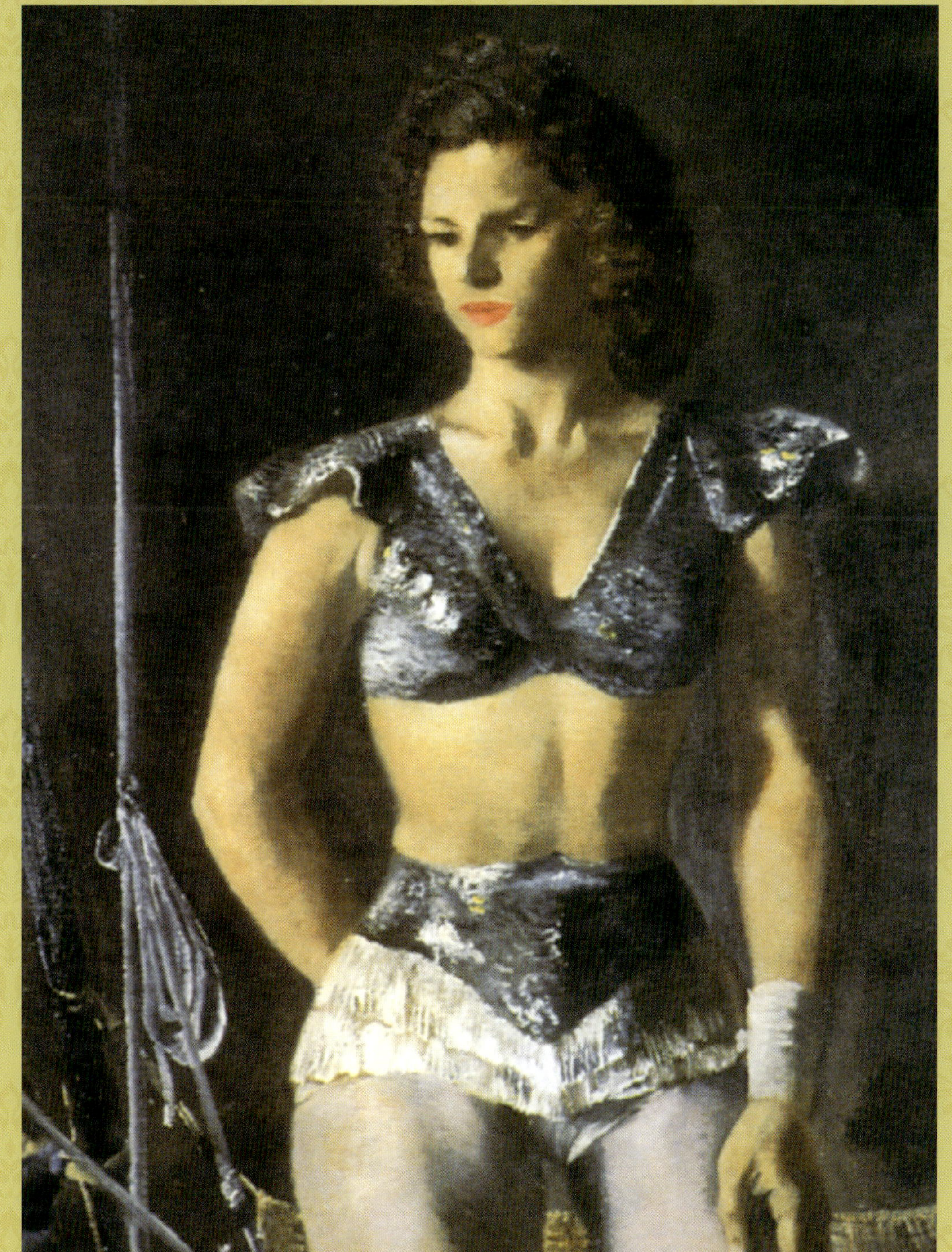

"Ringling Trapeze Artist" by Jerry Farnsworth

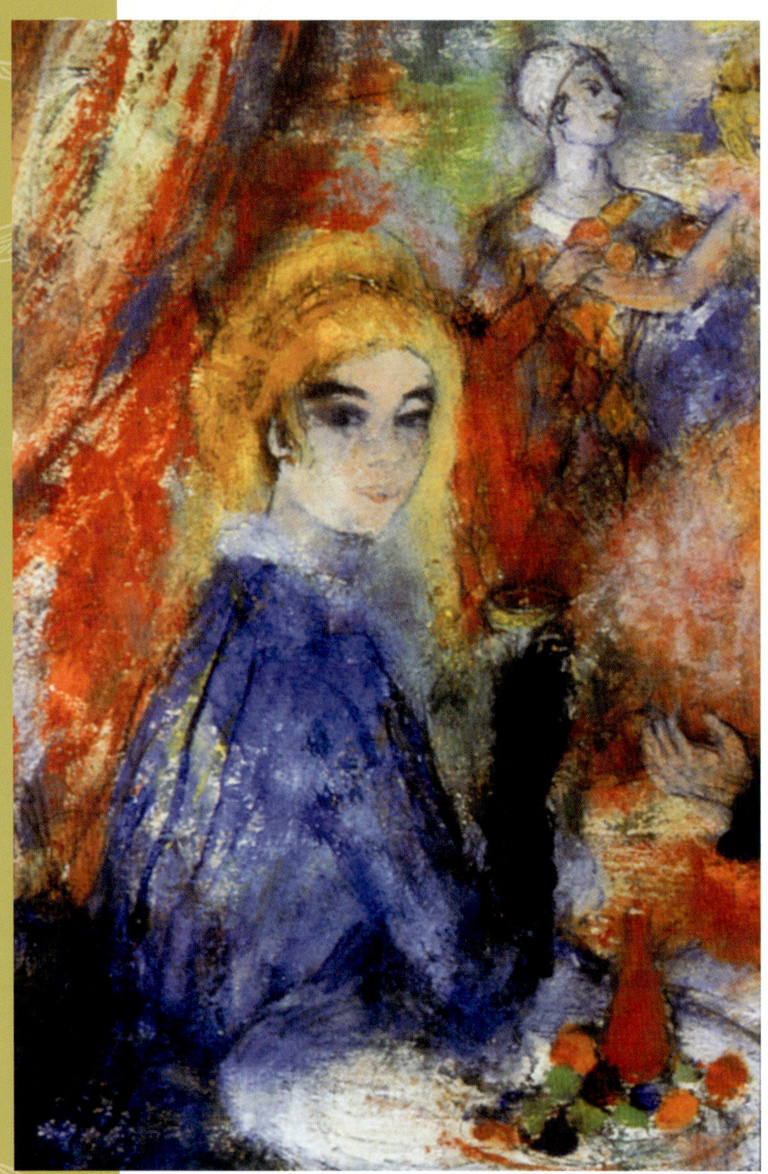

discovery that we followed the narrow two-lane road almost its full length to reach the North Truro area, where the Farnsworth Art School was located.

Our many years of happy association with Jerry Farnsworth, and his wife Helen Sawyer, also a well-known painter, began that summer. They suggested a place to set up the trailer in North Truro, behind a big house full of other students, and we settled in for a happy four months with perks such as growing a vegetable garden and picking high bush blueberries in a tangled area just below the trailer. We soon became close friends with Elsinore Budd and her dog Susie, who lived in the carriage house to which our electric cord was attached. Elsinore, a recent widow from Tarrytown on the Hudson, had come to The Cape, also to follow a dream, a long-deferred desire to return to painting.

The Farnsworths arranged for me to work for their friend, Robert Nathan, a Hollywood writer who summered a few miles away in Truro Center. Robert Nathan, a quiet gentle man who smoked a pipe as he strode back and forth puzzling over where to go next in the book he was writing, was exactly what I had imagined he would be when I read his many books at my office-sitting job before we left Cincinnati.

Elden and I went back to Cape Cod for many summers. But that first summer after World War II as part of the Farnsworth Art School group was a high point. Jerry and Henka (as they were called by us all with respect and affection) by example passed on their

"Entr'acte" by Helen Sawyer

love for their work and their place—Cape Cod. They had met as art students in the Charles Hawthorne School at Provincetown, famous art colony, some miles away at the end of the peninsula. Both of them approachable and appealing, Jerry was quiet and contemplative. Elden held him in very high regard and progressed rapidly with him as his teacher. Henka was vivacious and colorful. In 1995, not long before Henka passed on at over one hundred years of age, Marcia Corbino wrote a book, *Helen Sawyer, Memories of a Morning Star,* which depicts Henka's unforgettable unique charm as a person and an artist. The book is available at the e-Bay store of Lee, Marcia's daughter: http://stores.ebay.com/Lee-Corbino-Galleries.

We were sorry to see summer of 1946 end. The rainy days of nor'easters with the

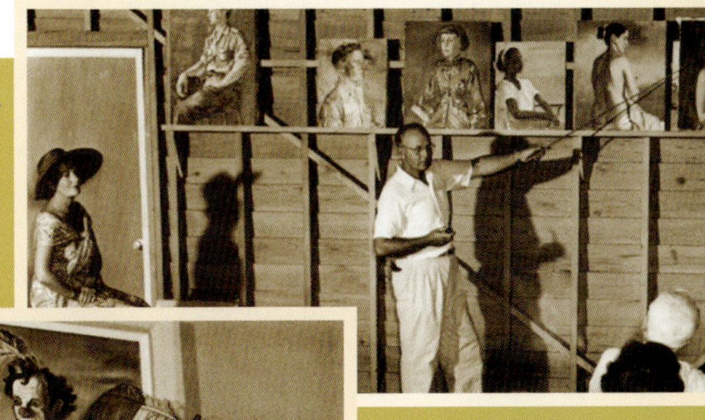

*Helen Sawyer &
Jerry Farnsworth
at critique*

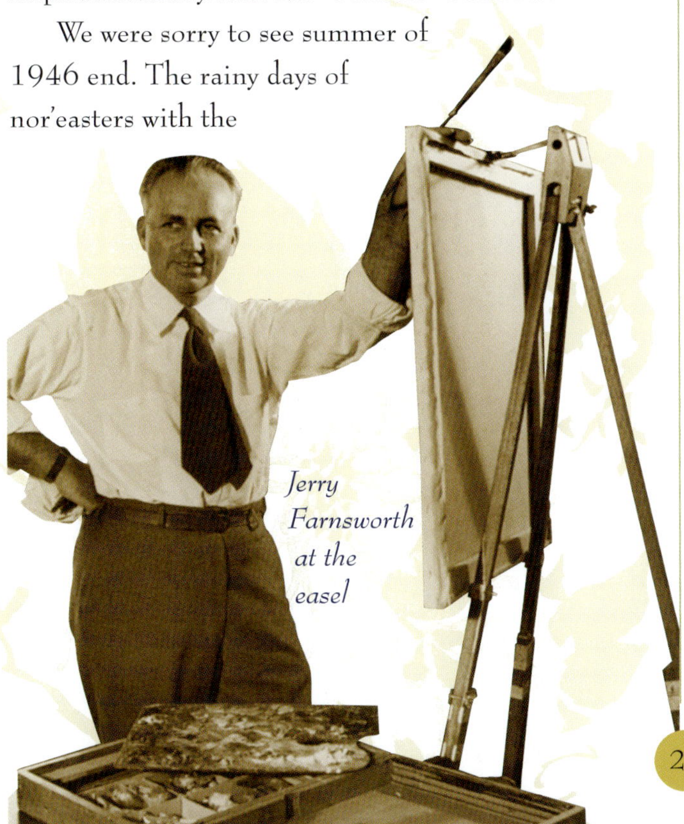

*Helen Sawyer
with "Buzzie
Potts and
Daisy"*

*Jerry
Farnsworth
at the
easel*

Highland Light fog horn blowing, were as memorable as the sunny days when the bright sun gave the light of The Cape the quality for which it was famous. We knew we would be back. In the meantime, we would spend one more winter trailer traveling, and the summer of 1947 in Noank, Connecticut, so Elden could study with Robert Brackman, and I could work in the stenographic pool of the Underwater Sound Laboratory at New London.

During that summer, we drove up to The Cape for a Saturday morning criticism at the Farnsworth School and while we were there Jerry asked Elden to be the monitor at the winter session of the school which would start in Sarasota on January 1st. So, back in Connecticut, when we pulled our peripatetic home out of its site in Mrs. Brown's cow pasture on Long Island Sound, we headed for Florida, with stops at New York City, Williamsburg, Virginia, and Tampa, so Elden could paint in the lovely fall weather.

Fifty *Sarasota* Seasons ● ● ●

When Elden and I reached Sarasota in the fall of 1947, we, and our trusty blue and grey Covered Wagon trailer, had a respite from traveling. Parked in the Pine Shores Trailer Park, it was jacked up off of its tires and put on concrete blocks, leaving our car free so Elden could take care of his duties as monitor at the Farnsworth School of Art.

I got a job as secretary to Ralph Caples, friend of the Farnsworths in the free-wheeling social scenes of the small city just beginning to expand. Ralph Caples, owner of advertising agencies in several Northern cities, was also a good will ambassador for the Seaboard Airline Railroad. He had a great Spanish style home on Sarasota Bay on the north side of town and helped to convince John and Charles Ringling to build their homes nearby. John Ringling had also built the John and Mable Ringling Museum and filled it with his collections of European art. Mr. Caples maintained an office on the second floor of a building he owned on Lower Main Street in downtown Sarasota but spent very little time in it. My job was to *be* there available to take his rapid-fire dictation the moment he came charging up the stairs. Then his chauffeur, Mose Ball, would take him in his prized Packard station wagon to visit with his cronies around town, and run errands, not the least of which was to buy a daily orchid for his petite wife, Ellen. I would transcribe the letters and have them ready for signature whenever he came back, be it that day, or next.

In the spring of 1948 I was introduced to Eleanor Treacy and Eric Hodgins by Henka Farnsworth and began what turned out to be a long and affectionate relationship with them and their daughter Patty. On Easter Sunday I typed an article for Eric, who was just returning from Hollywood where *Mr. Blandings Builds His Dream House* had been made into a movie with Myrna Loy and Cary Grant. Copy for an article describing his experiences had to be on a plane out of Tampa that night to meet the *Life Magazine* deadline— and we made it! Sixty years later, I recently re-read those pages and, although I have no memory of what I typed so furiously that Easter Sunday, I still find it fresh and interesting and filled with the subtle humor for which Eric Hodgins was noted.

When Eleanor was asked to be president of the Sarasota Art Association she agreed to serve if I would be hired as person in charge of the gallery. During that year I learned many invaluable things from her, one of them being: she taught me how to organize, a skill that was invaluable to me in later years in planning traveling workshops for painting and photography groups.

Eric Hodgins

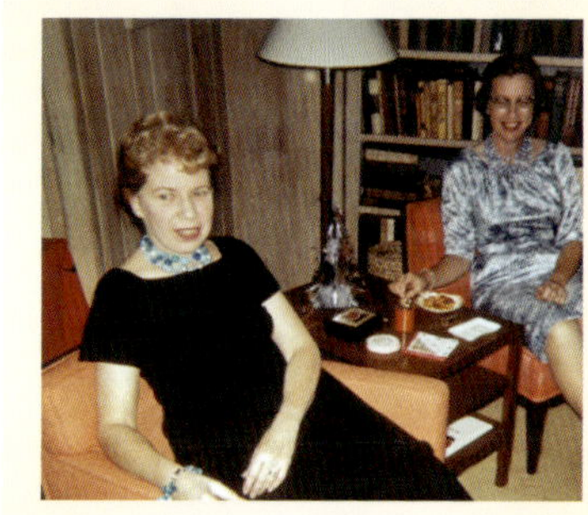

Eleanor Hodgins and Katherine

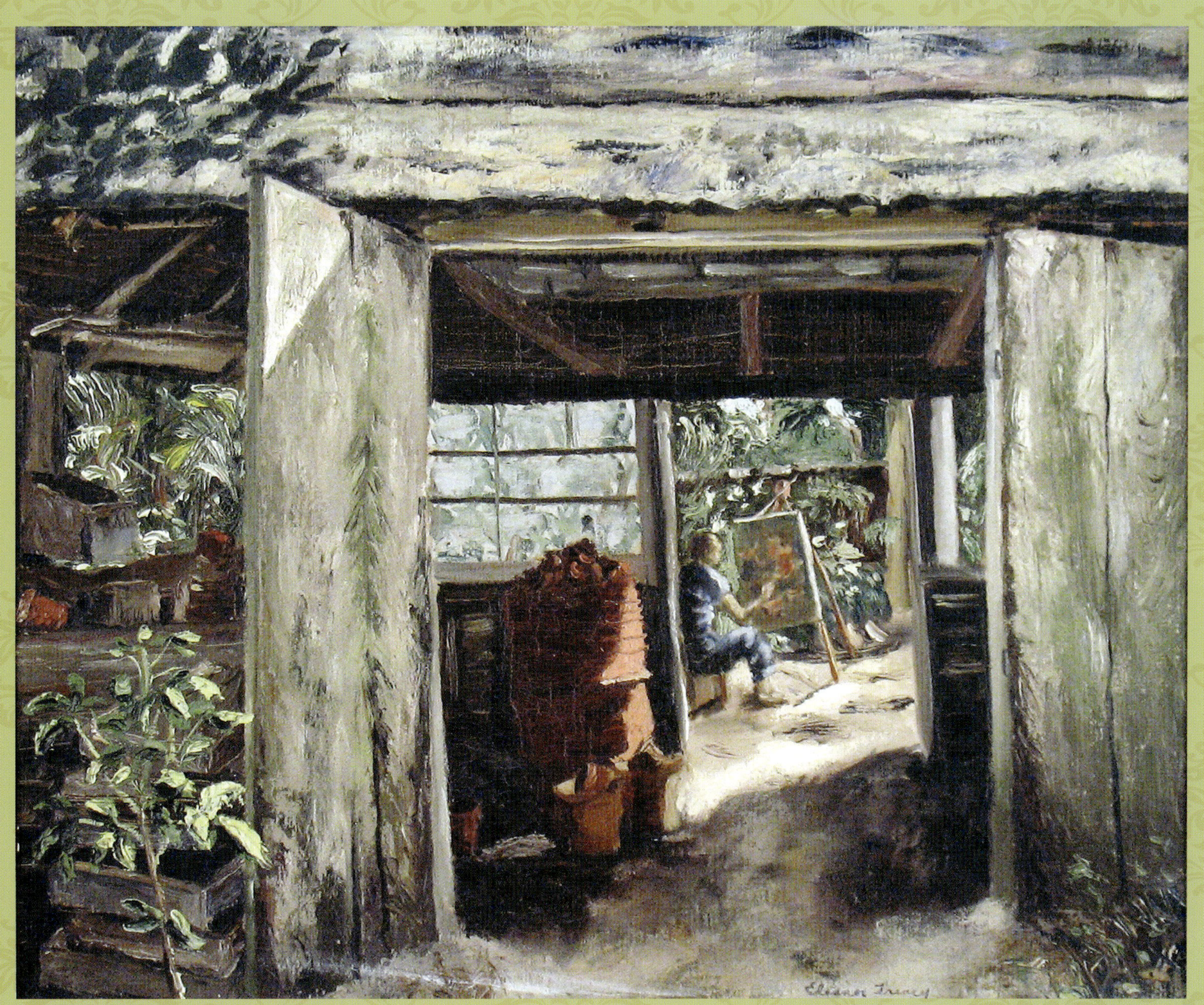
"Green Mansions" by Eleanor Treacy Hodgins

Cape Cod & Sarasota

Elden and I spent many happy summers on Cape Cod after the first summer in 1946 in North Truro when Elden was studying at the Farnsworth School. In the winters we began to establish ourselves permanently in Sarasota..

1948 was a banner year. We found a place for our trailer in Mr. Howes' hayfield overlooking Cape Cod Bay in East Dennis. Elden painted in a loft of Mr. Howes' barn and I worked for Eric and Eleanor Hodgins, who had rented a house down the beach a short way. Eric was working on a sequel to *Mr. Blandings Builds His Dream House*, although he was interrupted by many trips to New York. This left me free to pose for the series of "Girl-on-the-Beach" paintings which Elden originated that summer. The pictures of a timeless female figure sitting on a moody, mysterious

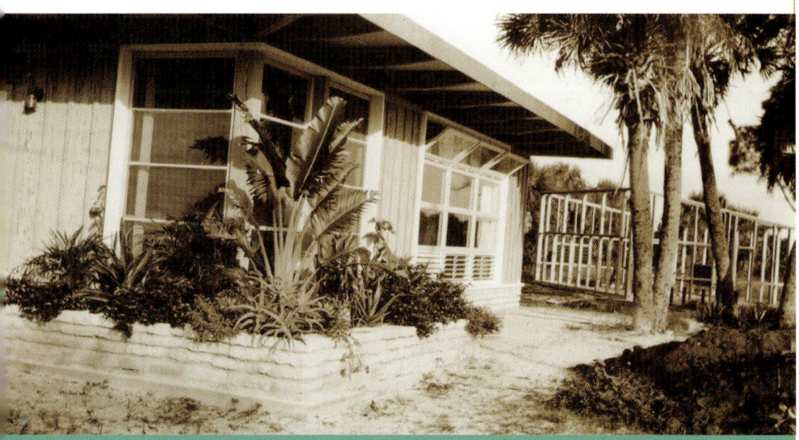

House, and studio under construction

beach became popular right away. The first one, "White Gulls Flying," was sold for $500 from the new Cape Cod Art Association at Hyannis, a banner happening for the Rowlands and the new art group as well.

1948 remained a memorable year when we returned to Sarasota for the winter. We purchased two uncleared lots on which to build a house on Siesta Key, just three blocks from a pristine white sand beach on the Gulf of Mexico. Elden worked with designer Harold Pickett to arrive at a plan and we contracted with him to build a unique little house using innovative materials for which Pickett Construction was noted. Taking advantage of a graceful grouping of five native palm trees at the center of the lots, and anchored by a large corner planter filled by the Hodginses as a housewarming present, the place soon began to take on a quality of "our home" which was to continue for more than fifty years.

Early the next year Elden and I cooperated in adding a separate structure to the rear of the group of palm trees as Elden's studio. My part was my $3,000 inheritance from Grandma Kittie Jameson Lollar, and his was his sense of design and skills in carpentry. As the house was being built, Elden had watched the Florida old timers as they coped with things like concrete slabs and hurricane straps and load-bearing beams and so was able to craft a north-light studio for himself. Although our next door neighbors bought the place from me in the year 2000 the studio is still, in 2008, used by an artist—Maxine Masterfield.

Maxine, a successful watercolorist well-known for her innovative techniques, first came into my life as an instructor in the Leech Studio Watercolor Workshops. Her buoyant personality and willingness to share her evolving processes for producing richly-colored creative results have made her a popular teacher in the studio and also in her two painting books. After Elden passed on I was using his studio for storage and guests until Maxine asked if she might rent the space to use

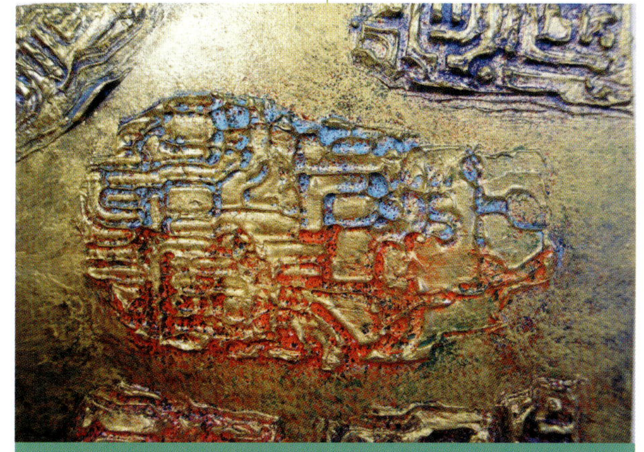

"Transmission in Gold" by Maxine Masterfield

for daytime work. As Maxine uses Elden's studio she feels a connection to Elden and his painting . When Elden was exploring the use of found objects, he tacked a small piece of his crushed-can art beside the studio door. Maxine has responded to it by attaching a piece of her own crushed-can sculpture to the wooden fence opposite the door and carrying the idea further by the use of images impressed in modeling paste on canvas highlighted with vivid colors. "Transmission in Gold" is part of that series. Elden's found-object pieces were in dark, earth colors. A triptych, "Transitions" was given a purchase award at the 1971 Berkshire Art Museum,

Pittsfield, Massachusetts.

After the summer of 1948 in East Dennis, Elden and I went to Wellfleet for our Cape Cod summers. Brownie's Camp, in the pines, under the Fire Tower was a very pleasant spot for the trailer one summer. Elden made a connection with Florence Rich at her Gallery just off the parking lot in the center of town. He painted in the loft and helped with hanging shows and met and enjoyed the other artists. I didn't have any secretarial work but with my overly-zealous work ethic felt I should be busy. So I was spending lovely Cape Cod days in the trailer laboriously hand-sewing curtains. However, I was soon rescued by a bouncy carrot-topped teacher down from Boston for the summer—Doris Campbell.

Doris had contacted Elden about taking art lessons and she and he conspired to get me out of my made-up duties at the trailer. She appeared at the door with the news that the tide was just right for a swim at Town Beach and that was the beginning of a rich, rewarding friendship, which she and I and Elden shared for many years. Her lively, warm, outgoing personality drew me to her immediately. We spent long

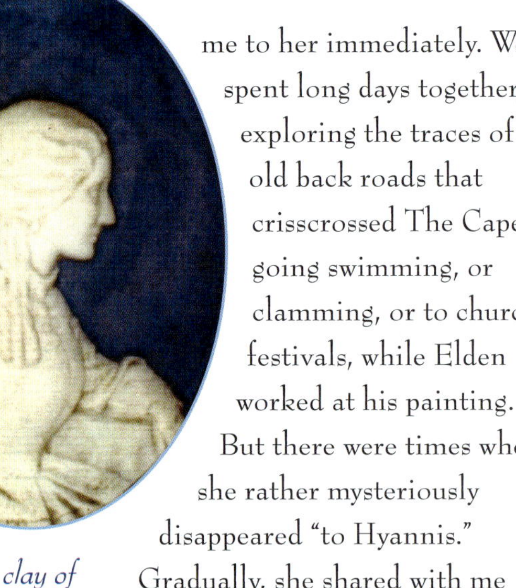

*Portrait in clay of
Mary Baker Eddy*

me to her immediately. We spent long days together, exploring the traces of old back roads that crisscrossed The Cape, going swimming, or clamming, or to church festivals, while Elden worked at his painting. But there were times when she rather mysteriously disappeared "to Hyannis." Gradually, she shared with me that she went to Hyannis to attend services of the Christian Science Church. Her attachment to her faith and what she was learning in the writings of Mary Baker Eddy in the First Church of Christ, Scientist, was so strong that she protected it from possible questioning by others to whom this out-of-the-mainstream religion seemed strange. I had never heard of Christian Science but immediately knew that whatever resulted in the happy, spiritual quality I had seen in Doris was something I would like to know about. I started going to church with her and became more and more grateful to her for introducing me to the principles of Christian Science, so much more comforting and joyful than the religion in which I had grown up. Years later, I was given an original clay portrait of Mrs. Eddy, which was made in 1913.

As Cape Cod summers followed one after the other, Elden and I sold the trailer and took various summer rentals around Wellfleet. Elden started to teach "Rowland Art Classes" in the old blacksmith shop, while continuing to show his paintings at Florence Rich's Gallery in Wellfleet, and Nieta Cole's in Orleans, and at the Provincetown and Cape Cod Art Associations. After spending a winter working at Barry's Art Supplies, in Sarasota, I opened a small art materials store in a corner of Elden's school. Elden started "Rowland Traveling Exhibitions," in which he gathered paintings from various artists and circulated shows to art associations and museums throughout the eastern United States and Canada. Two of his favorite shows were "Cape Cod Artists" and "Provincetown Painters." During the winters in the 1950s, Elden began to teach in different art classes on the West Coast of Florida. He continued to work in oils, notably the "Girl on-the-Beach" paintings, but still enjoyed Oriental ink brush techniques.

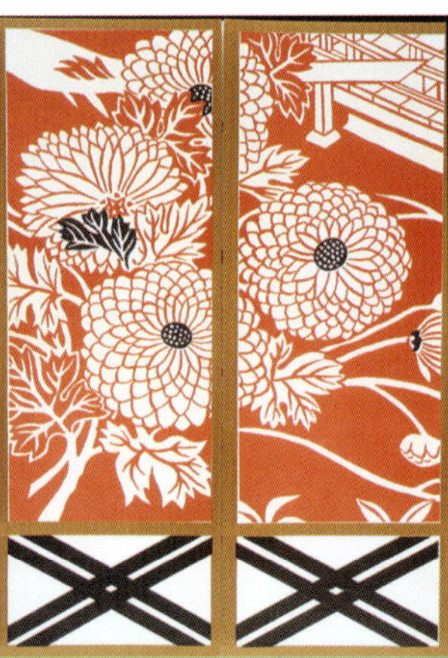

*"Invitation to Ikebana Show"
by Elden Rowland*

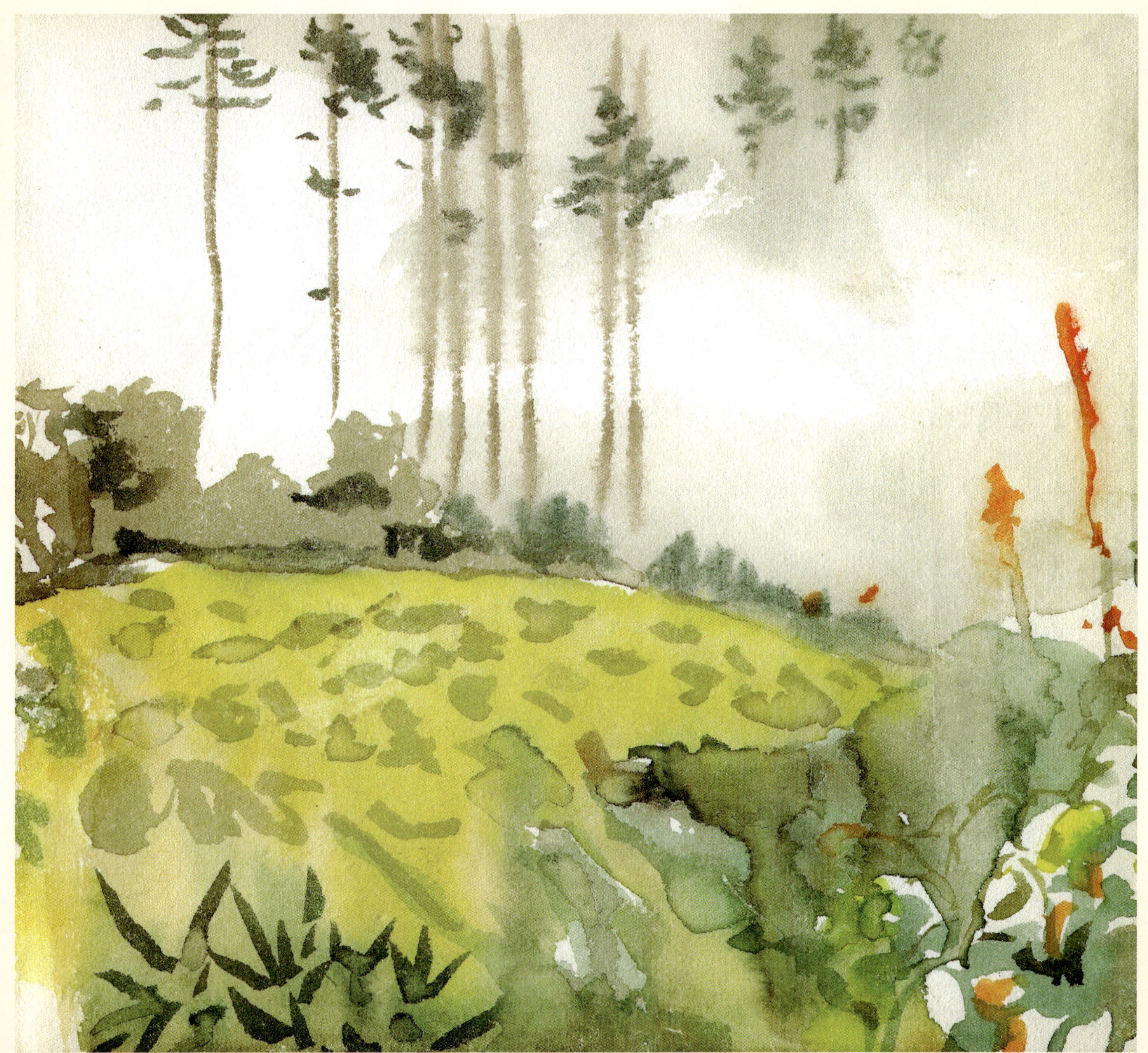

"Oregon Coast" by Elden Rowland

Hilton Leech Art School

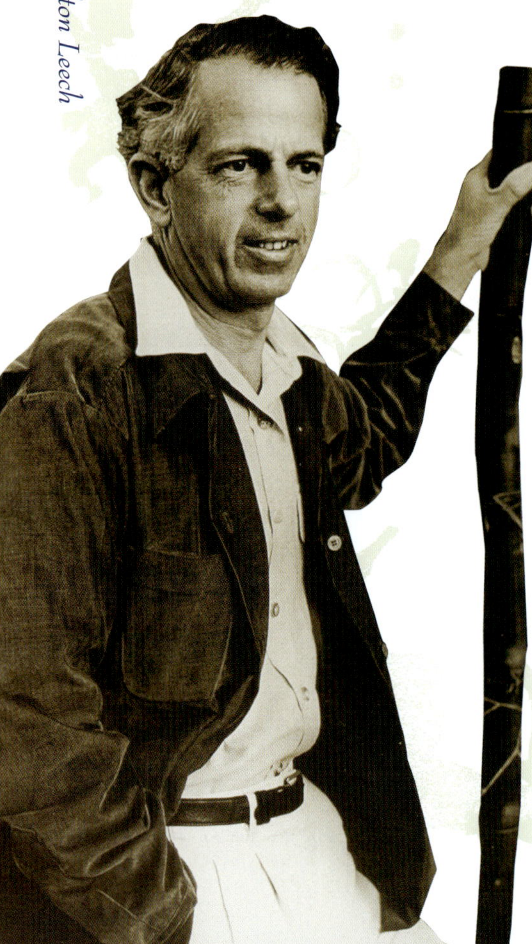

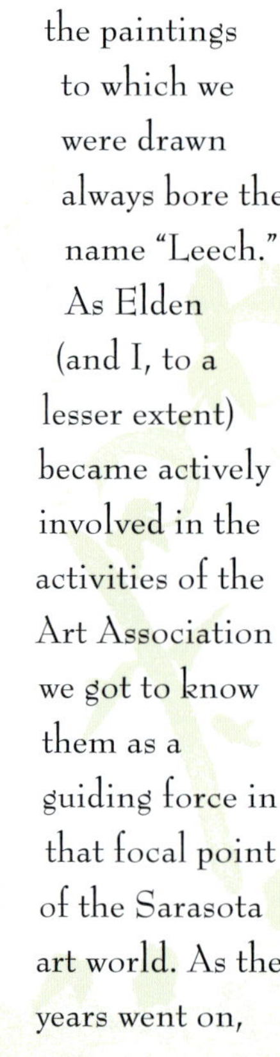

When Elden and I arrived in Sarasota in the late 1940s, Hilton and Dorothy Leech were already a well-established and much-beloved part of the burgeoning art community of Florida's West Coast. Hilton had come to Sarasota in 1931 to help start the Ringling School of Art and met and married Dorothy Sherman there. After World War II they started the Amagansett School of Art on Hillview Avenue. We had first become aware of the Leeches through seeing their art. It seemed that when we went to exhibitions, the paintings to which we were drawn always bore the name "Leech." As Elden (and I, to a lesser extent) became actively involved in the activities of the Art Association we got to know them as a guiding force in that focal point of the Sarasota art world. As the years went on, Hilton was president of the young Florida Artist Group and Elden was director of the traveling exhibitions.

Around 1960 the Leeches sold their property on Hillview Avenue to potter/sculptor Frank Colson, and his wife Diana. They bought a large wild tract on Phillippi Creek and built a school studio facing Riverwood Avenue, and later built their home on Pine Terrace, just to the rear of the school. Hilton Leech, always a person of wide-ranging interests, invited Roger Early, a popular television science lecturer and artist, to teach at the school. And soon other art teachers were added to the roster, including my husband, Elden, and Sally Hayden. It was at that time the name Amagansett was changed to The Hilton Leech Art School.

The new Leech Studio was a soaring avant-garde structure designed by Jack West, one of the "Sarasota School" of architecture gaining national recognition in the early 1960's. In later years, the Leeches told of the first time they took Jack West to see the big tract of native Florida jungle on which they intended to build. They, and their young daughter Jerry, were walking down an overgrown path toward the Creek when they happened to look back to see a fire in the scrub behind them. Fortunately, the fire was put out before it became a real Florida wildfire and plans went forward for the round, two-story masonry and glass building that was a center of art and learning through the remainder of the Twentieth Century.

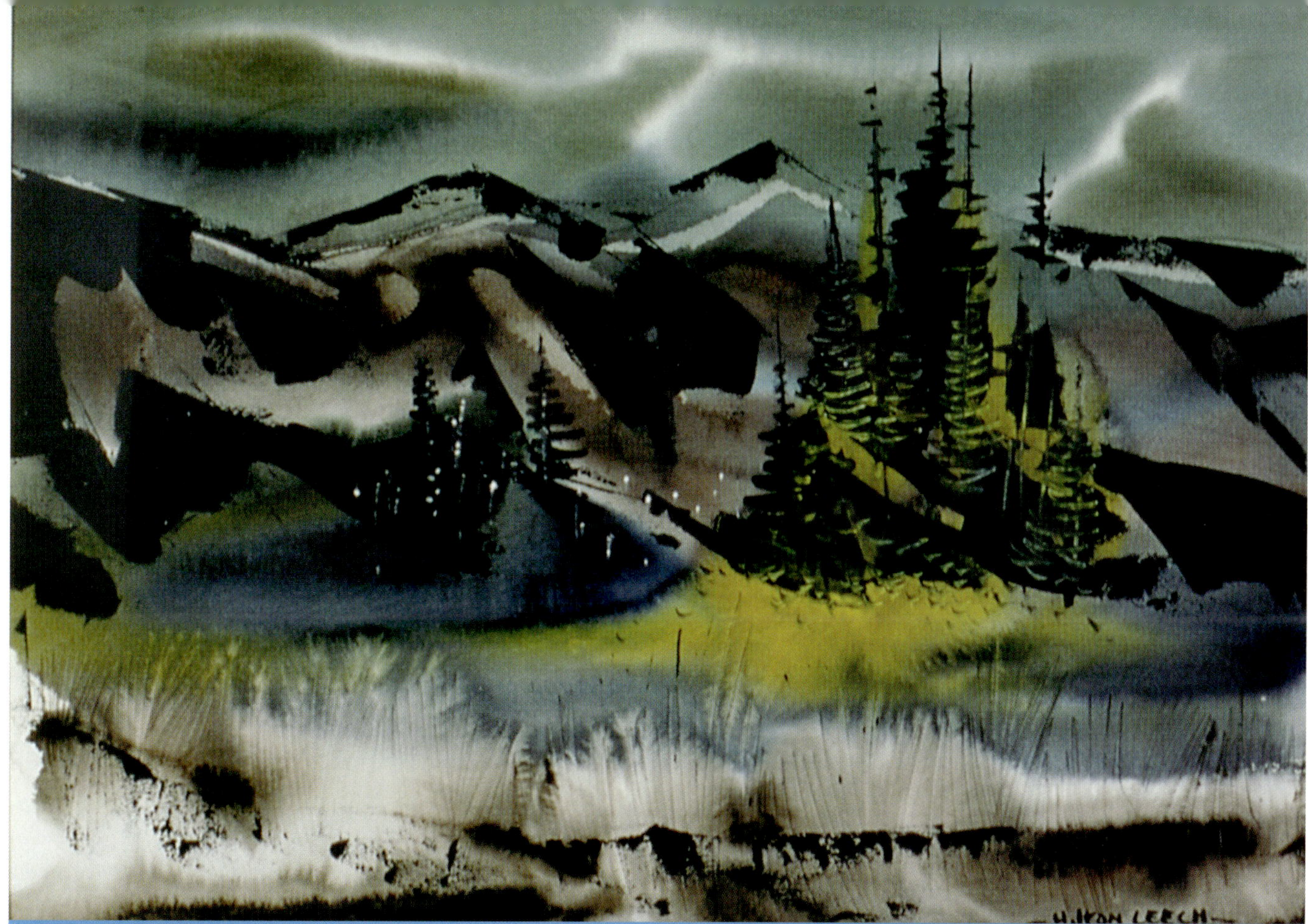

"Ruby Ridge" by Hilton Leech

A group of individuals, wanting to widen their horizons in all directions, began to gather around Hilton Leech and Roger Early. Attracted by Hilton's skill as an artist and his gentle charisma as a person, and by Roger's magic of being able to make the layman understand (or think they did) the intricacies of the new "Space Age," they began to meet at the Leech Studio. They purchased a 16-mm movie projector and started presenting a regular series of films on art, nature and science. In those days before television, it satisfied a yearning for help in trying to understand the changes that were taking place in their post–World War II world.

This group was chartered by the State of Florida, on March 7, 1963, as The Friends of the Arts and Sciences, a non-profit, educational organization. Elden and I were among the 77 charter members. Such was the enthusiasm of the members of the new organization that programs were held three nights a week for a six months' season: movies on Mondays, science lectures

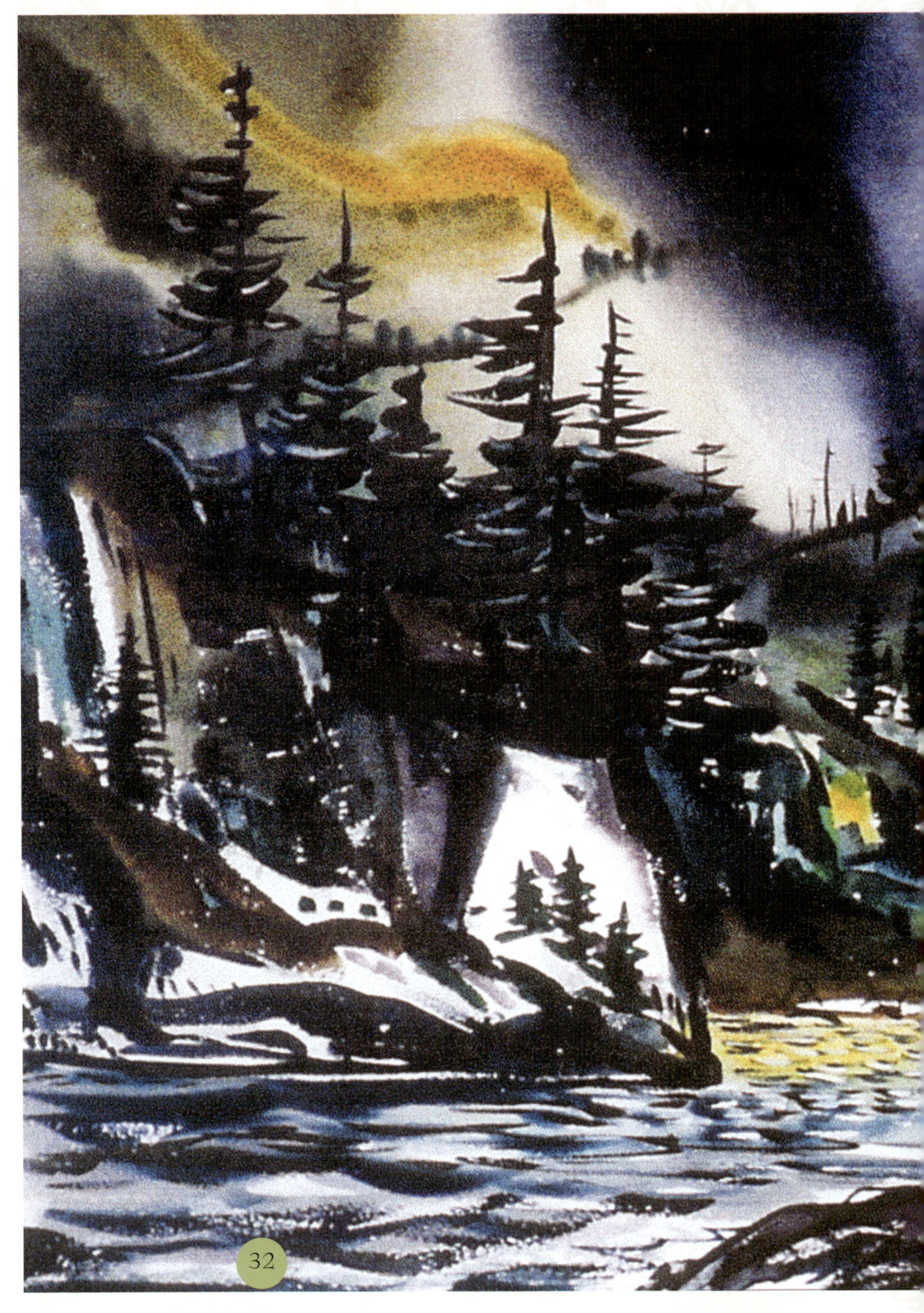

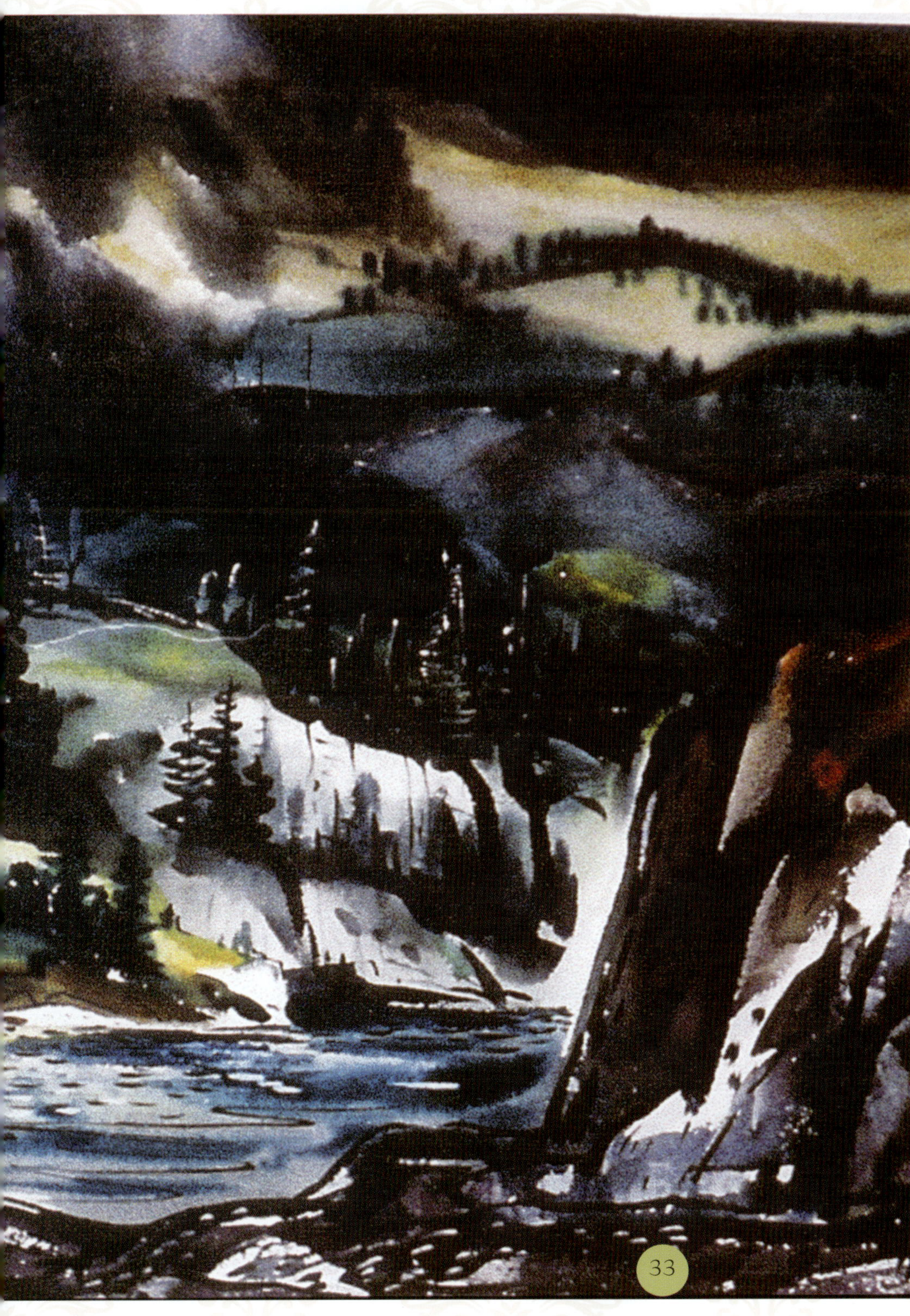

"Thunderstorm" by Hilton Leech

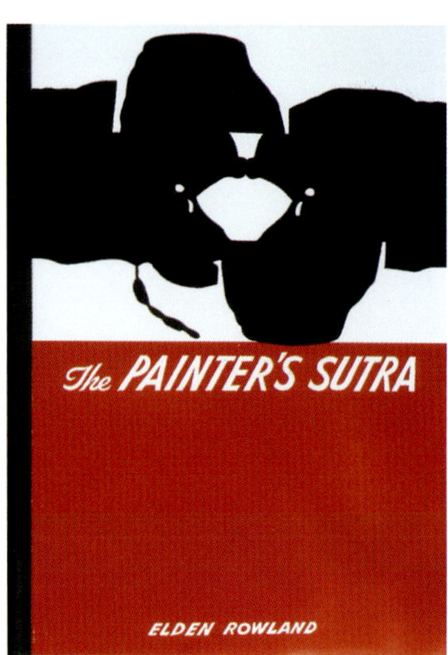

The Painter's Sutra, *cover of book by Elden Rowland*

on Wednesdays, and art demonstrations and a drawing clinic on Fridays. Field trips were also planned.

Activities of The Friends of the Arts and Sciences and the Hilton Leech Art School were separate entities both operating at, or from, the School Studio. I was the only paid secretary for both entities in those early days, the proud sole occupant of the neat little office space fitted into the center of the round building. The Friends of the Arts and Sciences paid my small stipend in a rather uneven exchange for all the space and utilities the School provided. Painting classes with instructors Hilton Leech, Elden Rowland and Sally Hayden (now Von Conta) were held daily. I was pleased to be a part of it all, but still felt left out when Hilton's sketching class went out to such interesting places as the Ringling Circus Winter Quarters or the abandoned Mary's Chapel on Mrs. Potter Palmer's estate at The Oaks.

Elden's classes at the Leech Studio were in oil painting, experimental techniques and sumi-e, or Japanese ink brush painting and calligraphy, thus, with Hilton's expertise in watercolor, covering a full spectrum of approaches to art. To help his students

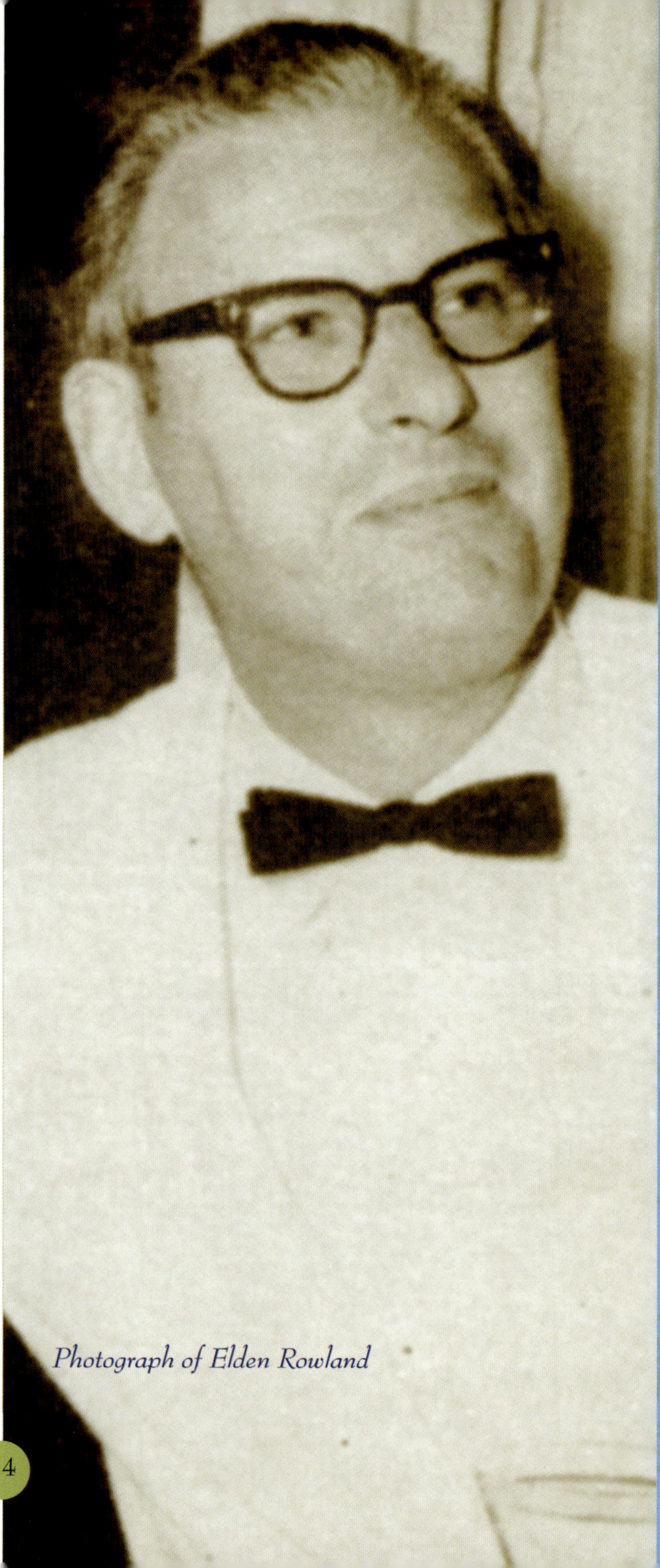

Photograph of Elden Rowland

have a happy painting experience, Elden originated workshops, such as "Intuitive Painting," and "Nature, the Inexhaustible Source," and wrote a small book *The Painter's Sutra*, based on his own study of Eastern art, philosophies and religions, in particular Zen Buddhism. He was a part of the Hilton Leech Studio from 1960 until his death in 1982, at the same time having his own classes on Cape Cod and teaching invitational workshops in Florida and elsewhere. He was as passionate about teaching as he was about painting. The sympathy notes I received after his death told me of the many ways he had quietly touched other peoples' lives of which I had not been aware at the time.

Sally Hayden Von Conta's lifetime in art began as a scholarship student at the Leech Studio. As a young adult she progressed in fine art and then went to New York City to work as an Art Director in Advertising Design for large retail establishments. She was happily married, but her husband, a photographer, died, and she moved to Santa Fe, New Mexico, to make her home and establish a successful fine arts career, now in plein air pastel painting. About her chosen medium, she says

"Plein Air Pastel Painting on site is heart work. It's always a surprise. It's a constant conversation between you and the land. At its best, you, yourself, dissolve into the landscape. Later you remember the heat on the rocks, the sound of the bees on the wild roses and the look of the light—it's all inside the painting."

Exhibitions changed regularly in the small gallery of the Hilton Leech Studio in Sarasota, the November presentation of the 1963-64 season being paintings by the three instructors. The February presentation was The Petticoat Painters Show, starting a long-standing tradition of the annual exhibition of that new group being held on a date close to Valentine's Day at the Leech Studio. The Petticoat Painters, an invitational group of 20 women painters, had originated a few years before at the gallery and school being operated by William and Martha Hartman in an old newspaper building in downtown Sarasota. Now, in 2008, the oldest continuous art organization of its kind, the Petticoat Painters' annual exhibition in recent years has been held at the Selby Gallery of the Ringling

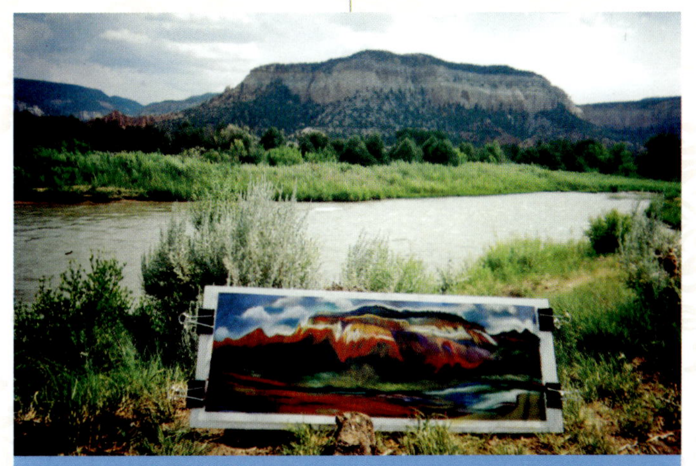
"Chama Light Setting" by Sally Hayden Von Conta

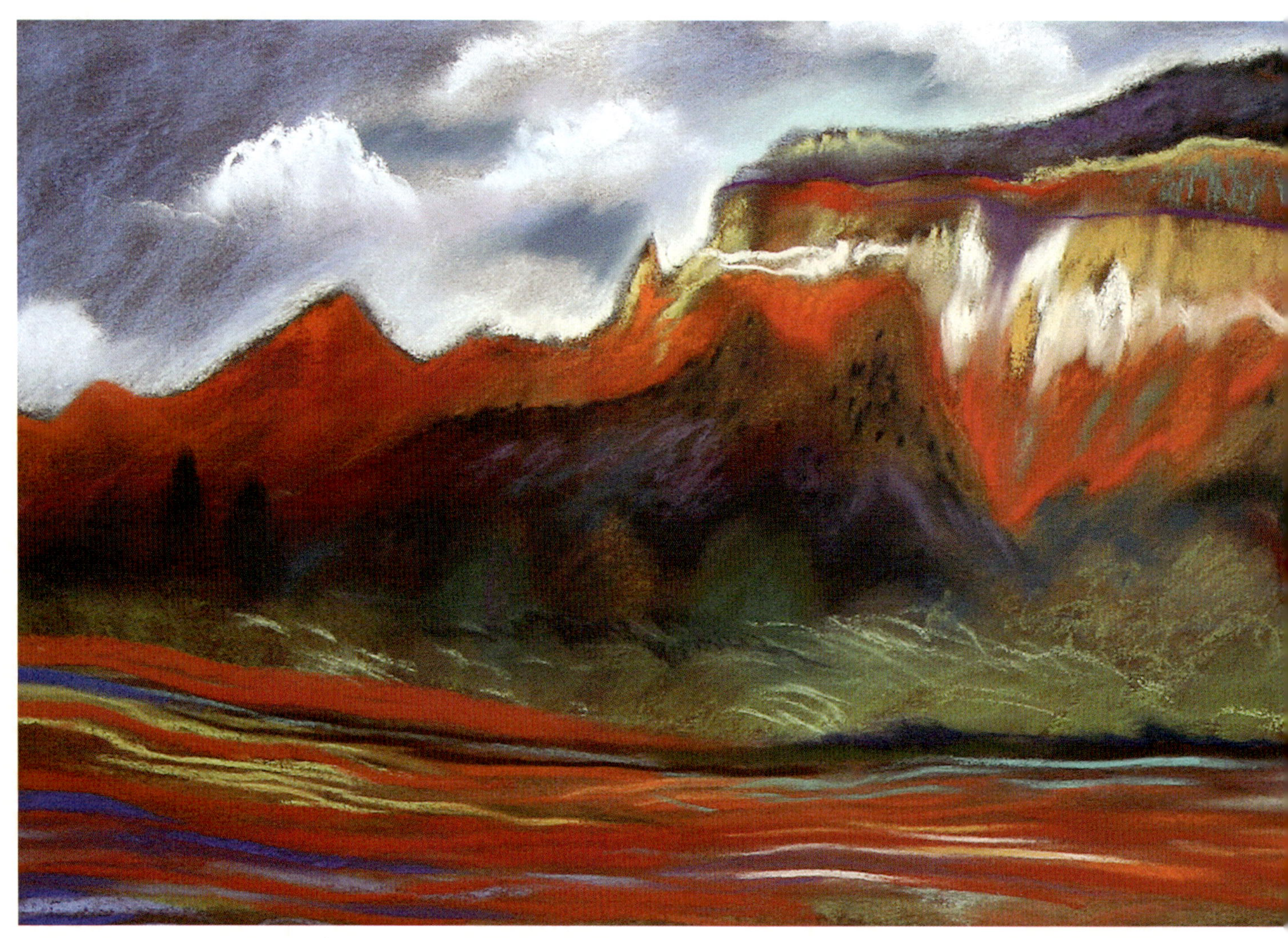

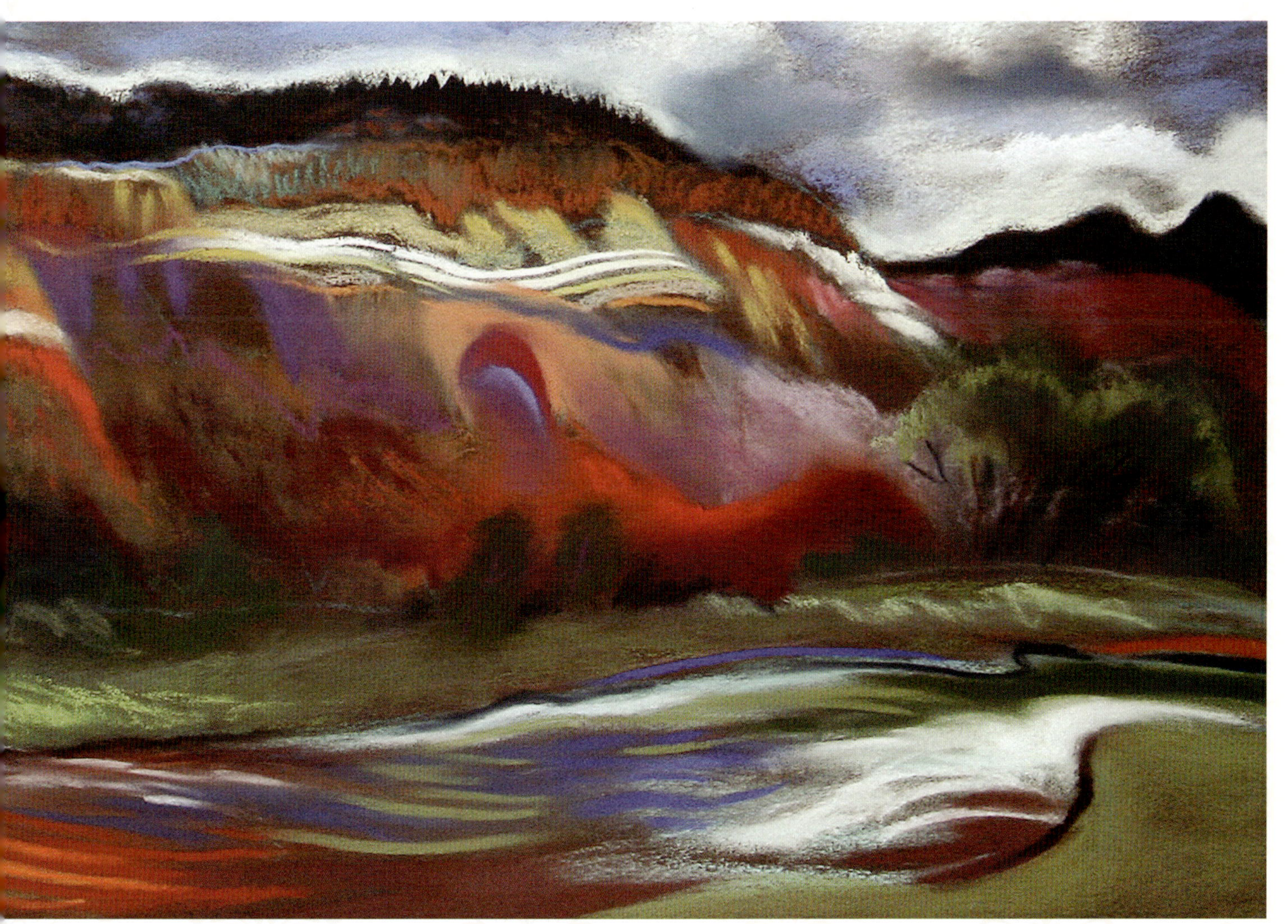

"Chama Light" by Sally Hayden Von Conta

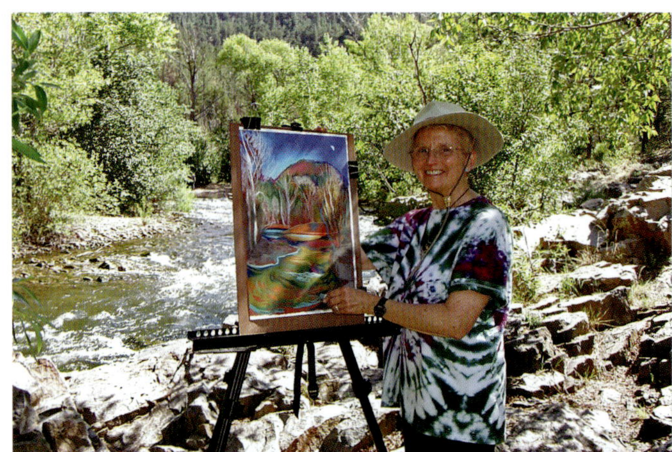

a reminder of our beautiful skies we saw in the Southwest." I was touched that she went on to say, "I shall never forget our workshops we did together in Santa Fe. Of all the workshops I have done, yours was the best, beautifully managed as only *you* can do."

• • •

School of Art and Design. I have been proud to have been made an honorary member of the group because of my close association with them during my twenty-six years at the Leech Studio.

In March, the final exhibition of the 1963-64 season at the Leech Studio was work by Beth Arthur, an early student of Hilton Leech, who became, and still remains, a successful and exceptionally-well-regarded painter in Sarasota where she is on the Faculty of Continued Education at the Ringling School. Many years after that show, I arranged workshops for her to present her creative teaching techniques in Michigan and in New Mexico under my own logo of "Katherine's World."

Of her painting, Beth wrote: "The blue cloud painting is called 'Sky Poetry,' my favorite, and

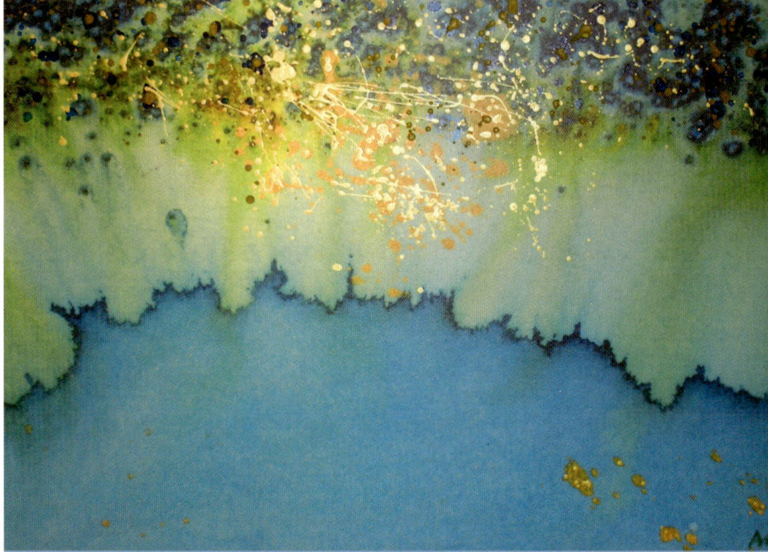

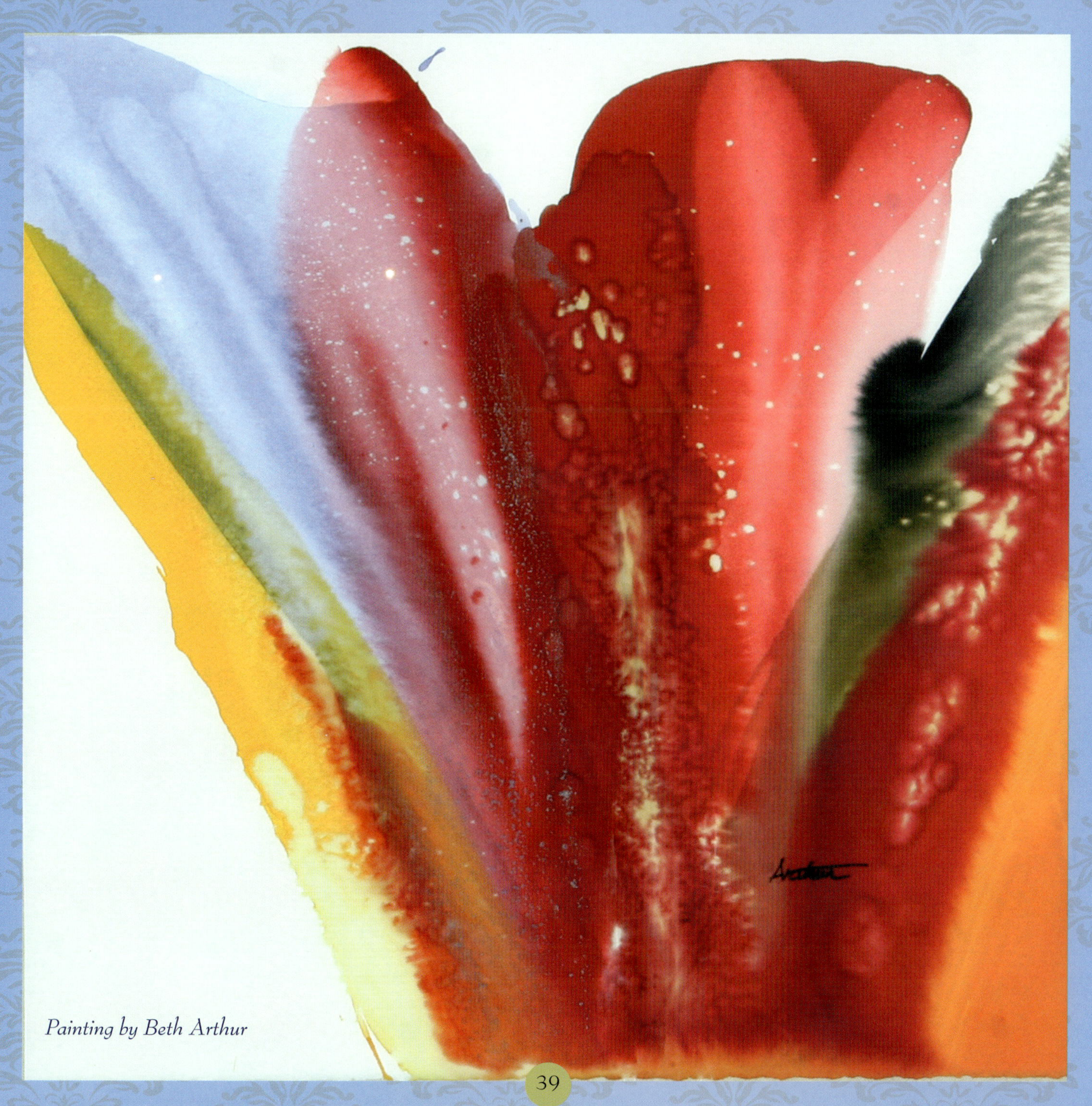

Painting by Beth Arthur

After Hilton Leech died in 1969, Leech Art School watercolor classes were taught by a series of visiting workshop instructors. The first of these was Marc Moon, A.W.S. A prolific painter and popular teacher in his home area of northeast Ohio, Marc won almost a hundred national and regional awards in his career of fifty-two years as an artist. His daughter, Lou Ann Moon Zimmerman, herself an accomplished artist with a gallery on Artists' Row in Augusta, Georgia, kindly let me use slides of her father's work for this book.

As the painting and photography workshops, at The Leech Studio, and abroad, grew in scope and popularity in the 1970s, I had a series of assistants to help me in the office. At least one of those, Helen Burkett, went on to become a career artist. Helen, who was originally from the Washington, D.C., area first came to the Studio as a student in 1975, and became my helper two years later. She, and her husband, Charles Marshall, became good friends of mine and Elden's. Charlie, whose father had been in the military, had lived in the Japanese island of Okinawa after the close of World War II. This gave him much in common with Elden and his interest in Oriental things.

Although always eager to learn more about color and composition, Helen, even at that time, had a unique vision of her own. "Harmony" is an example of the infinite variety of shapes and colors that make up the compelling mystery of the works in her early "Pilot" series. It is interesting to see how the earlier painting relates to a more recent work, "Magnolia Abstract." She says: "The main theme of my current work is an exploration in transparent watercolor of sunlight and shadow and the rhythm that evolves from the abstract design they create."

Helen and Charlie's life is a partnership devoted to art. Although keeping their residence in Sarasota, they spend much time on the road in their motor home, showing Helen's paintings - and winning prizes—at prestigious art festivals. Helen teaches and demonstrates for art groups across the country. Charlie handles business details, framing, photographing and printing. In spite of their busy schedule they take time out to visit grandchildren—and even a friend's Ninetieth Birthday celebration in Ohio!

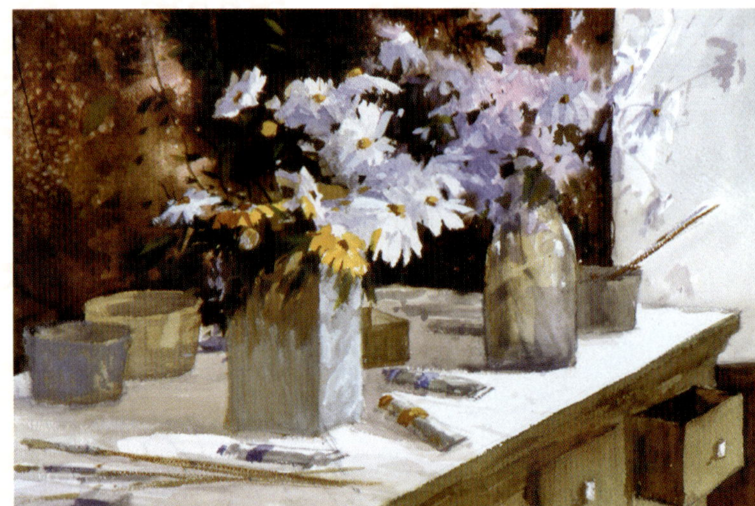

"Taboret" by Marc Moon

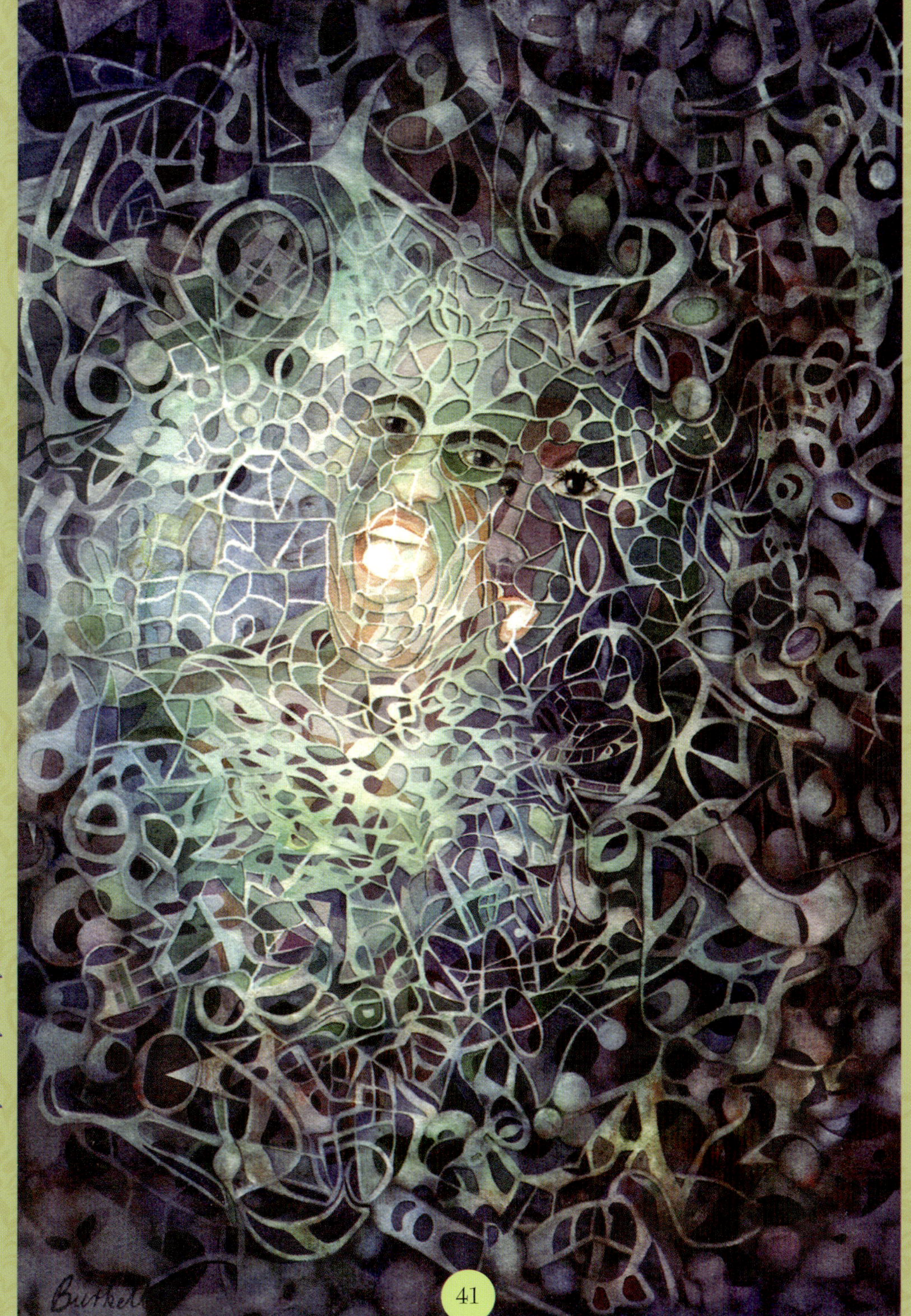

"Harmony" by Helen Burkett

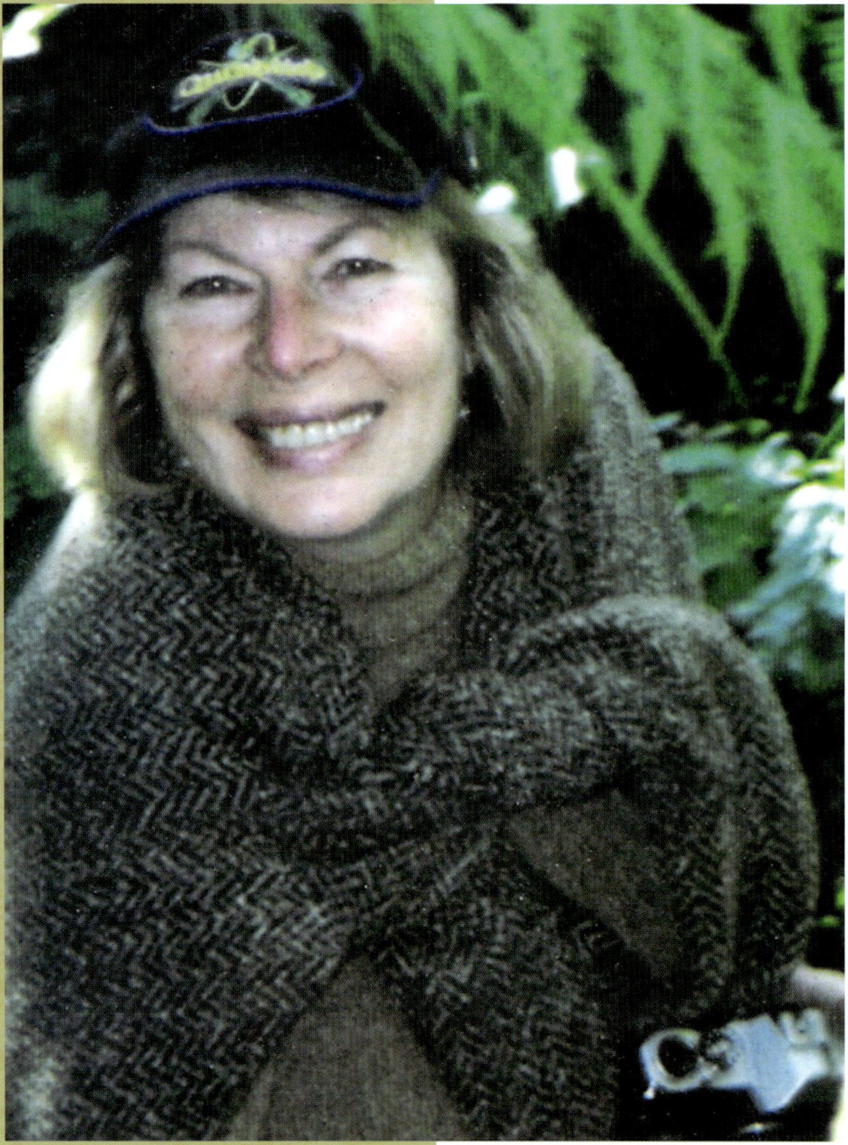

Photograph of Helen Burkett

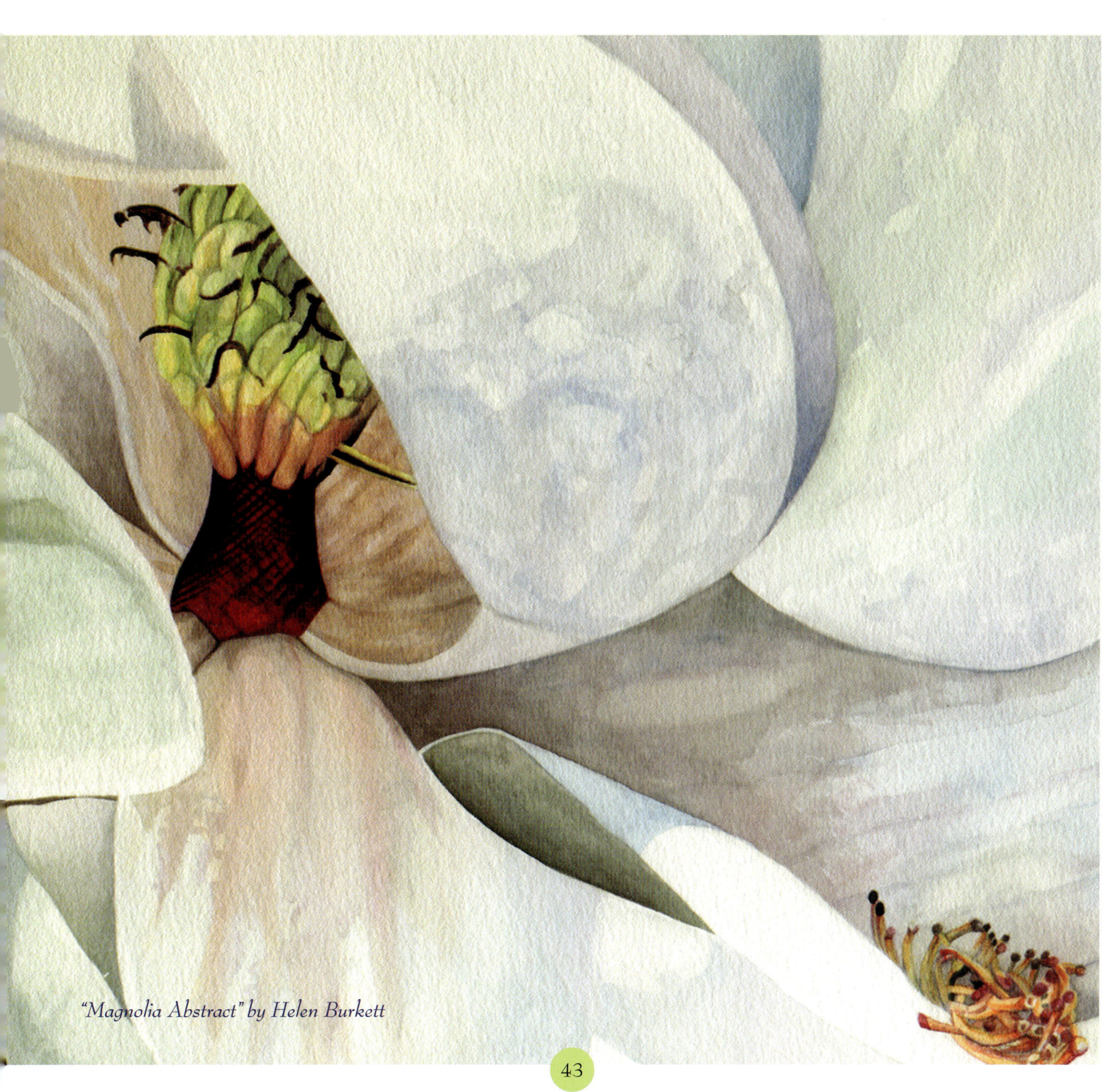

"Magnolia Abstract" by Helen Burkett

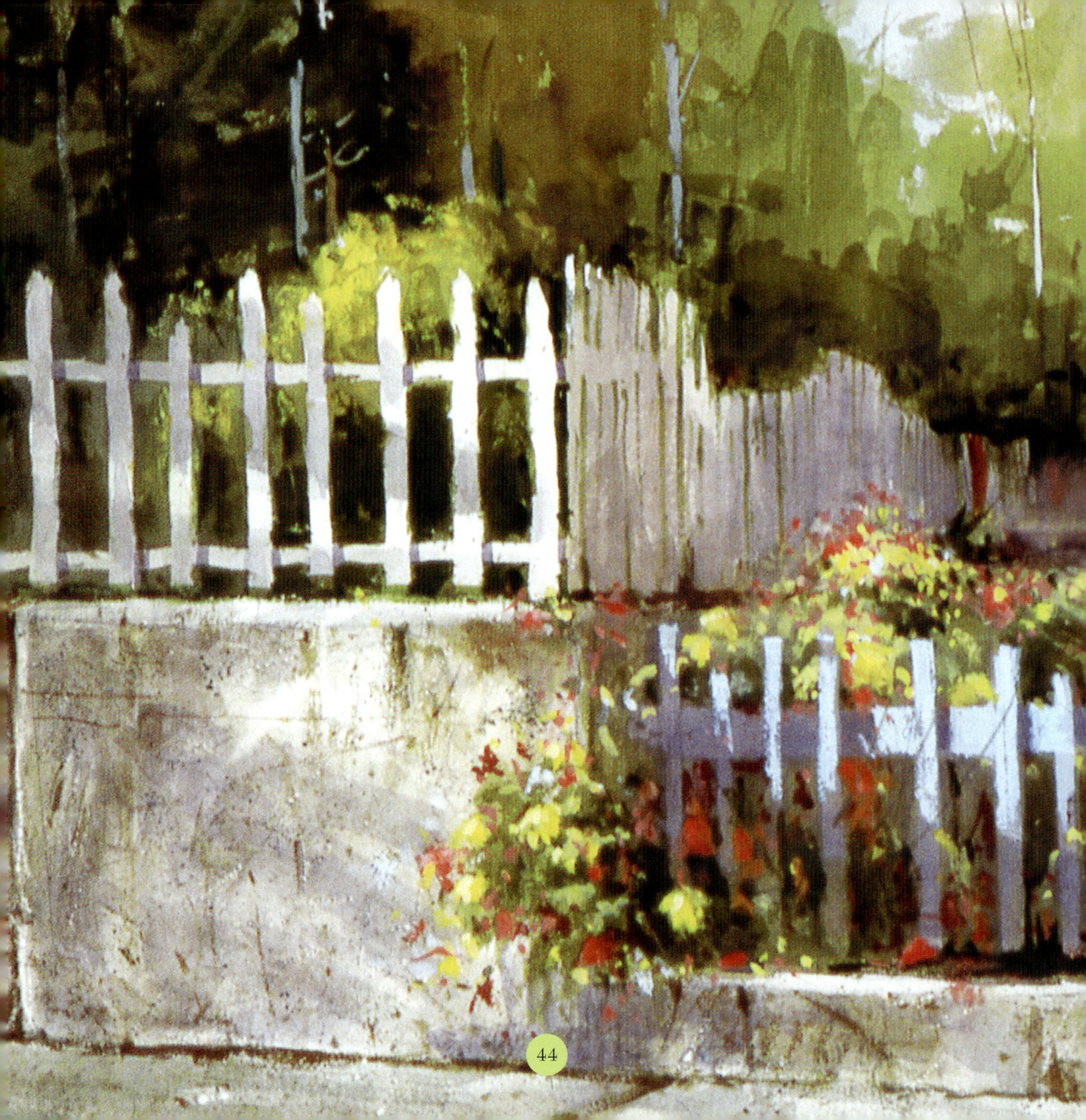

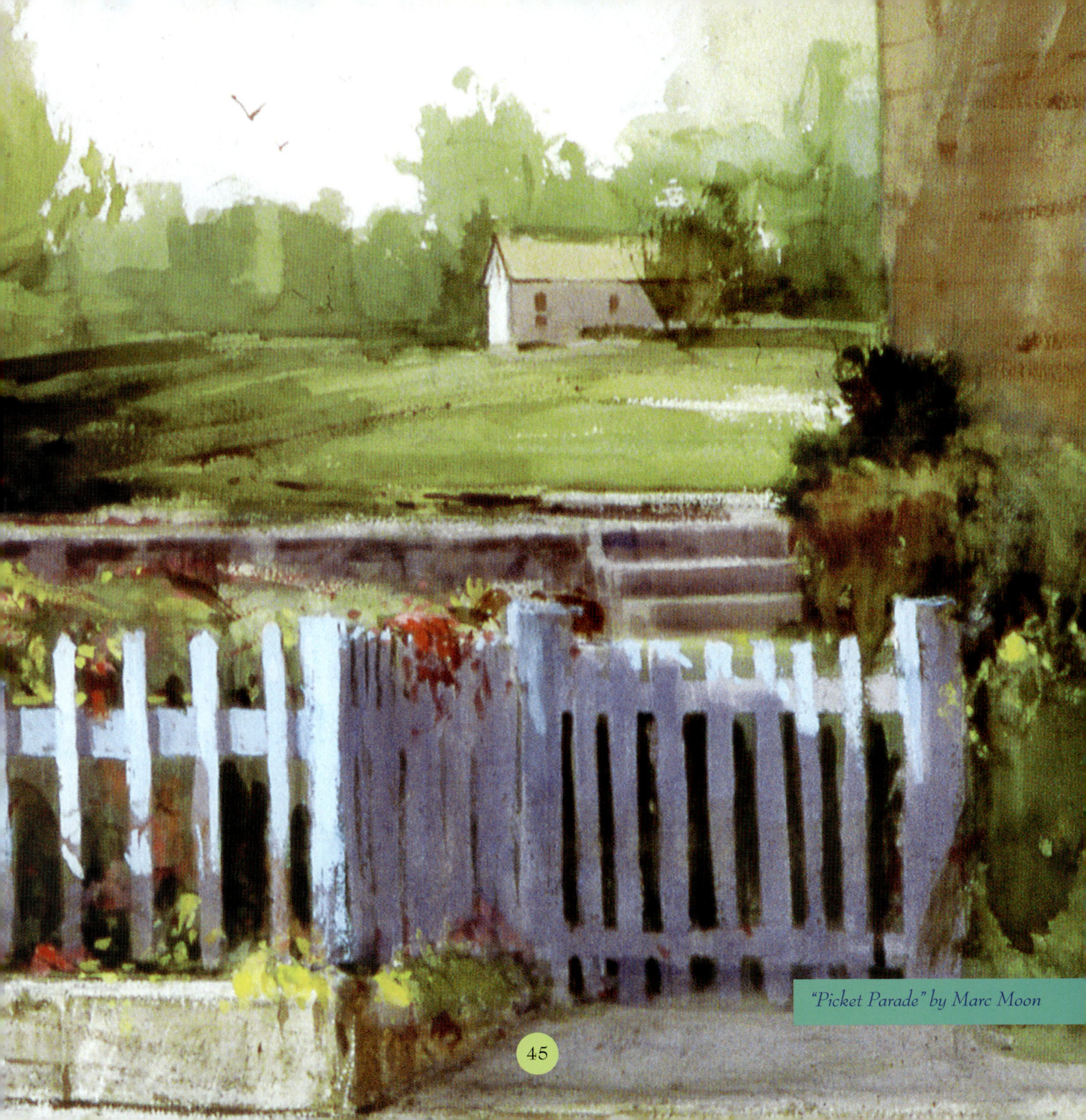

"Picket Parade" by Marc Moon

Montana Summers ●●●●

When traveling back and forth from Sarasota to Cape Cod each year began to seem burdensome to Elden and me, we decided to try the mountains instead of the seashore. One spring, with our friend painter Margaret Sturgis for company, I drove from Sarasota to Hendersonville, North Carolina, to search for a place for Elden's art school. I found a huge old three-story inn and we converted it into space for classes, with rooms to rent to students, as well as a gallery and craft store. When we hung an exhibition of paintings by Hilton Leech, he and Dorothy and Jerry came for the opening and spent the weekend with us in the inn. Through Eleanor Hodgins we met Ernest Hamlin Baker, *Time* cover illustrator, and had a show of his work. We enjoyed the mountain scenery with its waterfalls and misty valleys, but two indelible memories of the Hendersonville experience stand out: flatlander muscles shrieking from getting a three-story, 26-room, 6 bath, abandoned inn ready for occupancy; and the fun of buying baskets full of flowers and home-grown eatables every Saturday morning in the Farmers Market.

But I had always wanted to go camping and to see the American West, so the spring of 1960 we bought an umbrella tent and packed it and other camping supplies in our Nash Rambler and started out. Camping at that time was primitive, but delightfully uncrowded. Traveling at a leisurely pace, we went from state parks to national forests and parks of the Rocky Mountain West, exploring and getting to know our country. Our first stop was in Montana, to visit the Leeches. Hilton had art classes in the little town of Jeffers, across the River from Ennis, center of the Madison Valley ranching community, and famous for fly fishing. We took advantage of a campground set up for the fishermen in the tall cottonwood trees by the river to spend a few days visiting with the Leeches and enjoying a brief trip with Larry Lehman in his pickup to his ranch on Wigwam Creek. Larry, a student at the Leech Art School in Sarasota, had originally owned the land in Colorado which became the Air Force Academy. After selling that land, Larry became so enthusiastic about his new location in Montana that he persuaded the Leeches to follow him there. And, the Rowlands, too, as it turned out, for many decades to come.

That summer Elden and I, not knowing then if we would ever get out West again, camped our way through the Pacific Northwest and down to the Sacramento Valley in California to see his uncles and cousins, whom he had never met. Elden's impressions and memories from that trip resulted in large oil paintings, such as "Tioga Pass," "Monterey Cyprus," and "Yosemite," that became prize winners in the Abstract Impressionist Period of that decade.

In 1960 Elden and I went back to Montana to spend the entire summer and from that time on,

Montana has always had a happy feeling of "home" for me, a magical place to which I am anxious to return as often as I can. I hasten to say I have never spent a winter there, and I know they can be long and severe. But I do know that the landscape can be even more beautiful with an early spring or late fall blanket of wet snow than it is in the full bright sun of the summer months. Actually, the first time we experienced that fairyland of Montana covered-with-snow was on an August 19. It was so beautiful and exciting that the Leeches and the Rowlands rushed out to go to Ennis for chili and strawberry pie and then on up into the national forest to hike in the quiet of a pure white world.

But that's getting ahead of the story. The summer of the snow we were all in Virginia City, "living ghost town," high in the foothills of the Gravelly Range above the Madison Valley. Late in the summer of 1959 there had been a massive earthquake in the Yellowstone area, about 70 miles south of Ennis. There was danger of flooding from the Madison River so people were evacuated to Virginia City. The Leeches liked Virginia City so much that the next year they bought a log home on the top of a hill overlooking the town, and Elden and I followed them there.

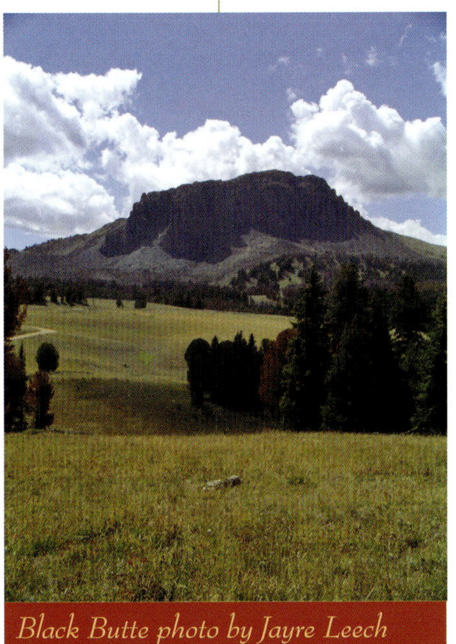

Black Butte photo by Jayre Leech

The center of the Alder Gulch gold rush in the 1860s, Virginia City was the second capital of Montana Territory. Old buildings still remained, many of them furnished as the stores and banks they had originally been along the boardwalk of Wallace Street. However, Virginia City was still alive and active. People lived there year round. The Madison County Court House stood grandly in the center of town. There was a post office, a library, a historical museum, a grocery store, and a place for tourists to rent horses to ride, in sometimes confusing juxtaposition to the buildings that were "museums." It was an interesting place from which to explore the surrounding mountains on the weekly painting excursions of the Leech art group.

When Elden and I arrived at Virginia City, Barbara Brook, monitor for the Leech Art Classes, after a valiant search, found Mrs. Gohn's house for us to rent. Mrs. Gohn's house, a weathered frame structure gently settling into the ground, had once been the home of a miner and his family. It had a bathroom, no hot water, cots in various bedrooms, all of which we supplemented with our camping equipment. Next to it was a fallen-down log cabin, surrounded by deep purple lilacs luxuriously

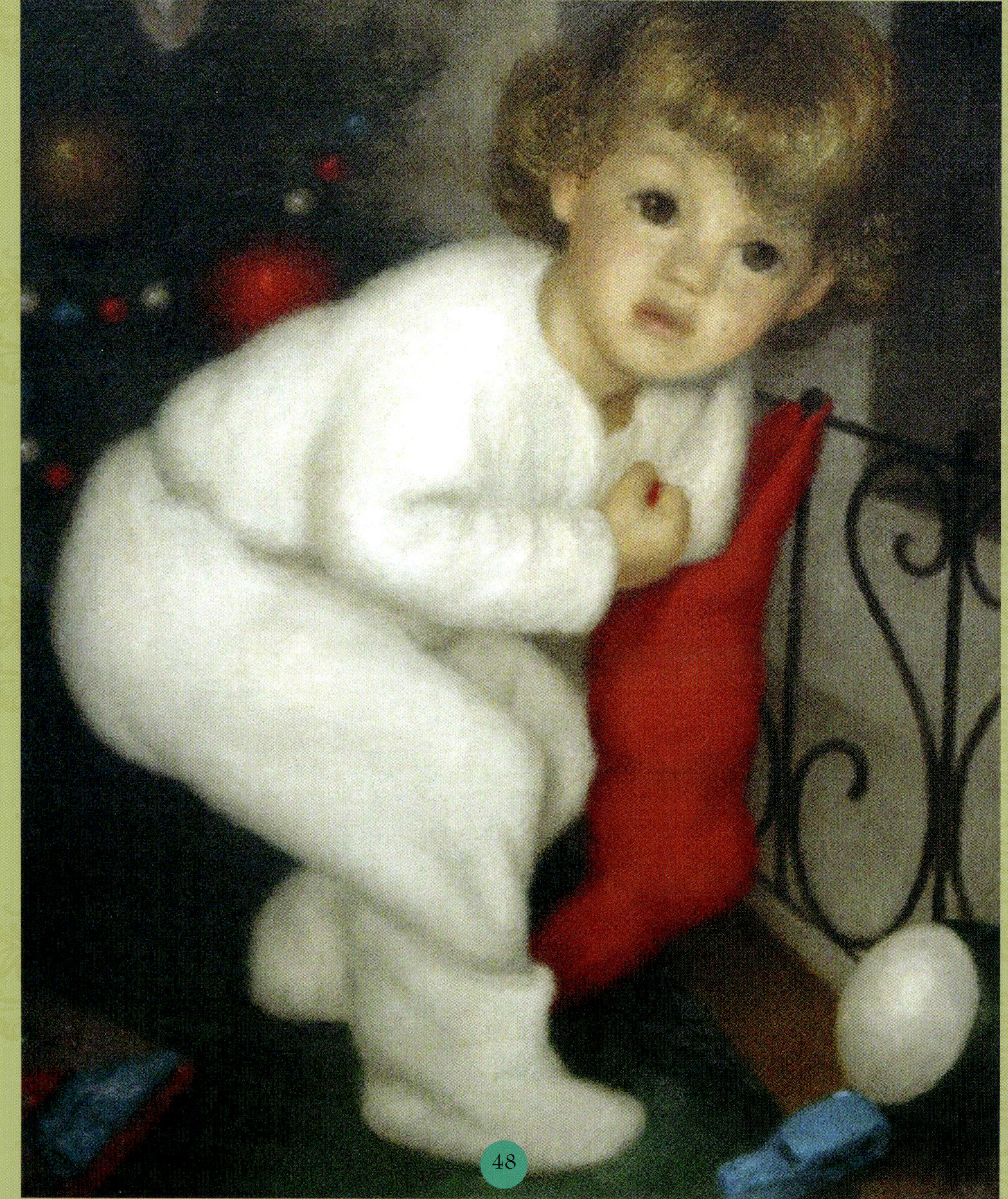

"Christmas Morning" by Dorothy Leech

48

blooming when we moved in. It was just down the hill from the Leeches' house. Mrs. Gohn's son, blinded in a mining accident, operated Bob's Place, the local bar located in the red brick building that had been the Territorial Capital. He could find by memory and touch any of the multitude of small items he had for sale, as well as faultlessly serving drinks.

Among Hilton's many interests were geology and minerals, artifacts of Native American peoples, and remnants of the rich history of mining around Virginia City. He had an easy rapport with people who sensed he was genuinely interested in their country. From the locals he was able to learn of out-of-the-way places to pan for gold or sapphires, or dig for amethyst, or search the tailing of the gold dredges for garnets. At that time, there were hardly any "no trespassing" signs at ghost towns or abandoned mines. He knew the owners of operating mines and learned the old rocky

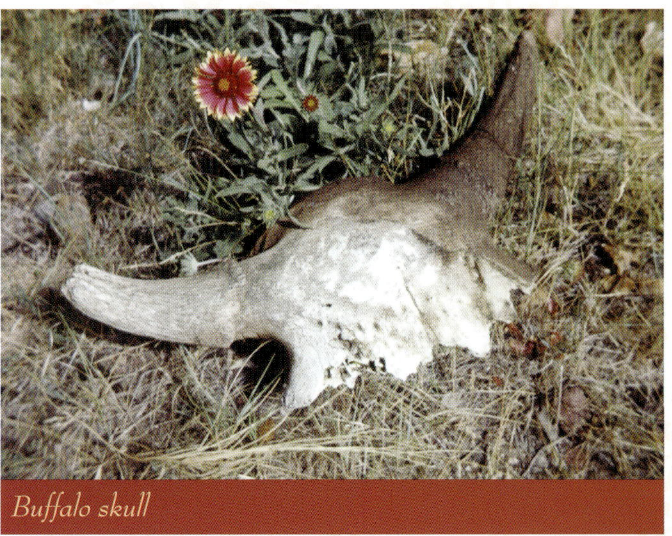
Buffalo skull

roads to follow exploring for good sites for the weekly artists picnic. Elden and I were privileged, often, to go with him on these exploratory trips, and then on the painting day itself we would take students in our station wagon. One of the favor spots was Black Butte, a volcanic core in the Gravellies. Dorothy enjoyed the excursions, too, but sometimes had to stay behind working on the covers she painted for her father's Dominion Steel Company Christmas issue. Her style was beautiful and unique, but time-consuming.

As we rambled the mountains we loved seeing wild animals and herds of free-ranging horses. We picked up "treasures," a dropped moose or elk antler, a cow or horse skull, or a curly sheep's horn, to bring home to suspend from an unused telephone pole behind the Leeches' house. Dorothy and I each found a prize—a buffalo skull. First, Dorothy found one and I yearned to find one, too. Then one evening, when I had driven Eleanor Fair up to Williams Gulch, Eleanor and I both had banner evenings. I wanted to get near enough to photograph a square-cut log cabin which I had seen from a distance and Eleanor was eager to have her first glimpse of a badger. Eleanor sat in the car listening to the evening calls of the many birds as I hiked up the draw to find the cabin. As I started back toward the car I spied the tip of a horn sticking up out of the gravel of the almost-dry streambed, and knew I had found a "buffalo." I dug it out with my bare hands and carried it, heavy and full of wet gravel, to the car and found that Eleanor had her wish. A badger had come

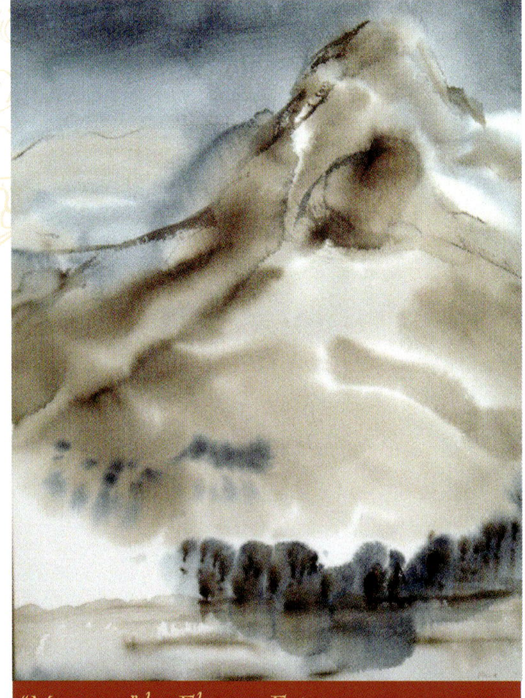

"Montana" by Eleanor Fair

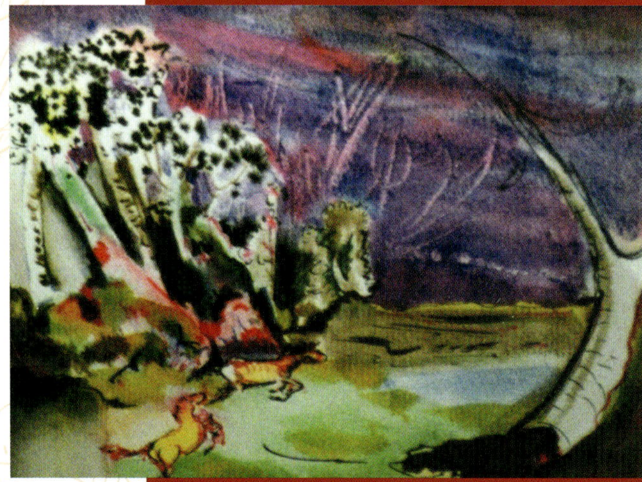

"Fantasy" by Bonnie Bausor Phipps

by, ambling quietly along while she watched the feisty creature from the safety of the car. Of such satisfying little incidents are large memories made—large enough to last a lifetime!

Eleanor Fair was from New York City, the librarian for a large life insurance company. She hoarded her vacation time to spend it with the Leech art group in the West. A gentle person, full of the wonder and joy of life, she had a very special natural talent for depicting her beloved Montana mountains in watercolor.

Although Elden enjoyed summers in Montana he felt more drawn to the seashore as a place to paint. After a few years he went back to spending summers teaching and painting in The East, getting to Cape Cod whenever he could. I sometimes went to join him there in the early spring and drove West across the northern U.S. One year I drove in to New York City and picked Eleanor Fair up and we, together with Bonnie Bausor (now Phipps, an Antioch college student who had been a helper at the Leech Studio in Sarasota) had hilarious travel adventures on the way West. Another summer, I drove Elsinore Budd, and her little poodle Susie, our friends from Tarrytown, New York, out to Virginia City and we shared a house there. Still another year, Dorothy Leech and I traveled from Florida to Virginia City in my new Open Road converted camper, the "Blue Beastie."

Sadly, Hilton Leech died suddenly in October of 1969 while checking out one of the old mining claims he had proved up on. A month or two before, he and

Dorothy had driven Jerry down to Fort Collins to start college at Colorado State. Jerry, and friends and family, came back to Virginia City for funeral services in the little Episcopal Church with the Tiffany windows. He is buried in the Montana he loved so much—in the little cemetery on top of the hill across Alder Gulch from their house.

I had been in Virginia City earlier in that summer but left for an adult session at Principia College, a Christian Science School at Elsah, Illinois, before going on to Sarasota to start planning for the winter season at the Leech Studio. At the end of October, when Dorothy was ready to come back to Florida, I flew out to drive her home in their station wagon. As my plane descended to land at Bozeman I was enthralled by my first aerial view of the patterns and textures of Montana covered with snow! I wasn't quite as thrilled with the snow as we drove the long way through

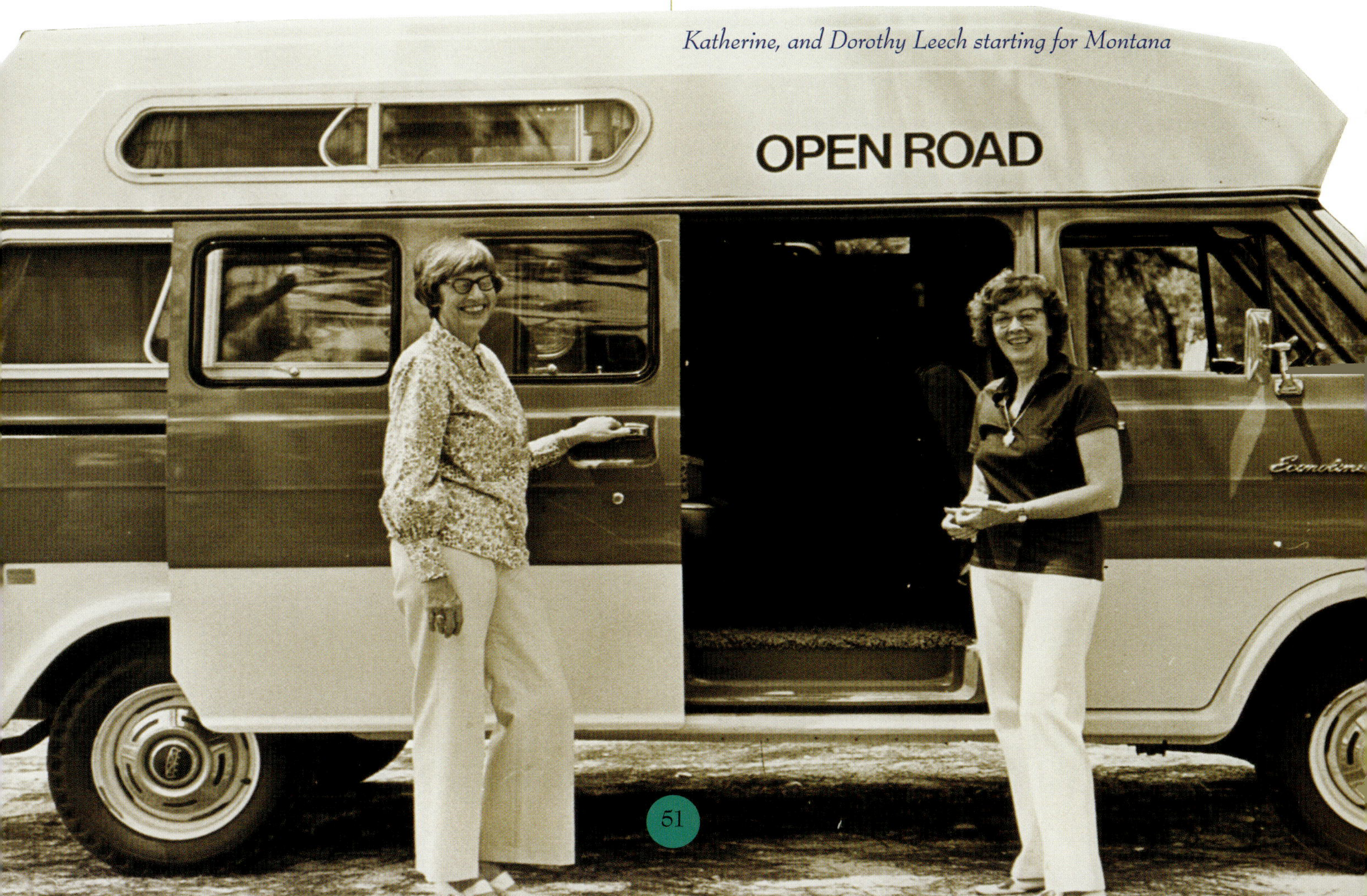

Katherine, and Dorothy Leech starting for Montana

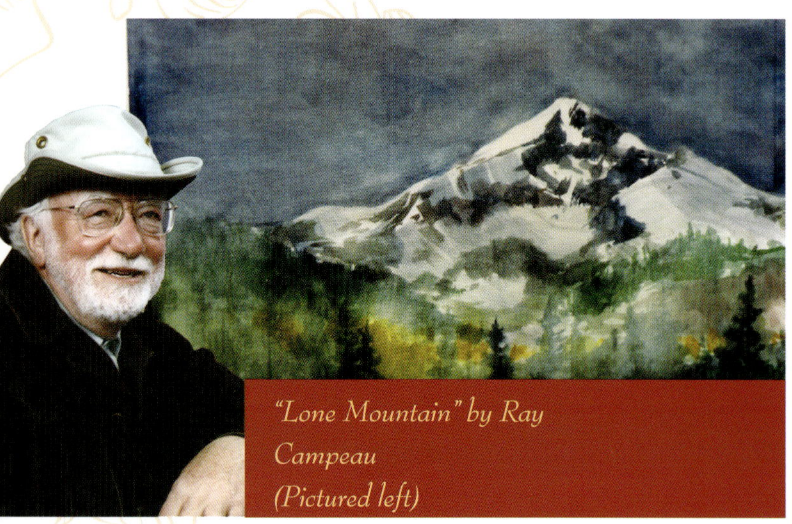

"Lone Mountain" by Ray Campeau (Pictured left)

Yellowstone Park because some high passes were closed. However, Dorothy's attitude of strength and calm was reassuring, as was a friendly truck driver's advice of "Hang Loose!", and we got over Togwatee Pass, our usual route out of the mountains to Dubois, Wyoming, without difficulty.

Hilton Leech's death was a blow, but everyone wanted the classes in Montana, as well as the Art School in Florida, to continue. In Sarasota, this was accomplished by setting up workshops with visiting instructors. In Montana, Ray Campeau became a continuing instructor, with occasional visiting teachers. Ray was born in Butte, Montana, and still holds strong ties to his native city. However, he and his lovely wife, Kay, lived in a wonderful big old Victorian house in Bozeman. Among his many other activities, Ray was head of the innovative art department at Bozeman High School where the students as a group bought

paintings for a permanent collection to hang in the corridors of the school. Ray arranged for a show of Elden's paintings to be held at the school in September of 1984. On the way home from the Canadian Rockies Two Arts trip, Alice DeCaprio and I stopped in Bozeman for the opening of the show and then drove to Denver for the National Carousel Convention. Kay was a school librarian. Now both retired, Kay and Ray continue to be active mainstays in the Montana art scene. Ray is busy with the Main Stope Gallery in Butte, and Kay is connected with the Symphony in Bozeman.

The spring of 1970, Elden went up to teach in New York State and I was to fly from Sarasota to meet him and we'd drive out to Montana together. It was fortunate I was not going to drive because a few days before leaving, while I was pruning a Brazilian pepper bush, the ladder fell beneath me and my right shoulder was broken. Although a broken shoulder cannot be put in a cast, by the end of the summer the shoulder was healed and all was well. I've continued to go to Montana, at least for a few weeks, for many of the summers ever since, most recently to visit Jayre at her ranch in the Madison valley.

Jerry Leech has made Montana her home. After spending a few years in Sarasota when her mother needed her, she took the Virginia City house and later bought land in the Madison Valley. Her first place was on Wigwam Creek, part of the same acreage that Larry Lehman had shown us in the summer of 1960. More

recently she has acquired a ranch on the east side of the
Madison Valley south of Ennis. She bought property which
had a great old double log barn and built a lovely modern
home called "Hagion," on Bear Creek Loop. She trains
horses, is skilled in horsemanship and roping, participates
in cattle drives, is an active part of community and church
affairs—a true Montanan. Part of her story is the change
of the spelling of her name from "Jerry" to "Jayre." She
was named Jerry Allyn, for Jerry Farnsworth and another
man painter. But when she went to college, a girl with two
men's names caused dormitory registrars problems, so she
changed it to "Jayre" a unique name for a strong individual.
She shares her love of her state, and her life, through
vivid e-mail descriptions and perfectly-focused digital
photographs.

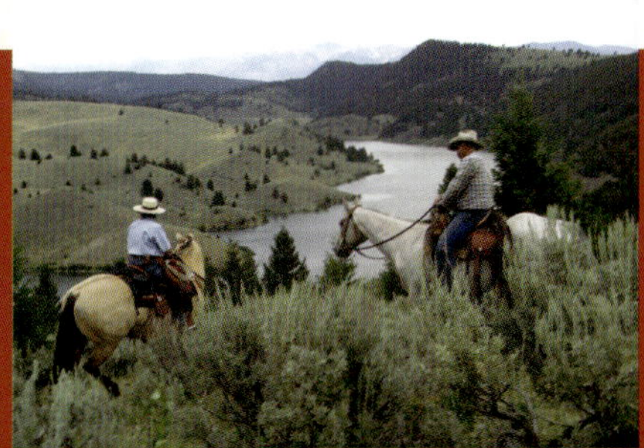

*Jayre and neighbor rancher
Kevin Boltz*

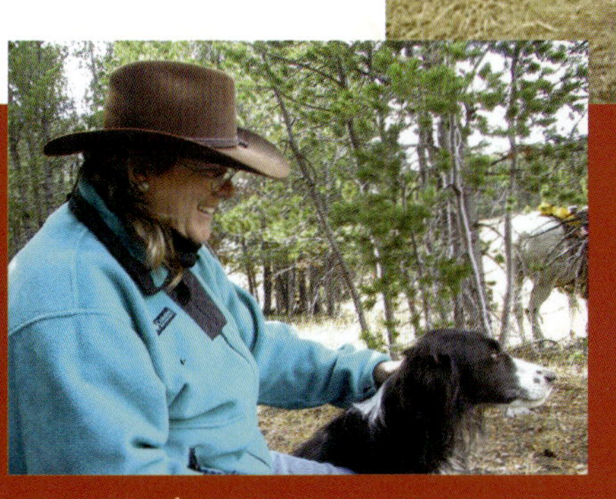

Jayre Leech

Jayre Leech on Gideon

Friends' Trips ● ● ●

The Field Trips of the Friends of the Arts and Sciences were immediately popular after that non-profit group organized in 1963 at the Hilton Leech Studio. Starting gradually with occasional local bus trips managed by members, the program expanded. And as the program grew, I grew into planning and managing the trips. Chartered as an "educational, non-profit arts and sciences corporation," destinations of The Friends' trips could include an endless variety of fascinating places. There seemed to be no limits, as long as the purpose was to be "educational." As the popularity of the Friends' activities and trips grew, the local Field Trips were expanded to include travels farther afield. These were known as "Foreign Tours." Defined, loosely, as "Field Trips," and "Foreign Tours," two membership committees were formed to choose destinations, "Field Trips" being bus trips in Florida and nearby states in the Southern United States.

In the Foreign Tours, members, and guests, if there was room, traveled world-wide. Being a small, private, organization we tried not to compete with the big commercial agencies going to tourist meccas in Europe and the big cities of the world, but chose far-out less-traveled destinations: The U.S. West, Canada, the Maya, Aztec and Inca civilizations in Mexico and Central America, the Galapagos Islands off of South America at Ecuador, the British Isles, and China. Three of these -the Maya ruins, first in 1966, the Galapagos Islands in 1969, and China in 1980, stand out as major experiences.

The Maya

The Yucatan Peninsula of Mexico, with its classic Maya sites of Chichen Itza and Uxmal, was chosen as the first Foreign Tour. Pat Matthews, a friend of the Leeches, through her agency, Travel Incorporated, planned and arranged the details. I, as office secretary of The Friends, publicized it, informed the members, and handled money and reservations. It was the custom that one free trip would accrue to an organizing group such as ours. It was decided that I, as part of the loose barter system under which the Leech Studio and The Friends operated, would be the one to go along on the trip and act as liaison. This set a precedent which endured for decades and led to countless learning adventures. Since Pat Matthews was not able to go on this first trip, my experience as Tour Escort began abruptly, and members of the group, and I, all began to learn together.

We had a memorable time, and later went back to many Maya sites, including Tikal in Guatemala. Elden overcame his reluctance to fly and went with the group on the Christmas trip in 1973. We flew from Miami to Belize for a few days and then to Guatemala City, for an overnight land tour toTikal. A few of our brave-hearted members climbed the steep stepped-stone surfaces of the pyramids that were so typical of the Maya civilization. But I sat and tried to calm the butterflies in my stomach as I watched them from a safe distance. However, at Tikal one of the huge, dramatic pyramids had not yet been cleared of the lush growth of trees and vines that covered it on all sides. Except, previous adventurers had left a path winding up one side, using banyan roots as toeholds and thick ropes of vines as handholds, making it possible to scramble up to look out from the top. With Elden (who definitely was NOT afraid of heights) as my moral support I climbed to that secluded spot and we sat marveling in the quiet. As we looked out at the tips of pyramids—those cleared and those still not excavated—showing above the dense tangled jungle, we tried to visualize how it might have been at the height of the Maya

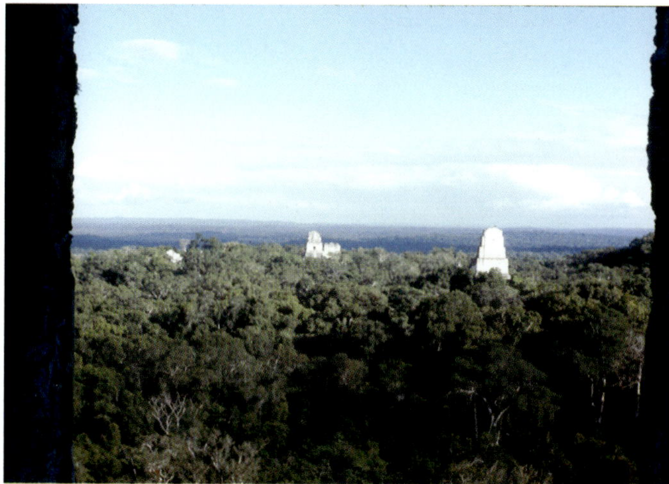

Tikal from top of pyramid four

civilization. Suddenly, the quiet was shattered by a grunting, growling, chorus close to us, answered by other piercing howls fading into the vastness of the jungle. Howler monkeys! A memorable experience for us, perhaps a small hint of what it was like for the Maya living there at the height of their civilization, before their collapse in the Eighth and Ninth Centuries, and Spanish conquest and colonization began early in the Sixteenth Century.

After we saw Tikal, Elden and I were part of a small group that traveled to Flores to spend the night on Lake Peten Itza. I could not have foretold that, many years later, my grandnephew, Kevin Robert Schwarz, would one day be staying at Flores while he led an excavation of a site in the Peten as part of his Ph.D. thesis in archaeology.

The highlight of the drive back over the "main highway" to Guatemala City the next day was being held up for hours while we all "supervised" the freeing of a truck stuck in the mud at a ford in the river.

Ecuador and The Galapagos Islands

The Friends' trip the spring of 1969 was in two parts: Ecuador, the beautiful high mountainous country on the west coast of South America, and the Galapagos Islands, 100 miles west of the mainland in the Pacific Ocean. Pat Matthews, always excellent in planning for groups, and accompanying them, was with us. She had previously been a flight attendant, in the days when it was necessary for them to have nurses' training. Charming and gracious, she, although petite, was a source of strength for trip participants, even though she did have health problems herself.

The group flew from Miami to Guayaquil, Ecuador's seaport, and was driven in cars to the capital city of Quito, high in the Andes Mountains. At an overnight stop, we visited the native villages of the Colorado Indians, who painted their bodies with the red dye of the achiote seed, believing that blood-red is a protection against evil spirits. As a gesture of hospitality which could not be refused, they offered the experience of having their faces and hands painted red to the two leaders of the group. In our case, that applied to Pat and me. Two things stand out in my memory of that "privilege" I was given: the cool sensation of that thick bright red paste as a dark hand applied it to my skin; and the look on the faces of the Indians as they began to understand that what they were hearing from a small recorder Hilton was holding was their own voices.

After a few days seeing the sights of beautiful and historic Quito (at 9,350 feet surrounded by volcanic peaks) and colorful crafts in native markets of surrounding villages, we left to return to Guayaquil by the "autoferro," a one-car electric train. As coordinator of the group, I was customarily given the aisle seat directly behind the driver of a vehicle. On the "autoferro," Dorothy Leech sat by me next to the window. These were fine seats for taking in the gorgeous scenery of the high mountains and seeing the small red steam engines approaching us on the same narrow gauge line our vehicle used. However, not so fine when problems with our motor required a mechanic almost literally sitting in our laps as he struggled to get us moving, and out of the way of those approaching steam engines. A brief look in 2008 at Wikipedia on the Internet shows that the ottoferro, which it describes as "an antiquated bus complete with brakes that feed on sand, mounted on a train's chassis and fitted with a diesel engine," is still running.

At the time The Friends' groups went to the Galapagos Islands in 1969, travel from mainland Ecuador was usually by boat. A few bunks for adventurous travelers had been put on the small freighter which went from Guayaquil to supply the needs of the Islanders. However, Pat Matthew, because of her Florida travel agency, was able to find air transportation to the Islands for The Friends' group. Once there, we went from island to island by small motor launches, and stayed at local accommodations ashore. We were well supplied with local guides, one of whom was young Tui DeRoy, who later became a famous environmentalist and nature photographer. We were able to roam freely among the animals but understood we should not take advantage of their lack of timidity, even as we marveled at it.

It had been planned that some of our members would return to the U.S. at the end of the mainland portion of the trip and I would escort that group, thereby missing the Galapaos Islands. However, plans changed. Hilton Leech had not been feeling well and it was decided the Leeches and Pat would leave and go to New Orleans. Pat's husband, Dr. Lamar Matthews, had arranged for Hilton to be treated in a famous clinic there. This meant that I needed to go to the Islands to escort that group back to the U.S. when the time came. I was delighted to have the Galapagos experience, although I did not have proper boots for the rocky volcanic trail that led to a farm in the hills to which we were invited for lunch. Nonetheless, I chose not to ride a horse as the others did.

A vivid memory remains of the last days on the Galapagos of Hilton sitting on the beach engaged in one of his enthusiasms—hunting rocks! The volcanic sand contained small polished bits of peridot—a translucent green semi-precious stone, often used for jewelry. Hilton was first to find them, as he always had been, whether it be fossil hunting, or looking for Indian arrow heads, or sharks teeth on a white Florida beach, or panning for gold or sapphires in a cold Montana stream.

China

President Nixon's trip in 1972 opened the People's Republic of China to visitors from the United States and competition began among groups and agencies to be the first to visit the country that had been so long closed. Mary Duncan, Chairman of the Friends' Foreign Trips Committee, already a world traveler, was eager to add China to her list. In 1979, she contacted a world class agency in West Palm Beach and began to work out an itinerary. I felt it was too ambitious for our small organization. However, with Mary Duncan in charge, things moved forward. A China Study Group met at the Leech Studio with China scholars as speakers. Soon twenty-five persons were signed up to leave May 3, 1980, on a three-week China Classical Tour arranged for the Friends of the Arts and Sciences by Lindblad Travel, Inc. I went in my usual capacity of Tour Escort. Elden did not want to go and we were told single rooms would not be available so Ione Shriver and I shared a room. Ione was a fine artist, an experienced world traveler, and a long-standing friend of mine and Elden's.

The trip to China was a dream for me as a tour escort. I shepherded the group to San Francisco, and then on to Hong Kong. There we were met by a skilled Lindblad escort, who stayed with us for the entire three weeks. We also had a full-time representative of the Chinese national government for the entire trip, and local guides joined us in different locations. Most of the hotels were clean and comfortable, but not yet Westernized. The food was bountiful; a variety of dishes of vegetables and rice with fowl and seafood, each person served himself/herself from a Lazy Susan so meals were satisfying, but not too heavy.

At Hong Kong The Friends group was given a

welcome dinner at the Lindblad Apartment on Victoria Peak with its spectacular view of the Harbor ablaze with lights far below. After two or three days of sightseeing at the British Colony and an evening trip to Kowloon on a Chinese junk we entered the Republic of China by train.

From Canton, on the way to Kweilin, we had what was one of the most fascinating air flights of my life as we flew over the amazing land formations of the Li River Valley. There they were—the distinctive geologic Karst formations rounded and softened by lush greenery and encased in misty light—which I had seen so often in Chinese paintings. I had always thought such ethereal landscapes had to have come from the artists' imaginations. But here was the real thing! And they were no less enchanting the next day from a small boat on the river itself—a whole day of leisurely watching the farmers at their huts along the banks and the fishermen tending their cormorants as they practiced the age-old art of letting the birds do the fishing for them.

From that memorable beginning we traversed from one historic city to another: from water buffalo guided by farmers knee-deep in watery rice fields in the southeast to the Forbidden City in Peking in the northeast, there was something new every day. (At that time, the capital city was just beginning to be referred to as Beijing.) There were throngs of people everywhere, people moving purposefully about on foot and on bicycles, with the only cars being a few official Government limousines. The people on the streets gave the impression of being lean and strong, pulling carts and rickshaws and carrying heavy burdens on their backs. The people were friendly, young people, especially, wanting to try to practice their English by talking with us. Parents would hold up their cute babies for us to photograph. We were taken to see their highly-advanced hospitals and shining kindergartens where the children lustily sang for us. On one memorable morning I came out of our hotel in Shanghai and happened upon a large group of Chinese people practicing Tai Chi in a small park. The peace and quiet and calm beauty in the midst of the big city was, indeed, memorable.

I was surprised that we were, in that time still under the rule of Mao Tse-tung, not restricted in moving around by ourselves. We were simply told to carry a letterhead with us from the hotel in which we were staying. If we became confused and didn't know how to find our group again we were to show the letterhead as our identification. During one afternoon sightseeing by chartered bus one of our members wanted to go to a certain shop to which she had the directions. The guides encouraged her to do it on her own and she got off and disappeared, one head of white hair, in a sea of black-haired people surging along the wide sidewalk. She got back to the hotel for dinner, with no adventure to tell about except that she got the precious treasure she needed to find for a friend.

Shopping was sandwiched in between visits to

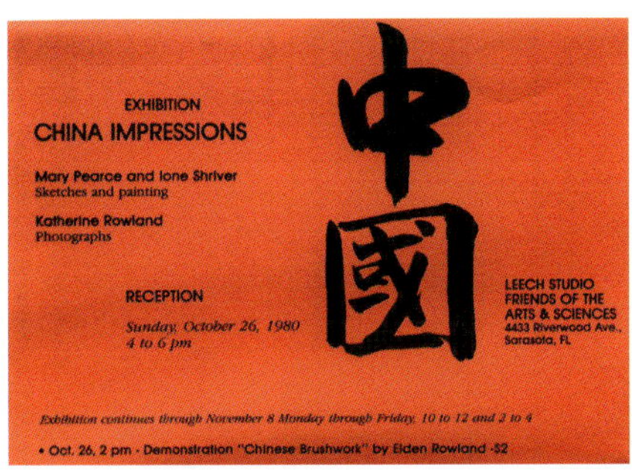

China Impressions

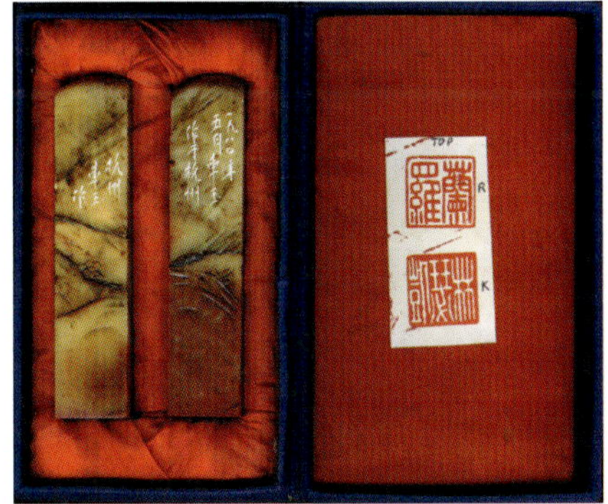

Chops

beautiful gardens, and pagodas, and Buddhist temples, and a visit to the zoo to see a panda, and the avenue of animal sculpture leading to the Ming tombs, and a ride on the Yangtze River, and to artisans making the famous Chinese cut-outs. And, of course, the Great Wall of China! Some of us climbed the steps in its wide expanse along with other hardy tourists and were rewarded by looking back and seeing our tourist bus a tiny speck at the point of entry.

Although not an enthusiastic shopper, I could not resist the fascinating array of art materials in the government stores as the perfect souvenirs for Elden, with his interest in Chinese calligraphy. Five-inch wide flat Hake brushes, and a mammoth pointed brush, ink sticks, and a box of paste vermillion ink, were beautiful as well as practical. And beautifully carved seals called " chops," signature stones, one that says "Rowland" and one that says "Katherine," cradled in soft red sateen in a decorative box, to this day remain treasured reminders of The Friends' 1980 trip to China.

Elden designed the invitation for "Impressions of China," an exhibition of sketches by Ione Shriver and Mary Pearce and photographs by Katherine Rowland that was held at the Leech Studio Galleries the following season.

The Caribbean

The Caribbean islands were good destinations for trips over the Christmas holidays. On a trip to Trinidad and Tobago, an evening small boat trip gave us a close-up view of waves of elegant scarlet ibis floating down to spend the night in great rookeries among the deep green of the mangrove islands. Back at the hotel, the lobby Christmas tree was decorated with flocks of red origami ibis, repeating the festive color scheme.

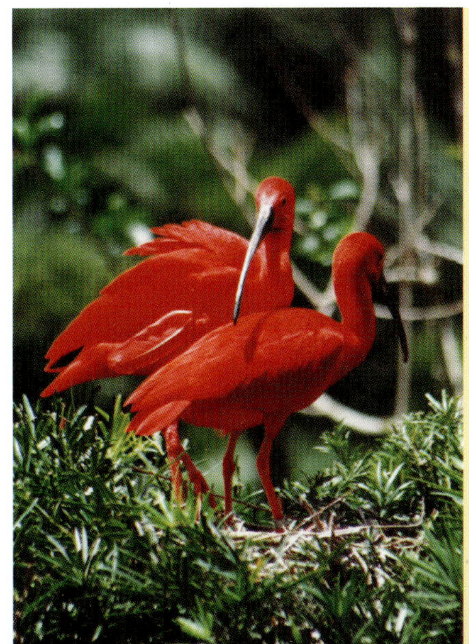

Scarlet ibis

Two Arts Travels ● ● ●

It was a happy scene of good camaraderie when forty-two painters and photographers gathered at the home studio of watercolorist Valfred Thelin in Ogunquit, Maine, in late September of 1981. The group was nearing the end of its Two Arts in Nature Traveling Workshop to Maine, Nova Scotia and New Brunswick, of which I was the Tour Director. We were all buoyed up by the events of the past two weeks painting and photographing and enjoying the beautiful scenery of that dramatic and historic part of the United States and Canada. It had all been so excitingly different from what we were used to in sub-tropical Florida whence we had come.

Comments and reminiscences flew back and forth as several of us worked husking fresh sweet corn for a "Down Maine" picnic at Val's house. Even the prospect of husking more than eighty ears of corn (at least two apiece) did not daunt us, it was so pleasant on the cantilevered back deck near the pines that framed the view toward Perkins Cove. We remembered the trip getting off to a hilarious start when Val and his friend Deidre O'Flaherty (later his wife) had turned up two weeks before at the Portland Airport in bright red lobster suits to meet the Sarasota contingent of the group .

Val, a renowned artist and member of the American Watercolor Society, had been the painting and sketching instructor for the workshop and James H. "Pete" Carmichael, nationally-recognized nature photographer whose work appeared regularly in *National Wildlife Magazine*, had been the photography instructor. They chose locations in which to work, gave help in the field, and presented demonstrations at our over-night stops. I, as tour director for the Hilton Leech Art School of Sarasota, had planned and publicized the workshop and went on the trip to keep everything moving smoothly and pay the bills. The instructors' assistants were Flo Singer and Margarette Mead, both skilled in their fields and helpful to students and instructors alike.

My assistant was Shirley Hummel. Shirley met every occasion with cheerful peppiness, from corralling luggage so bus departures could happen on time, to playing lively music on any piano that became available. She was also a photographer, later became an instructor

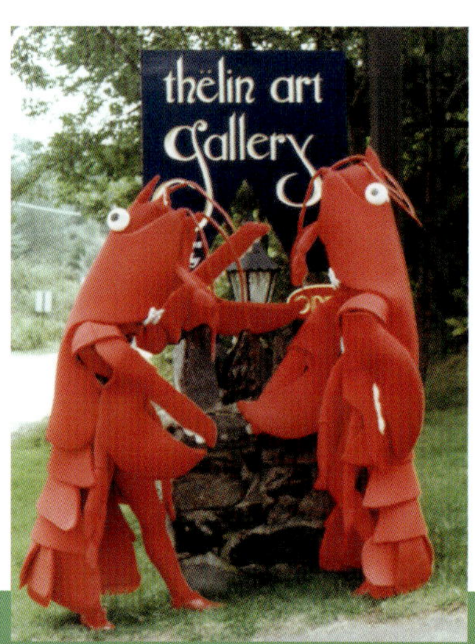

Red lobsters

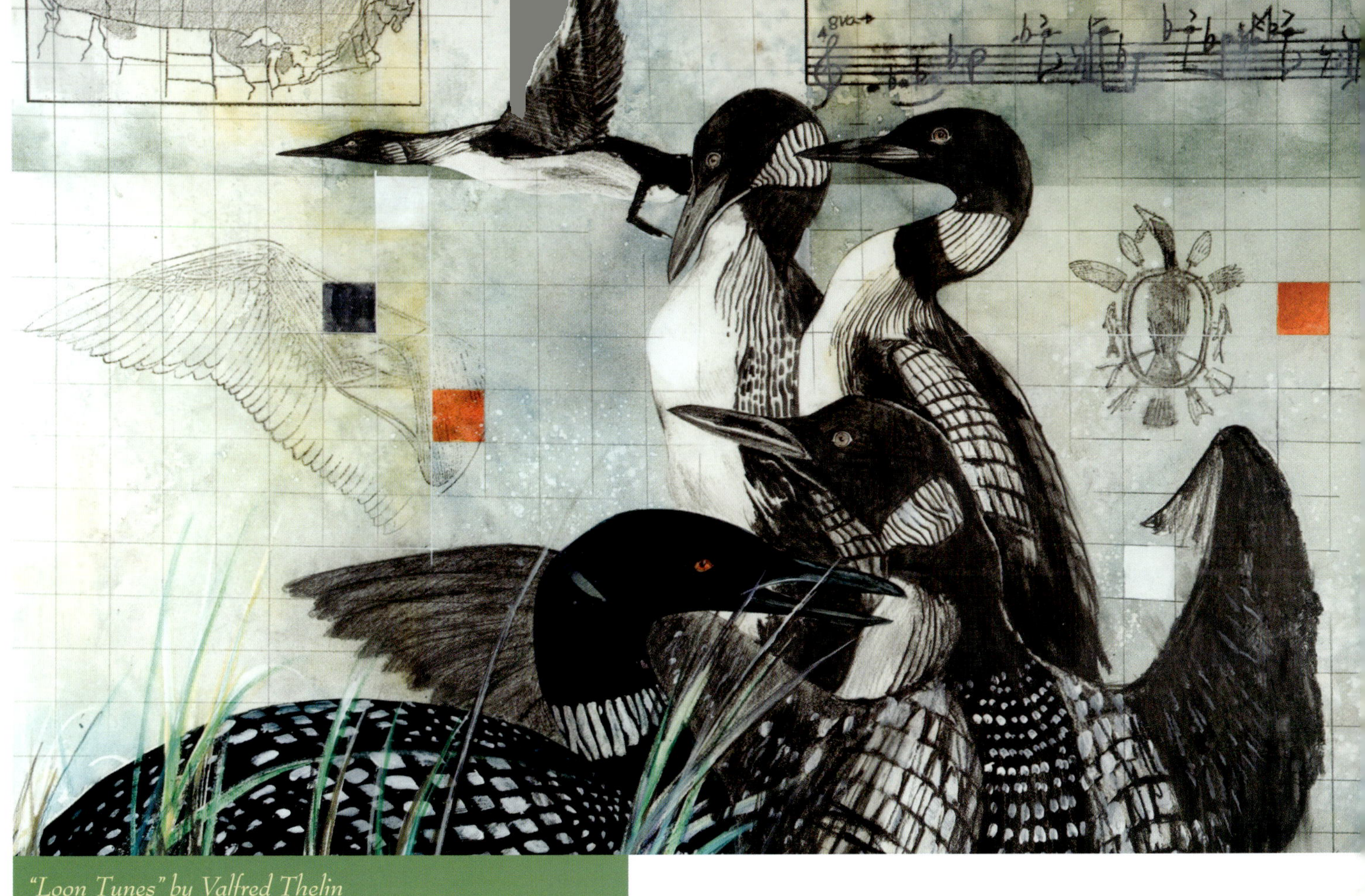

"Loon Tunes" by Valfred Thelin

in the Leech Studio, and went on thirteen of the Two Arts Traveling Workshops. For this book, Shirley has graciously provided me with many images taken from her website http://www.pbase.com/maranda1935, amazing galleries of the beauties of the natural world.

On the Down East trip, Margarette Mead was a photography assistant, although she soon became an instructor herself. Margarette had first come to the Leech Studio photography workshops to learn to take pictures of Amity, her small daughter. When

Margarette began to teach she often used slides of Amity to illustrate fine points of focus, depth of field, composition, etc. So, as I watched the mother grow in confidence and success with her photography I also vicariously watched the daughter grow from a toddler to a very attractive young woman.

Margarette and I grew in mutual respect and affection. She was extremely thoughtful and helpful during Elden's last illness. After Pete Carmichael withdrew as the instructor on the Two Arts Traveling

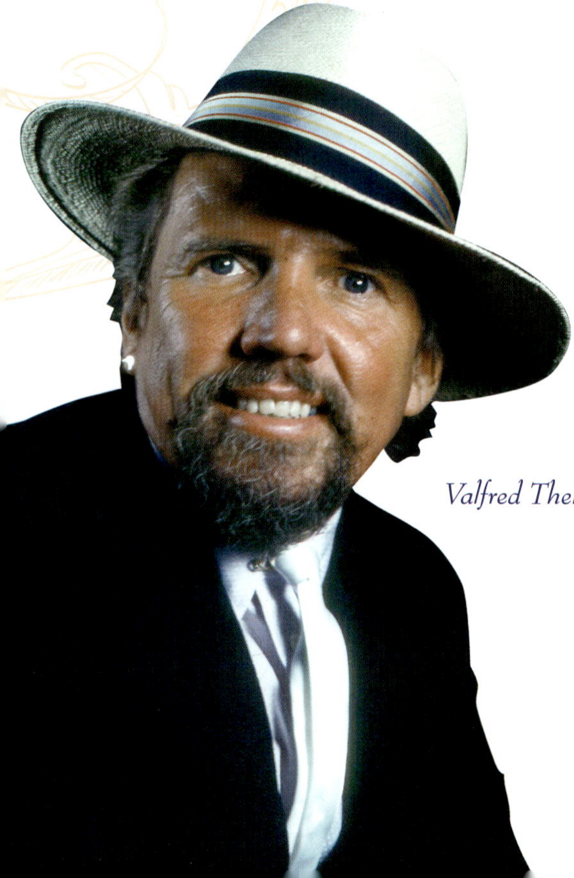

Valfred Thelin

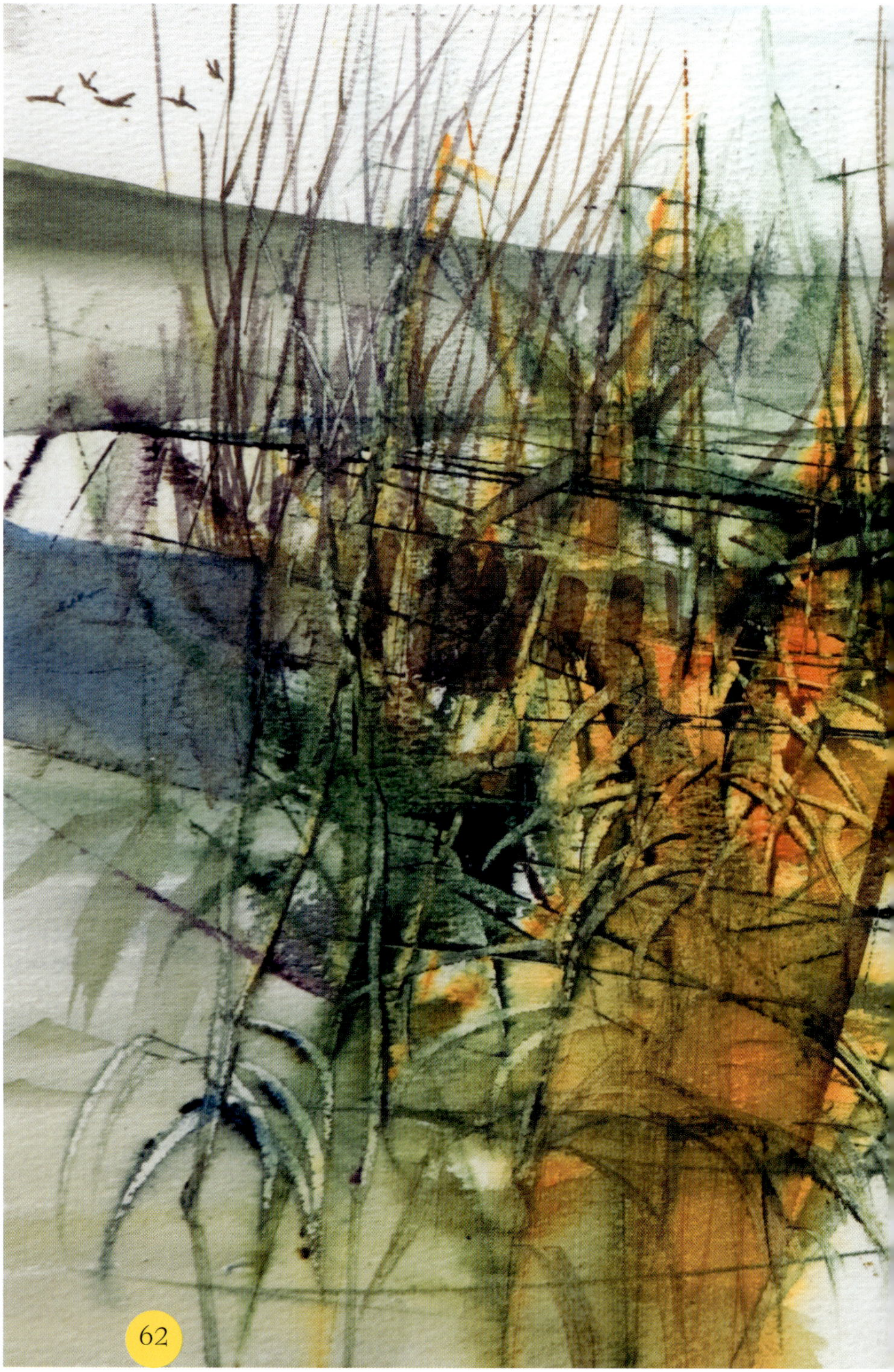

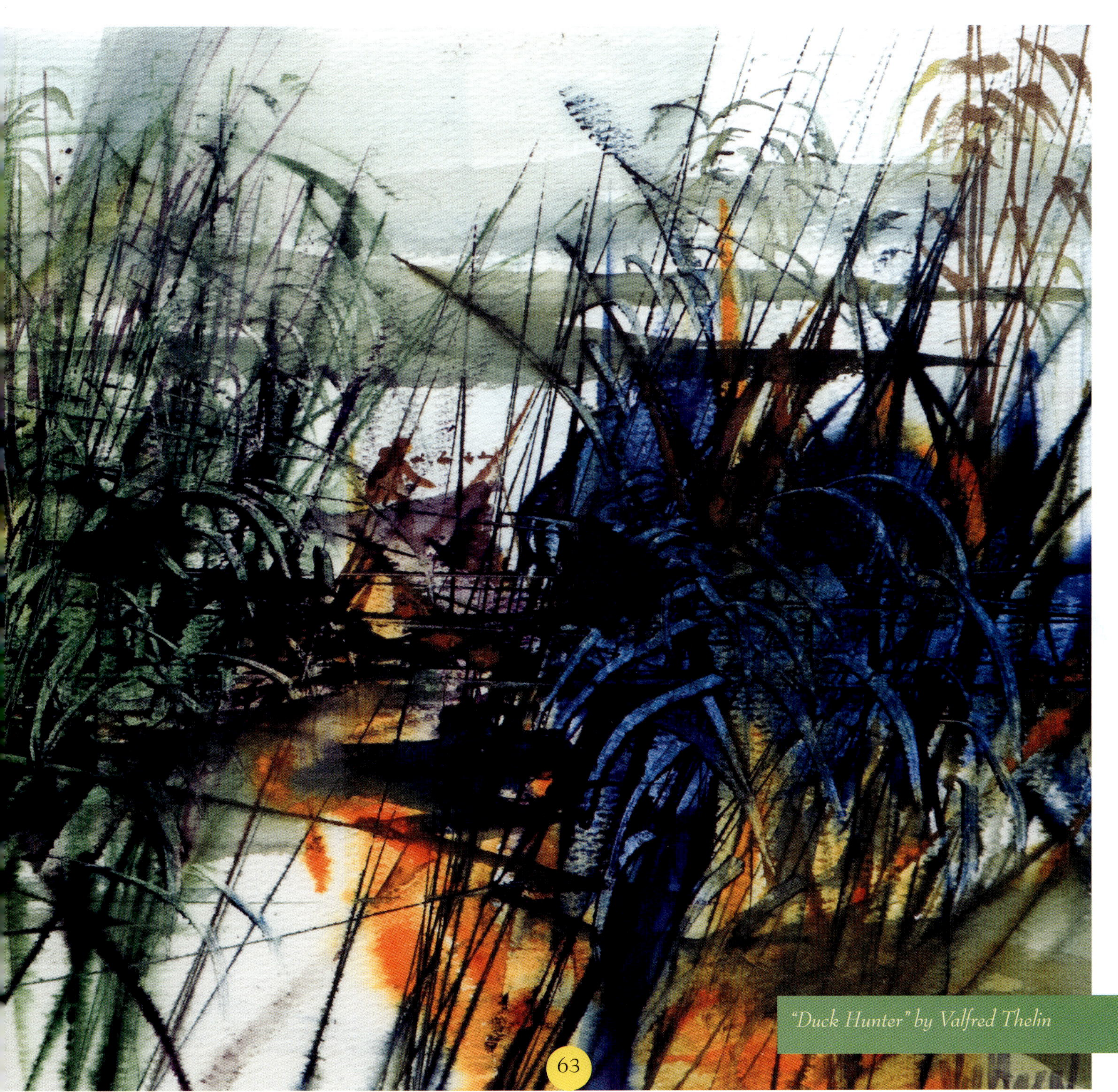

"Duck Hunter" by Valfred Thelin

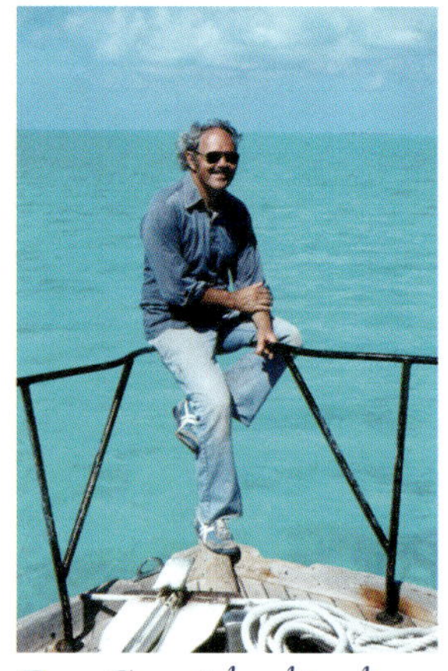

Pete Carmichael in the Bahamas

Workshops, Margarette took over that position and she and I shared many experiences, until, sadly, she was diagnosed with a life-threatening illness. In Amity's first year of college she had taken a year abroad and gone to Spain. I was extremely grateful that I was able to persuade the airlines to accept my Frequent Traveler miles to help Margarette go to Europe to spend some time with Amity. Not long after she returned home, Margarette died. A memorial service was held under the spreading banyan trees at Selby Gardens in Sarasota, a lovely spot which Margarette had often photographed. As it happened, I was driving north at the time of the service and so missed the closure that kind of service gives. I was happy, as I began working on this book, to be able to contact Amity, now living in California, and have her contribution of photographs to this tribute to her mother.

Since the Down East group was from Florida, most of our participants were from mid-to-retirement age. But there was one younger participant. Nicholas Simmons, a young musician from Iowa had seen Val's work in Sarasota and been so inspired by it, and Val's personality, that he added watercolor painting to his activities. Since that time, he's made steady progress with his painting and in 2007 his powerful "Fresh Sushi" won top award in the National Watercolor Society's Annual Exhibition, one of many honors he has acquired. He lives in the Washington, D.C., area of Maryland, and is married to Olga, from Ukraine, with whom he fell in love on a trip to Russia. They have a daughter, Larissa.

At the picnic at Val's house I was feeling elated that everything had gone so well. The only hitch had been an extremely cold and rainy passage in the small mail boat to Monhegan, the only way to reach the popular island art colony off of Port Clyde. However, everyone took that in stride.

My own joy that night watching my husband, Elden, husking sweet corn and wearing a German military cap from Val's collection of men's crazy headgear, was bittersweet because I knew that he was gravely ill. Elden was a painting instructor at the Hilton Leech Art School but had gone along on this trip just as observer. I had marveled as he gamely struggled up and down the rocky beaches wanting to be a part of the activity but not even carrying a sketch pad. We did have one more Christmas together after we got home to Florida before he passed away in February of 1982.

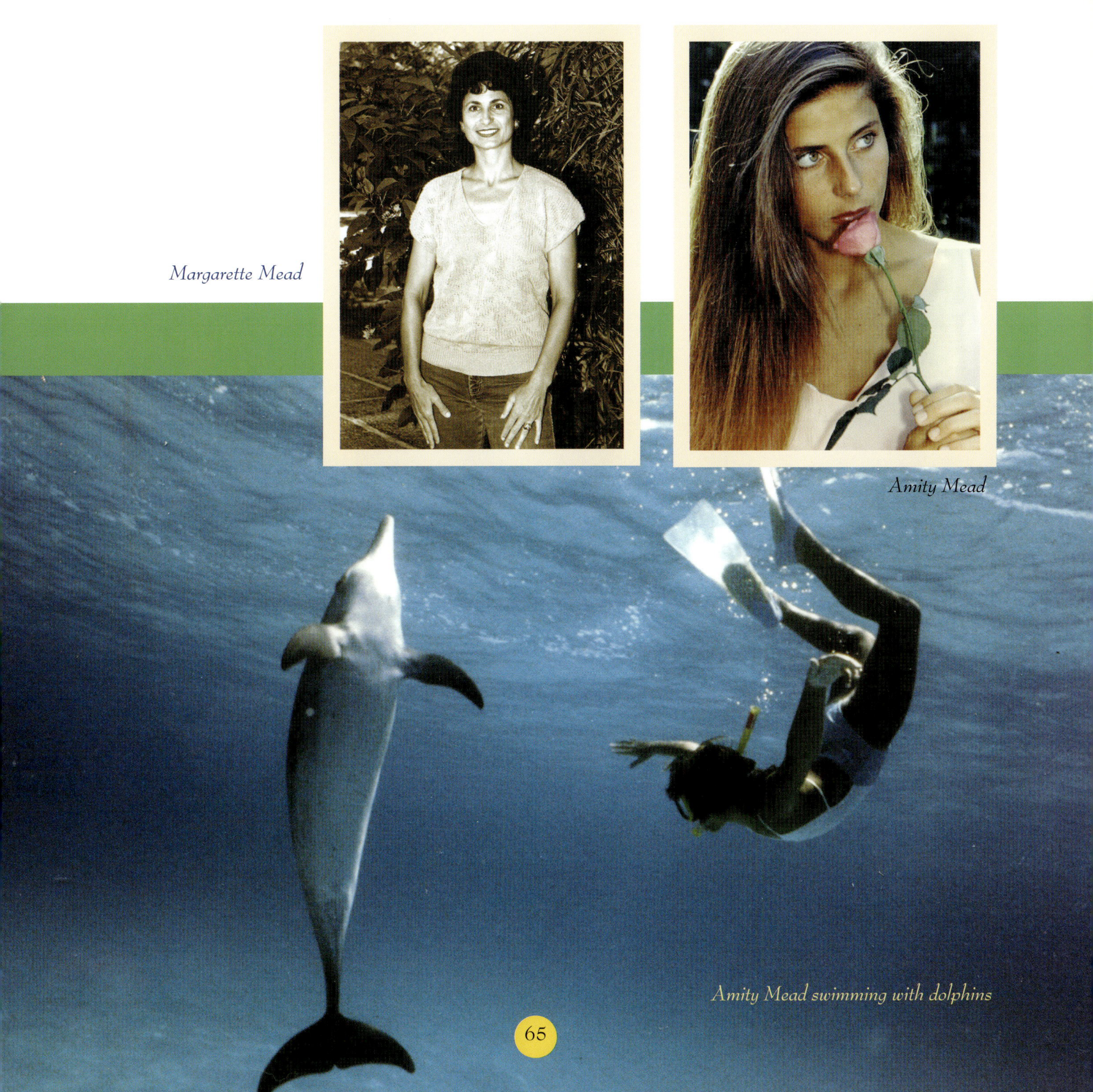
Margarette Mead
Amity Mead
Amity Mead swimming with dolphins
65

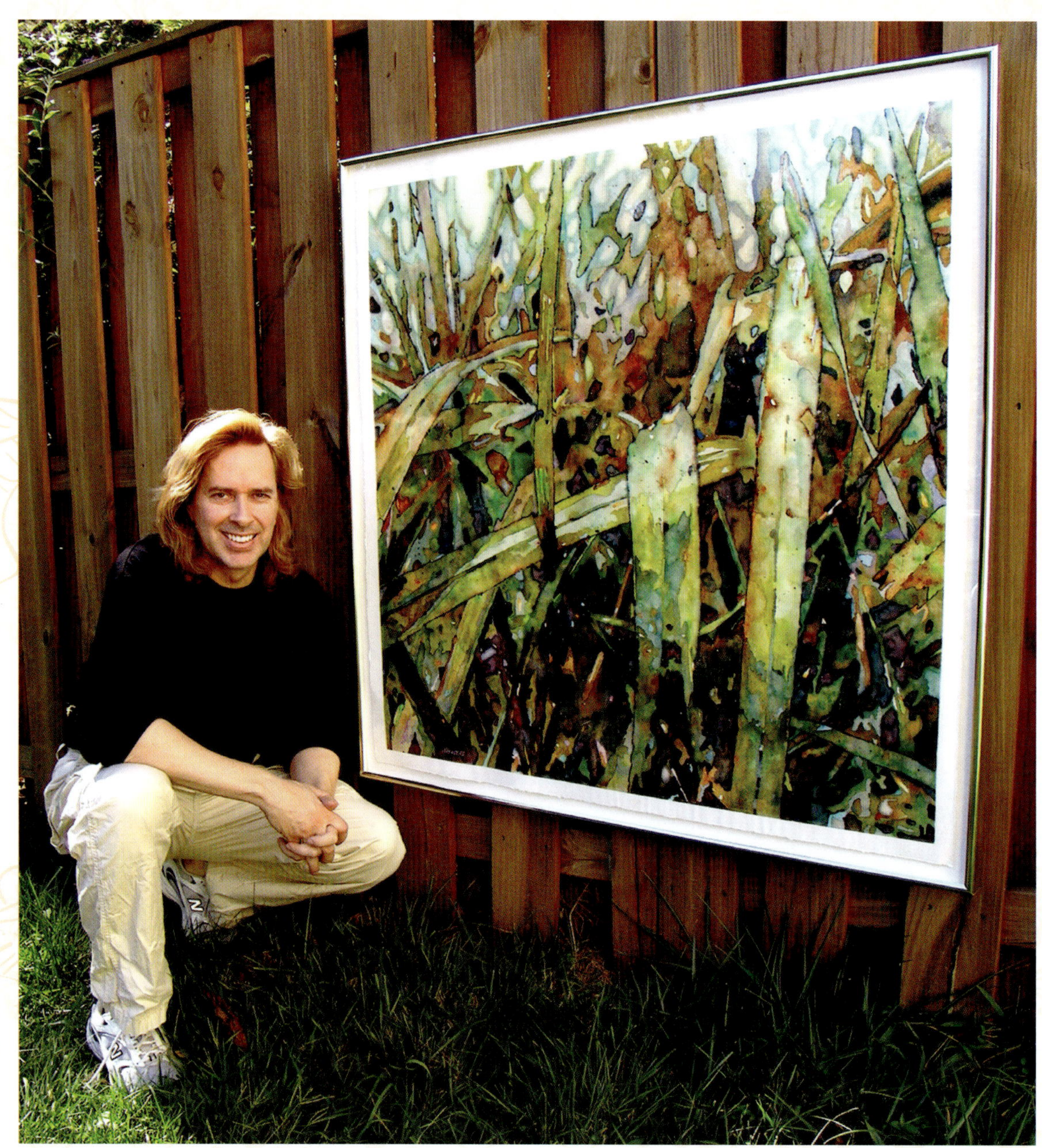

"Summer Sonata" and Nicholas Simmons

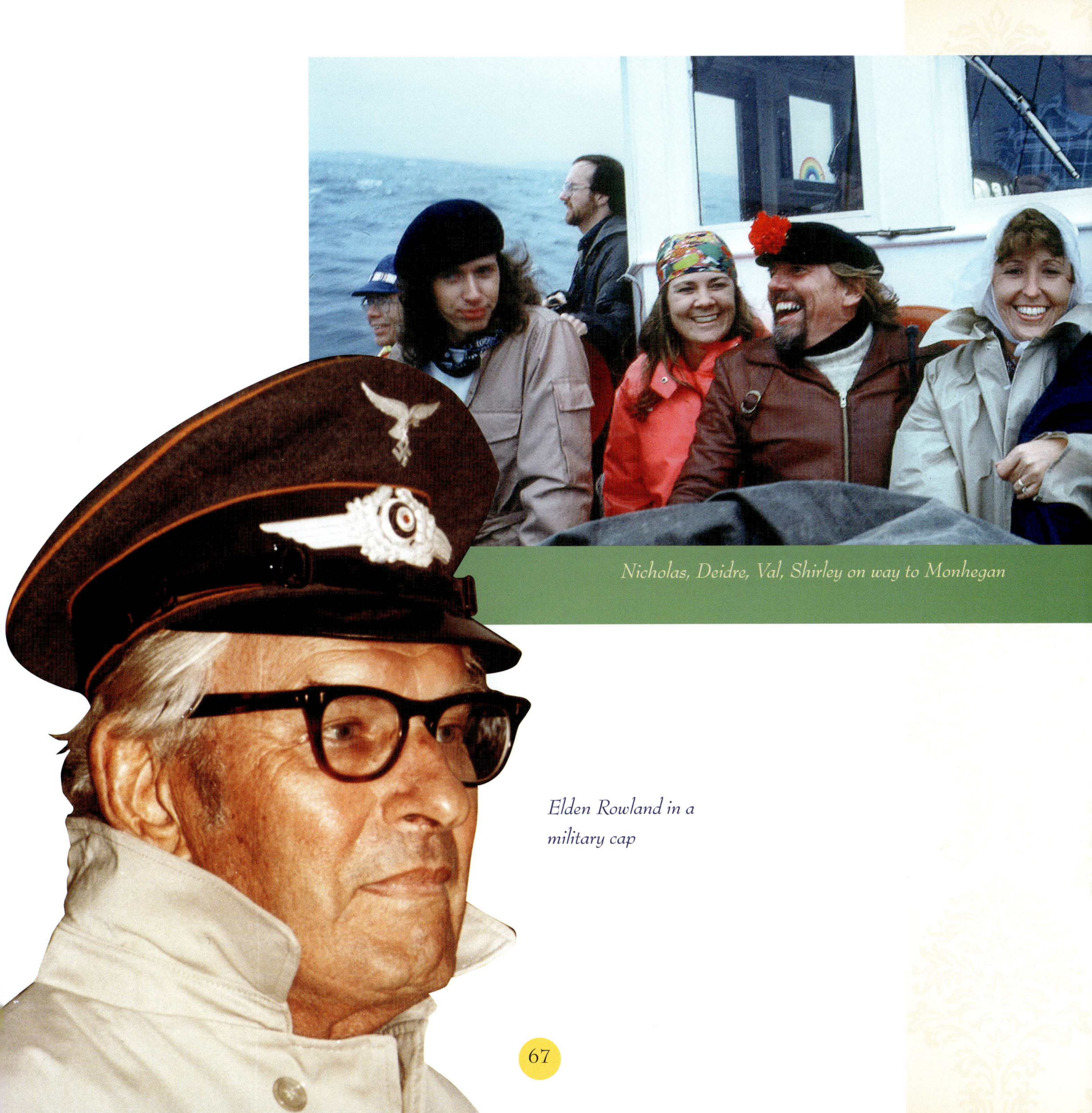

Nicholas, Deidre, Val, Shirley on way to Monhegan

Elden Rowland in a
military cap

Canadian R o c k i e s ● ● ●

Nicholas Reale, A.W.S., was the instructor for sketching and painting on the Two Arts Canadian Rockies and Glacier Park trip August 20/September 3, 1984. Well-known in the New York area, Nick was a renowned watercolorist who had come fom his home in New Jersey to teach at the Leech Studio the previous winter. His enthusiasm and involvement in his demonstrations and teaching were so appealing he was a popular choice to lead a fun excursion to such a gorgeous part of our continent as the Canadian Rockies. Among many awards, Nick received the 1971 Silver Medal of Honor from the New Jersey Watercolor Society.

Because Alice DeCaprio had first told us about Nick Reale, she was chosen to be his assistant on the Canadian Rockies trip. Alice had known Nick since they were both members of art activities in New Jersey. In World War II years, Alice had been one of the first three Michigan women to be selected for officer's training in the then-new women's branch of the Navy. After Alice moved to Sarasota she became an active

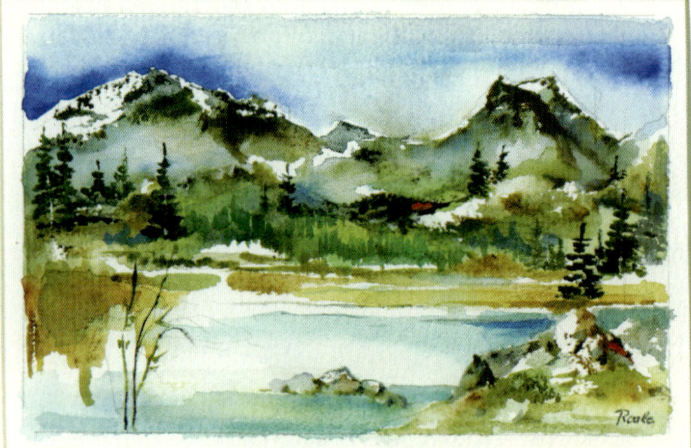

"Mountain Lake" by Nicholas Reale

and valued part of the Leech Studio activities and was the instructor on a group trip to the Chesapeake Bay area. She became interested in carousel animals and participated in International Trade Shows of the Amusement business with her pastel drawings and a line of circus memorabilia she designed. Always one to progress, she moved on to doing enhanced photographs, one of which, "Little Dove of the Desert," is from another Two Arts trip in which she had participated. Alice became, and still remains, my very special good friend.

The photography instructor was Margarette Mead, with Shirley Hummel, as assistant. We flew from Sarasota to Great Falls, Montana, where our chartered bus met us. Janet Harris, Siesta Key resident who was president of the Friends of the Arts and Sciences, was my assistant, as she had been many times before. Whenever possible, rather than interrupt work in the field, we would have picnic lunches. Providing picnic lunches for as many as forty persons in the wilds of a national park was a

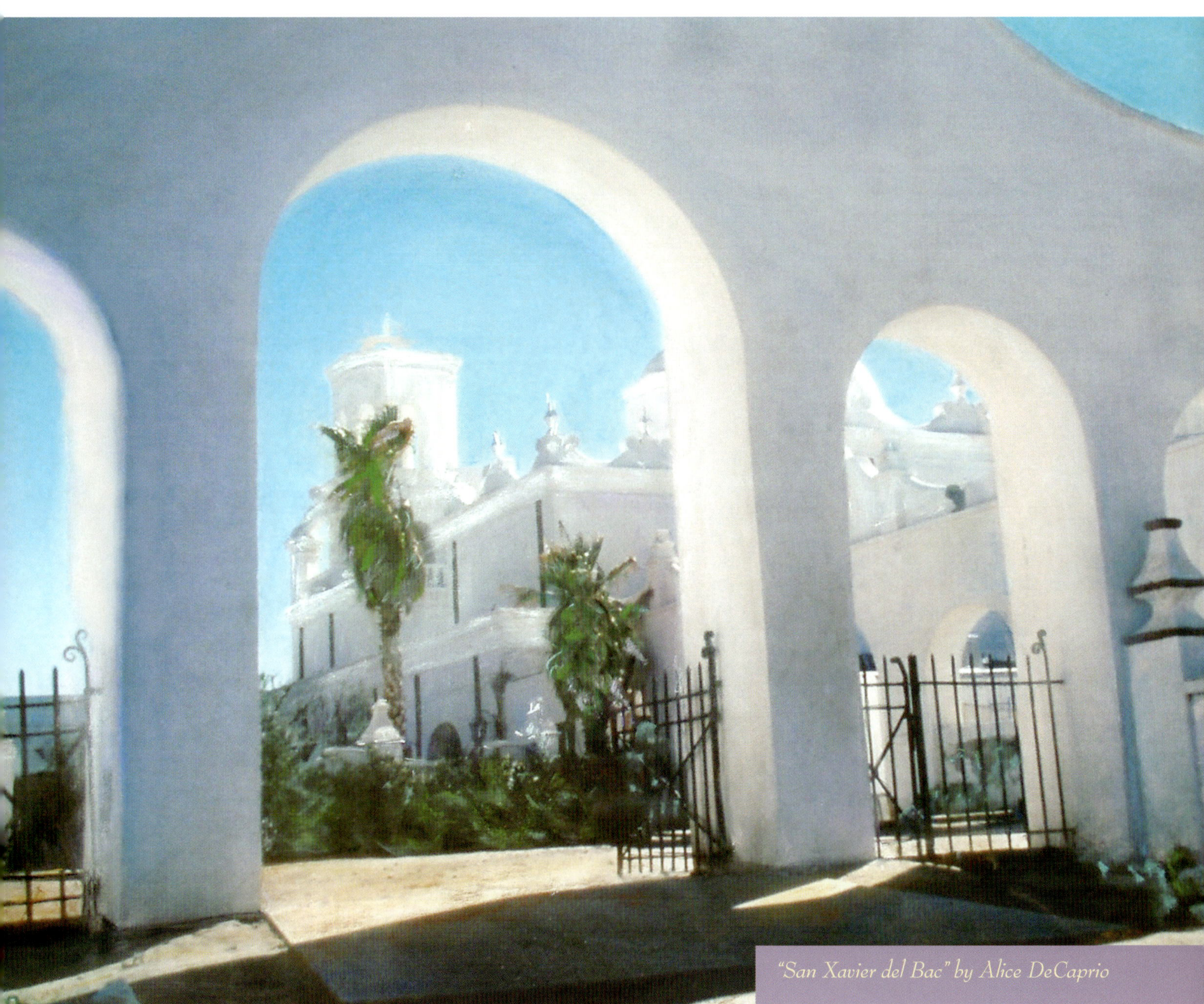

"San Xavier del Bac" by Alice DeCaprio

fun project, although a challenging one. After the students settled down to work in the morning the driver and I would take the bus and find a grocery store to get everything from sandwich makings to ice-cold watermelon and spread it out while students compared notes on the morning's work. It was my practice to make an exploratory trip as I started to plan travels for the groups. On the one to the Canadian Rockies, Sally Von Conta had gone with me and we had a fine time checking essentials and details, such as driving times, accommodations, rest stops, places to sketch and photograph, where to find picnic supplies, even to a birthday cake!

At the end of the travels, Ray Campeau joined us for a farewell dinner. He and Nick talked about Nick's coming back to Montana to teach a workshop and agreed they would work out details later. Later, when Ray called Nick's New York number he was shocked to learn that Nick had suddenly passed on! We, in Sarasota, were also shocked at the news which Ray relayed to us. In 1999 the Nicholas Reale Memorial Award was given at the 132nd International show of the American Watercolor Society. I have treasured the lovely little watercolor Nick did for me as a memento of our Canadian Rockies Two Arts Traveling Workshop.

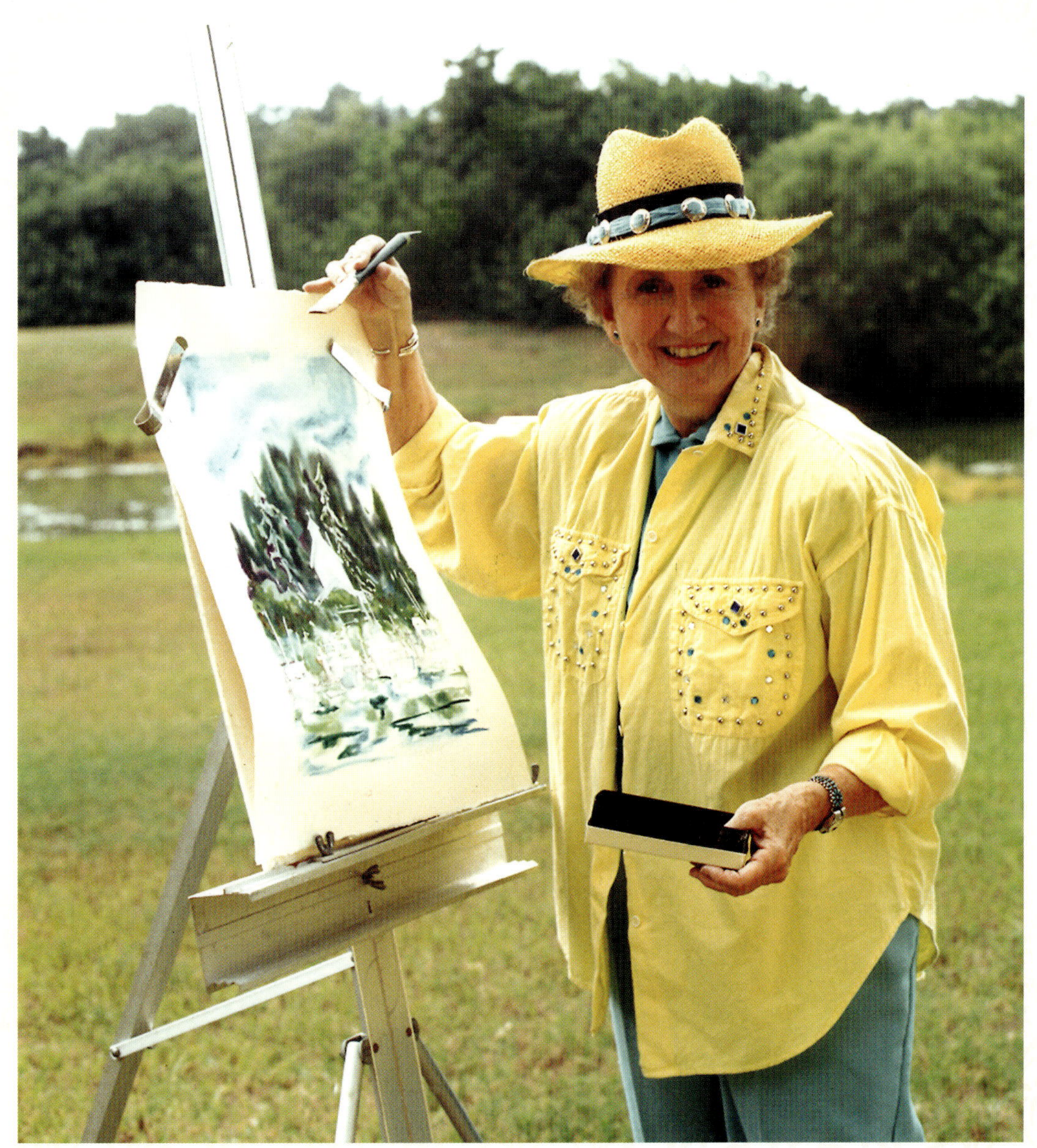

Alice DeCaprio

Barbara Nechis

Alaska is such a natural choice for Two-Arts-in-Nature-Painting-and-Photography-Traveling-Workshops that we went there more than once, not repeating, just exploring different parts of the vast state. I have chosen to include two of the trips in this book as a sampling, one with Barbara Nechis as painting instructor, and the other with Emily Holmes. Margarette Mead was photography instructor on both of them. Julee Docking and Pat Hanberry were assistants.

The Southeast—August 11/27, 1986, with Barbara Nechis

I had first gone to Alaska many years before to take a summer short course at the University in Fairbanks. The material in "Geography of Arctic Lands" was fascinating, in spite of sitting on the lawn in the mosquitoes for class sessions because it was so hot. On June 21, the longest day of the year, the day there was no night, the University sponsored a flight in an old DC3 north of the Arctic Circle. The outgoing flight was memorable for enabling me to take pictures all night long out of the window of the plane; the returning flight was memorable for the take-off from the "airfield" at Arctic Village, the Indian settlement at which we had landed. As the old plane shuddered and shook, and slithered from side to side, I was not the only one that strained in my seat to help it lift off before we reached the end of the run-way of gravelly earth supported only by permafrost.

I started going to different colleges and universities in the summer of 1967 when I went to The University of Colorado at Boulder, and took two courses that sounded interesting. Since I had not gone to college I took these courses for credit, naively hoping to pile up enough for a degree some day. "Biblical Archaeology" was a breeze; I struggled with "American Poets," without it occurring to me I could just audit the course. Since the summer short sessions were planned for teachers working to keep their credits current, the courses were of graduate level. Only years later did I learn from Manatee Junior College in Florida that graduate level credits could not be used for an undergraduate degree! Nevertheless, I learned and enjoyed, in places as far apart as Arizona and Vermont and Montana and Florida. Before Elderhostel, it was the "real world."

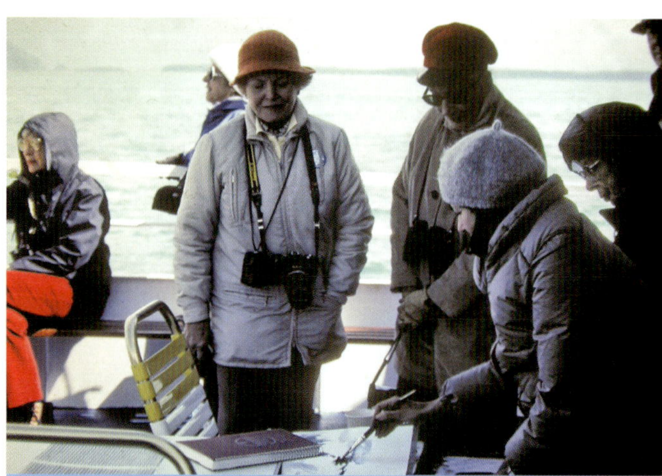

Barbara Nechis demonstrating on deck

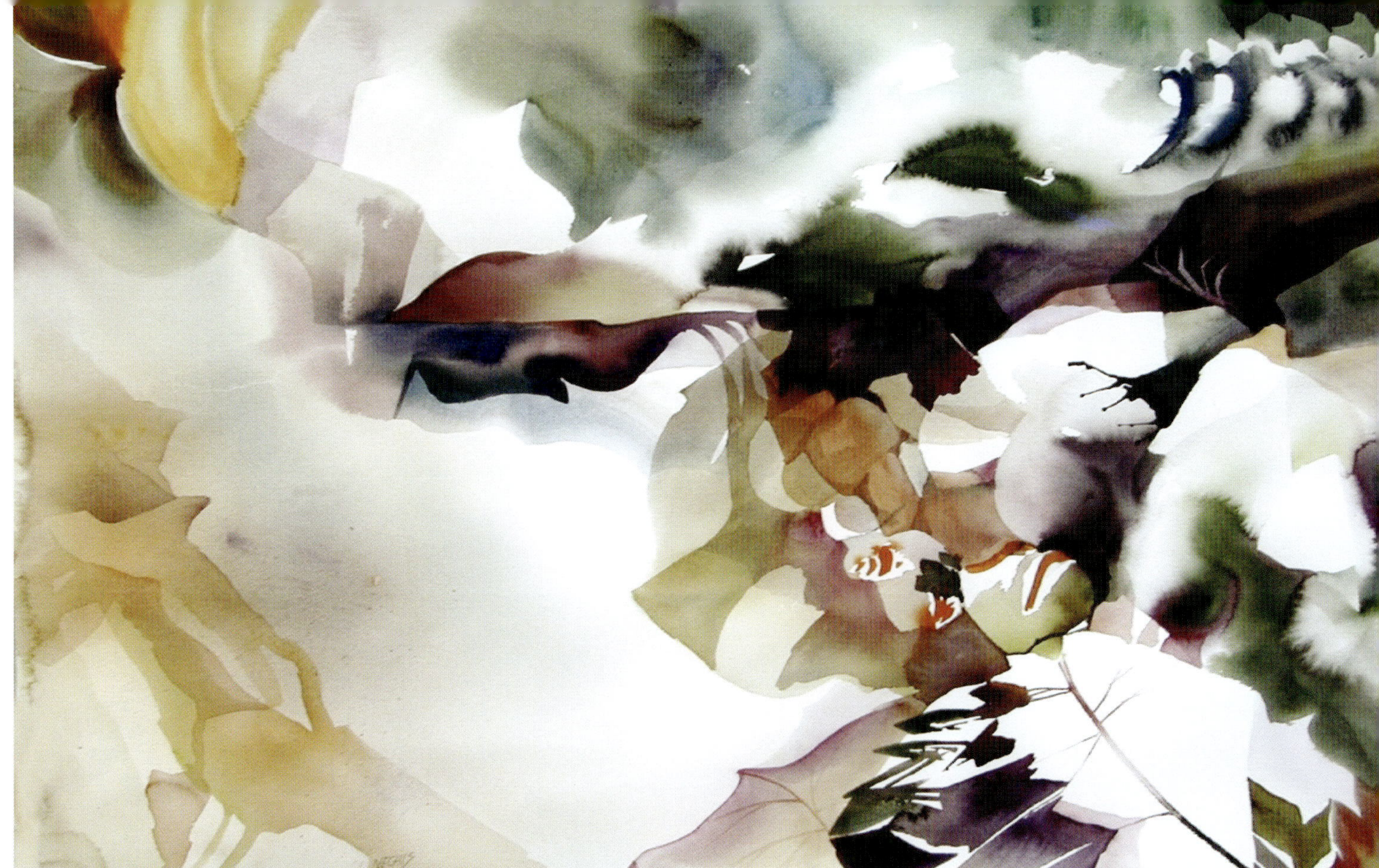

"Glen Alpine" by Barbara Nechis

I met people from all walks of life, especially in the Southwest where there was a wonderful mixture of Native Americans, African Americans, people of Spanish descent, and just plain folks like me.

Compared to the Lower 48, Alaska is expensive and hard for a small group to compete with the huge travel operators. But the summer of 1985, before the trip with Barbara Nechis, on my exploratory trip I pleaded my case and managed to get a contract with the hotel chain owned by former Governor Sheffield in Juneau and Anchorage. These served as our base as we traveled in the Southeast, took a cruise on Glacier Bay, flew to the island of Sitka, and back to the mainland to Homer at the tip of the Kenai Peninsula. All the while, members of the group were sketching and photographing, and the instructors giving demonstrations.

Barbara Nechis' credentials are impressive: with a BA and MS in art, she has taught at well-known art schools in New York, and throughout America

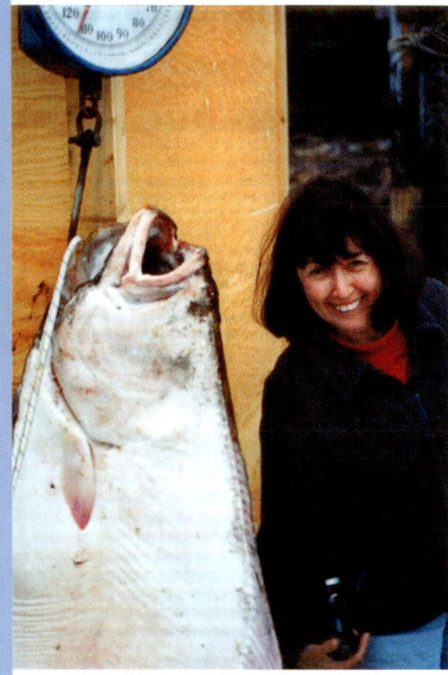

Barbara Nechis with halibut

and abroad. Her work is in many collections, such as Butler Institute of American Art, IBM and Citicorp. However, *Watercolor from the Heart*, and *Watercolor the Creative Experience*, the titles of her two books, say more to me about her inspirational style of teaching and her warm personality. She lives among the vineyards of the Napa Valley of Northern California. In a statement of her creative process, Barbara says: "My experience of Alaska continues to permeate my paintings. My work is an exploration based on my response to the entire experience of nature. I use the fundamentally abstract patterns of nature both as a source of inspiration and as a compositional element."

As a result of my exploratory trip, we had a special treat while we were at Homer. After I learned of Diana Tillion, an Alaska artist who lived in Halibut Cove in Kachemak Bay and painted in octopus ink, I arranged to take the group to see her. The small *Danny J* took us out to her charming home and studio hidden away in the greenery of Ismailof Island. A painter in many media, a sculptor, and a printmaker, Diana traveled to the remote reaches of Alaska capturing the people, scenery and wild creatures that make the state unique.

A member of the Governor's Growth Policy Council, she was the wife of Alaska State Senator Clem Tillion. She showed us how she worked in octopus ink, telling us how she caught her own octopus "for the rich range of warm tones in its ink." Her brochure also stated that she was the "best sautéed octopus cook anywhere in the state." Although we didn't taste Diana Tillion's sautéed octopus, we followed the boardwalks and had a memorable lunch of sable fish chowder, home-made bread, and "outrageous" chocolate cheesecake at the tiny Saltry restaurant, run by her daughter and serving only for special groups like ours, enchanted to have a glimpse of their unique way of life. In the intervening years her daughter, Marion Tillion Beck, has also become a prominent artist on the island which is now a charming art colony.

As the

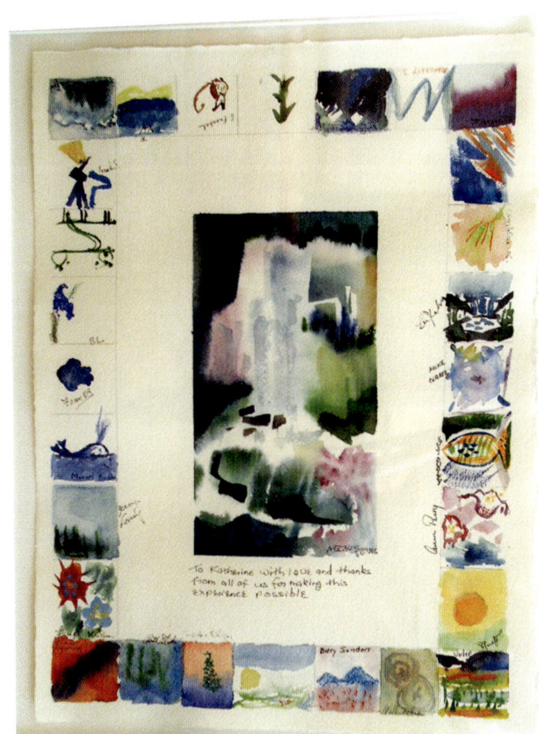

Katherine's memento

result of an event of another kind while we were at
Sitka, I have an unusual memento which I treasure.
People who were not painters or photographers often
went on the Two Arts trips because they liked what we
did and liked being with the artists. In Sitka, one of
the non-artists had a heart attack and was taken to the
hospital. Fortunately, the attack was not too severe,
the hospital was excellent, and her sister and brother-
in-law were also in the group to stay with her. As a
"get-well" gift for her, Barbara did a central painting
and had each person add a small square of color around
it. I knew about this, even added a little upside down
pine tree as my contribution. However, I did not know
that Barbara was having two of the pieces done, and
one of them was for me! Another lovely memento
was a beautiful painting of Portage Glacier, south of
Anchorage, by Julee Docking, the assistant.

It might be interesting to note that in all of the
hundreds of trips I managed, there were only three
times when participants became incapacitated and had
to leave the group.

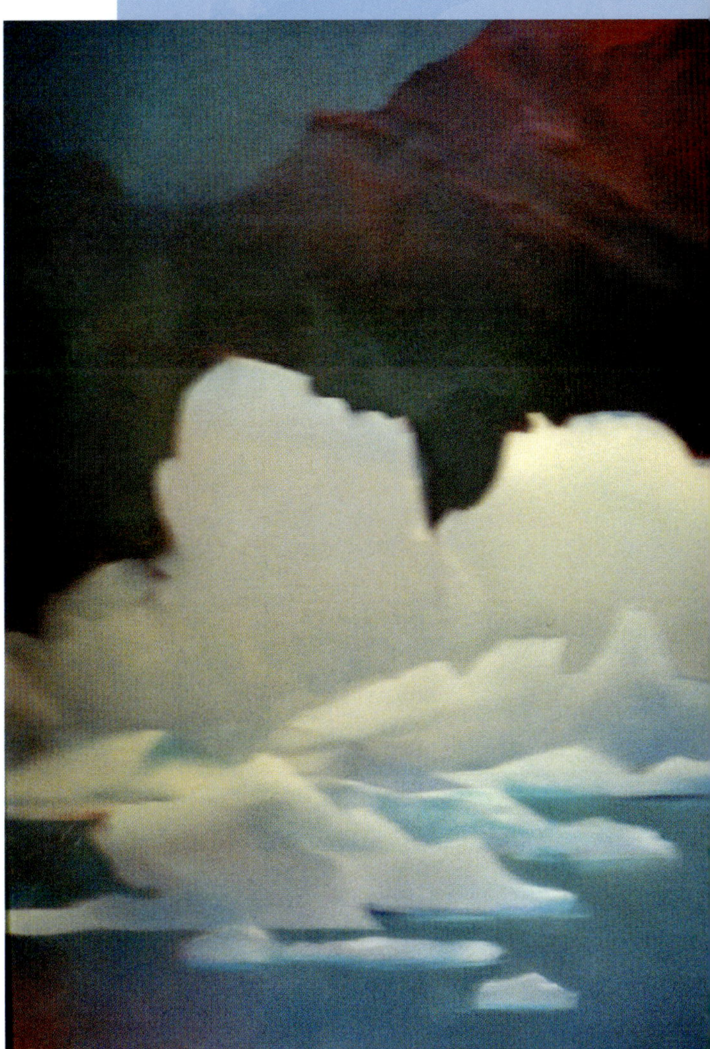

"Portage Glacier" by Julee Docking

$Emily$ Holmes ● ● ●

The Last Frontier—June 15–30, 1990, with Emily Holmes;

Extension to the Pribilof Islands—June 30–July 5

Emily and Gordon Holmes, so valued both in the Leech Studio activities and also in my personal life, did not often go on the Traveling Workshop trips. But they did go on the Alaska trip called "The Last Frontier," in 1990, on which Emily was the sketching/painting instructor.

Emily and Gordon became a part of activities at the Leech Studio soon after they moved to Sarasota from Winter Park, Florida, in 1960. Emily, who had a bachelor's degree in art from Western Reserve University in Ohio and had continued her art education at the Cleveland Art Institute, first became a student in Hilton Leech's art classes and later worked with him on a book he was writing when he passed on. Emily completed the book titled, *The Joys of Watercolor*, and readied it for publication. She was one of five women who founded the Fine Arts Society of Sarasota. Gordon, educated as an electrical engineer, led the development of the ultra violet data

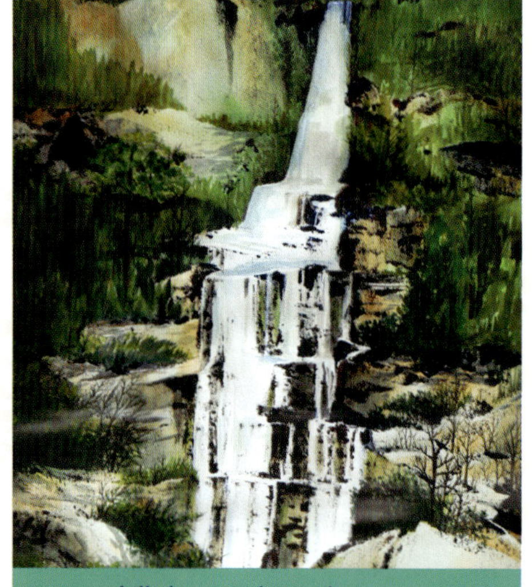

"Waterfall" by Emily Holmes

collection satellite system for the orbiting astronomical electrical observatory when he was with EMR (Electro Mechanical Research, now Schlumberger). Also knowledgeable about investments, he later became a full-time business advisor, whose expertise in many fields is invaluable to all of us in the art world.

There were at least two times in my life when I felt I could not have gotten through without the friendship of Emily and Gordon Holmes: when my husband, Elden, was ill and died; and when the board of the Friends of the Arts and Sciences decided they wanted to manage the workshops in the Leech Studio, rather than have me handle them as I had for so many years. Memories come back of two nights when Emily and Gordon were there when I needed their steadfast support: in Sarasota Memorial Hospital during Elden's surgery; and at the Leech Studio as we manhandled my desktop computer and other personal office furniture down the narrow winding metal steps from the balcony when I moved out of the Studio to carry on the traveling workshops from an office I set up in the laundry room of my home.

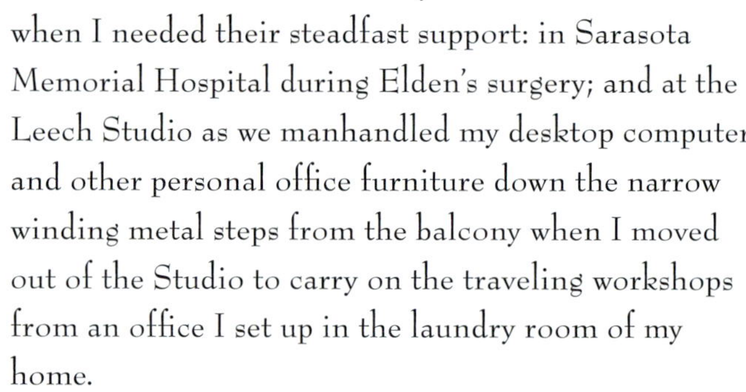

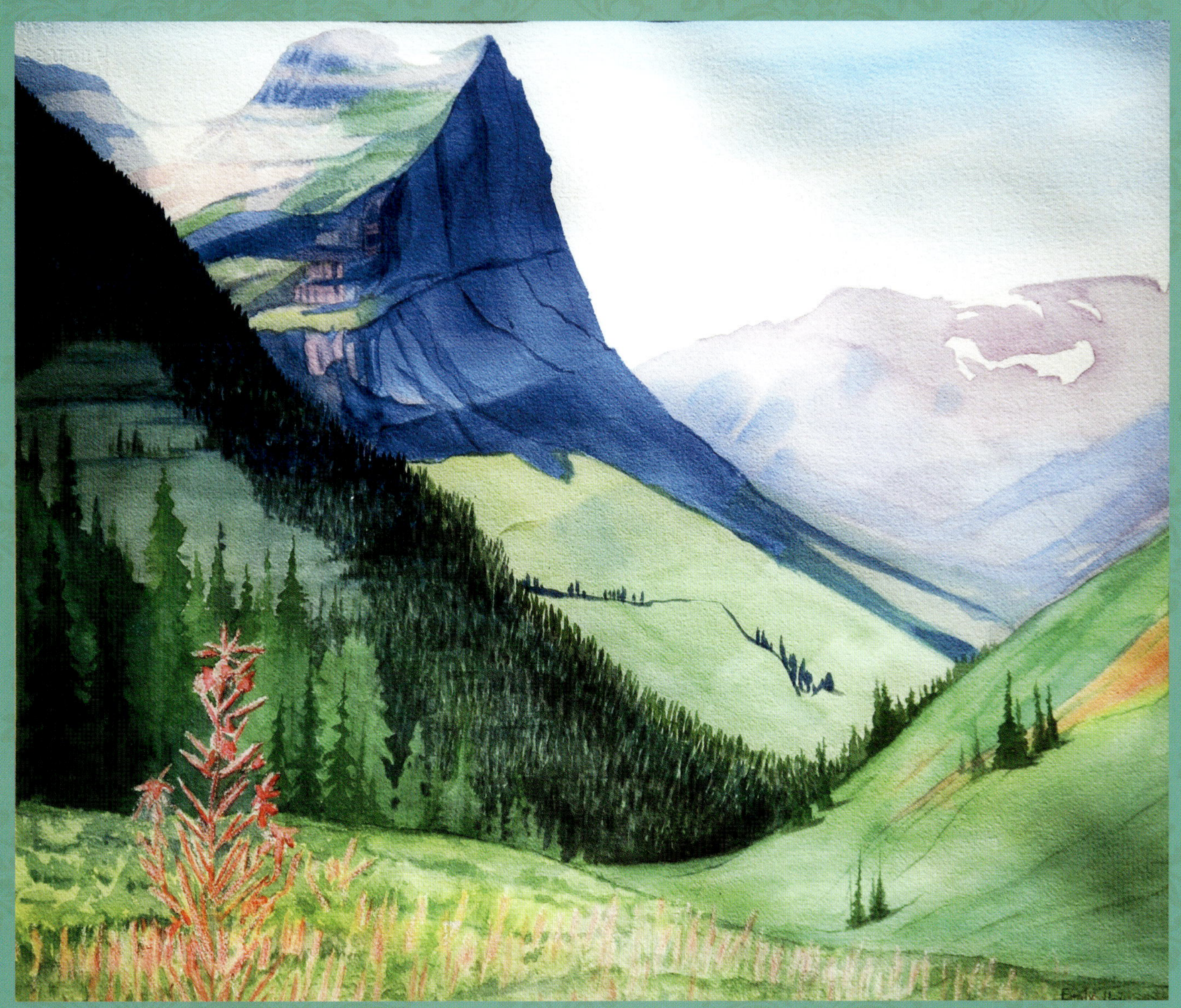

"Logan Pass" by Emily Holmes

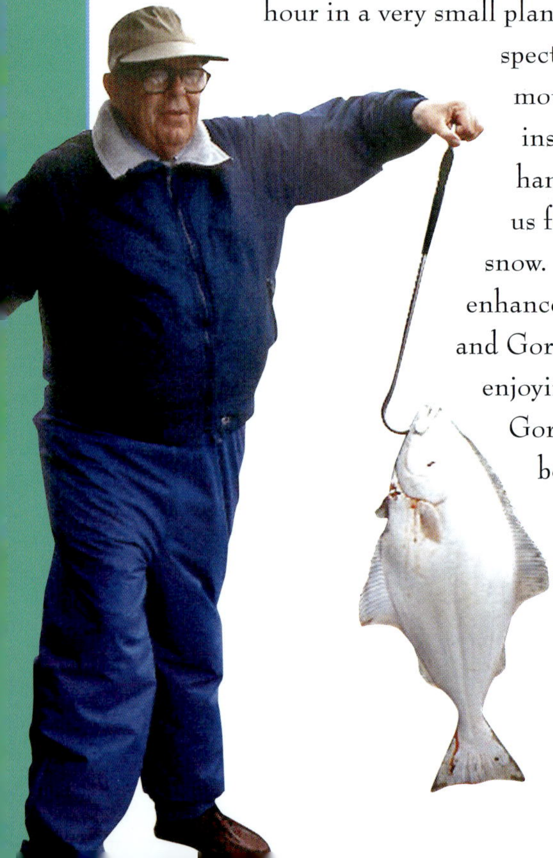

Emily and Gordon's enthusiastic participation was, as always, invaluable in the Two Arts Trip to Alaska in 1990. The previous summer I had taken the Inside Passage ferries from Washington State, stopping to explore each island as we traveled north, and decided on Haines, as the one at which to start our "Last Frontier" trip. The itinerary description said: "Surrounded by snow-covered mountains, fjords, glaciers and rushing mountain streams, the historic town will be our base for four nights—friendly people, native dances and Indian art are highlights.—Optional one-hour ferry to Skagway, colorful old mining town."

Another option out of Haines was a "Glacier Bay Flightseeing Tour," a never-to-be-forgotten hour in a very small plane flying just above spectacularly glaciated mountains, so close I instinctively put my hand out as if to keep us from touching the snow. My experience was enhanced because Emily and Gordon were evidently enjoying it so much, and Gordon had up to then been reluctant to fly. On Two Arts flightseeing tours we often had helicopter doors removed so the photographers could have clear shots. But none of these flights ever quite compared with the small plane tour over Glacier Bay out of Haines.

Next stop after Haines, was Anchorage, with side trips to Kodiak Island and Portage Glacier, and climaxed by a 75-mile school-bus drive back into Denali National Park for four days at North Face Lodge. Mt. McKinley is often hidden by clouds and haze. But for the full time we were there, the majestic mountain was visible in all its glory, giving us "bragging rights" among other tour groups.

Emily and Gordon went back to Florida with the main Two Arts group, and I went on with seven photographers to St. Paul's in the Pribilof Islands. Situated well out in the Bering Sea, the Pribilofs are volcanic outcroppings, home of Aleut natives, sea birds, Arctic foxes, reindeer and thousands of fur seals. There was a hotel of sorts. For our meals we were bussed across the island to a factory making artificial crab meat. The island had a lovely feeling of remoteness, yet, of history, too, evidenced by its old domed Russian church, still being used by the residents.

When I began preparation for this book, I wrote Emily asking if she would like to be a part of it, and was happy to have her acceptance, with her usual enthusiasm and encouragement, a few months before she died in April of 2008.

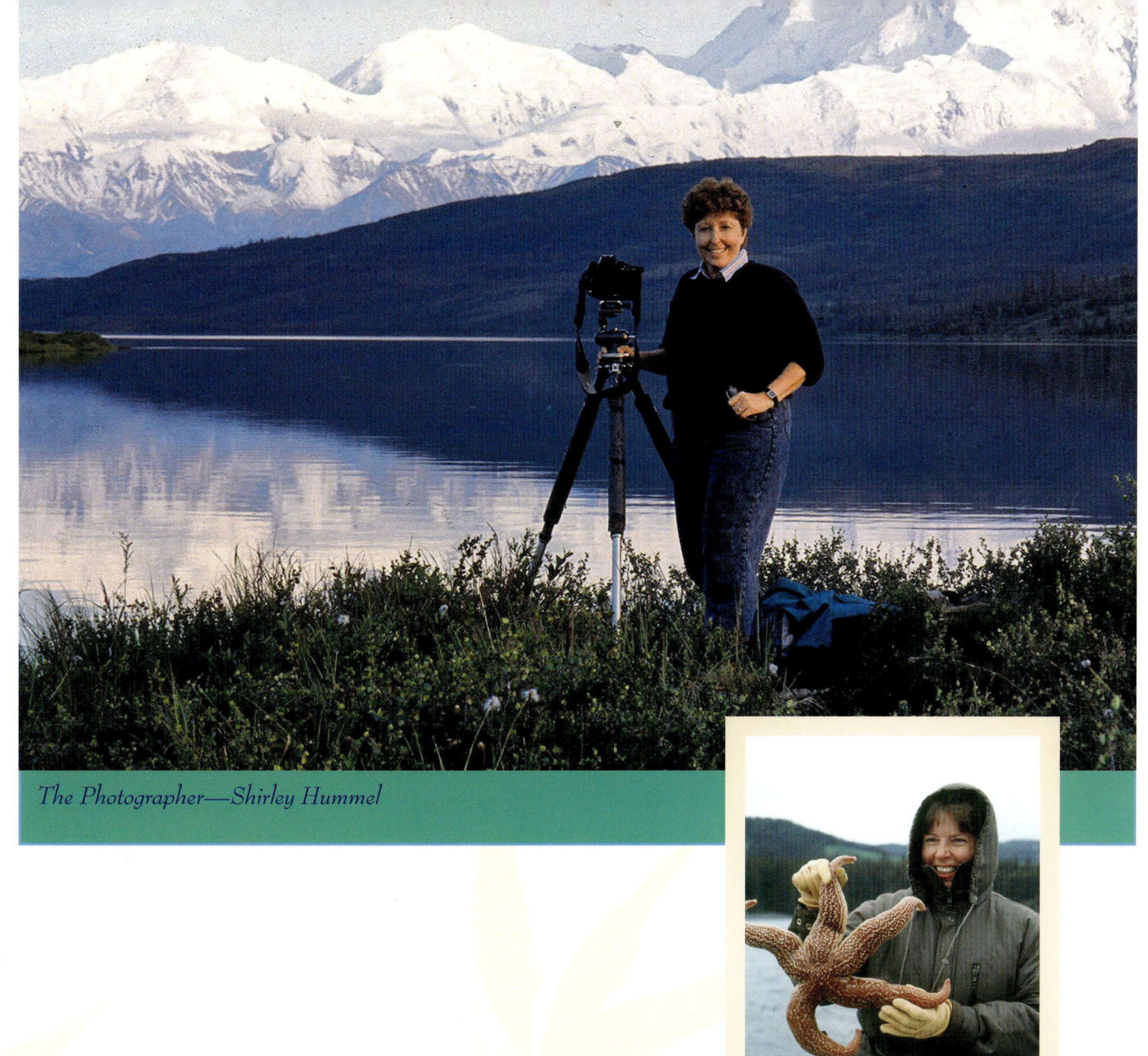

The Photographer—Shirley Hummel

Pat Hanberry with starfish

Judi Betts

Hawaii, like Alaska, was such an ideal destination for traveling workshops that I took groups with Carole Myers, Bruce McGrew and Judi Betts. On the Oahu & Kauai Tour from August 23/September 7, 1988, Judi Betts was the sketching/painting instructor. Margarette Mead was to be the photography instructor but could not go because of an emergency in her family. Fortunately, Shirley Hummel was able to arrange to get away from her new Sarasota photography studio and go in her place.

Judi Betts, A.W.S., N.W.S., is an internationally-recognized painter, instructor, juror and author of two books, *Watercolor…Let's Think About It!*, in its 5th printing, and her latest co-authored book, *Painting. . . a Quest toward Xtraord!nary*, which has won 5 major awards. Pat Hanberry, a photographer, was our assistant.

I went to Hawaii twice in that summer of 1988. Hawaii, although a part of the United States, has an exotic quality to it. With its unfamiliar street and place names, and the many intriguing sites on the different islands, plans didn't fall into place with the certainty that they did on the Mainland. So I went out from May 4/17 to work out all of the details. I immediately fell in love with Hawaii. It seemed something like traveling in a foreign land but with the assurance of being in my own country. It was all beautiful—the people in their casual clothing, the dramatic scenery of sea and mountains, the rich history of what less than a century ago was an independent kingdom, the balmy breezes.

For the group's August trip, in Honolulu I found the Pagoda Hotel and Floating Restaurant. Owned by an "old" (having come there generations before) Japanese family, it had an authentic Oriental ambience. Running through the lobby and winding its way through the lush green foliage was a stream of sparkling water, stocked with colorful, lazily-swimming fish, some of the largest carp I ever saw.

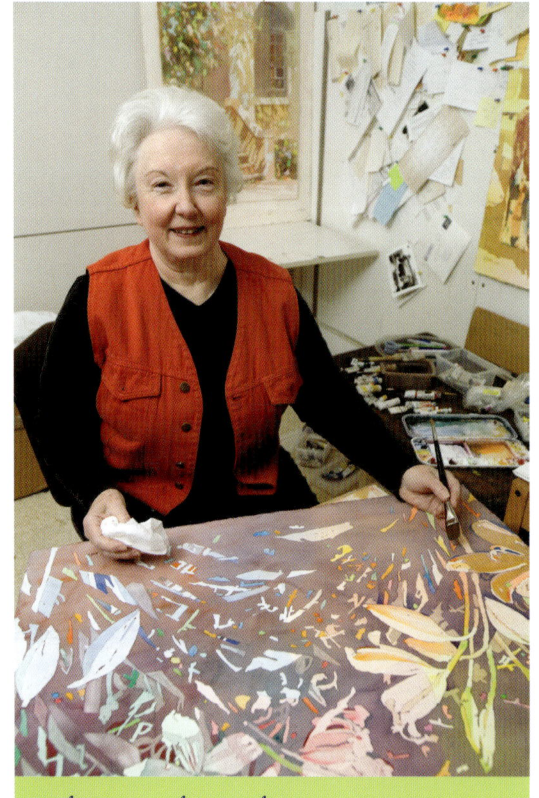

Judi Betts in her studio

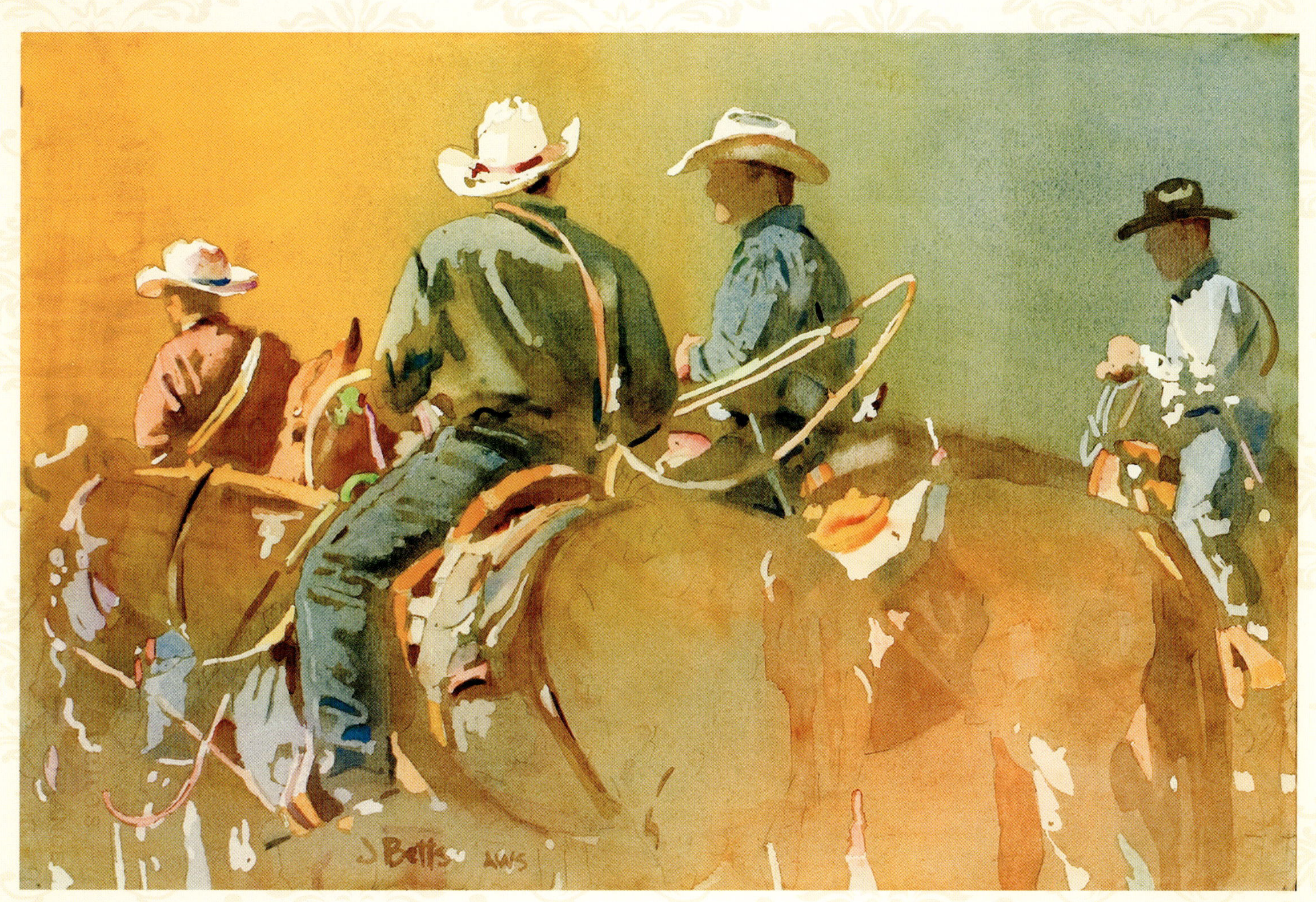

"Professionals" by Judi Betts

The Pagoda was our headquarters for a leisurely four days of sketching, photographing, and enjoying Honolulu and Oahu. One day, chartered transportation took us through the pineapple fields of central Oahu to Waimea Falls Park and the Polynesian Cultural Center, at Waimea Laie, a living museum project of the Mormon Church. Judi Betts painted the endemic chickens which roamed freely at Waimea Park, and later used the images of the colorful fowl in a line of silk scarves, one of which I still treasure. One evening we went to the Pacific Beach Hotel, on Waikiki, to have dinner at their Oceanarium Restaurant, where the walls were spectacular floor-to-ceiling fish tanks filled with brightly-colored tropical fish of many varieties.

We left Oahu to fly to Lihue, on the island of Kauai, to spend the latter half of our Hawaii adventure. The first five days were spent at the Beach Boy Hotel, on Waipouli Beach, where individuals were able to explore on their own. Or go with the group to see such well-known spots as Waimea Canyon, the Na Pali Coast, the Kilauea Point lighthouse, Wailua Falls, Kilohana Plantation, and the Fern Grotto. A special treat for some was a helicopter flight over Waimea Canyon, whose dramatic cliffs have been called the "Grand Canyon" of Hawaii.

On my exploratory trip in May I had fallen in love with the Coco Palms Resort, not very far away from the Beach Boy. This long-established resort, set among a great grove of towering coconut trees, had such an atmosphere of authentic Hawaii that I took the chance of moving the group for the last two days. And not one of them complained! Situated on small lagoons at the point where the Wailua River joins the sea, its evening torch lighting ceremony and our farewell dinner in the Queen's Audience Hall, made all of them agree it was worth making the change.

On the way back to Florida we extended our flight change-over time to include a day in San Francisco. I had the fun experience, as I stood at the desk of the Holiday Inn Fisherman's Wharf, to hear a man's voice say to me, "What are you doing here?" I quickly replied the same, because it was my brother, Bob, who happened to be passing through San Francisco at that time on a business trip.

Later, Judi Betts taught workshops for me in Colorado and Montana as part of my Katherine's World Workshop series. She continues her unique way with watercolor, exploring subject matter in depth, and then moving on. Presently she is working on her "Cowboy Series."

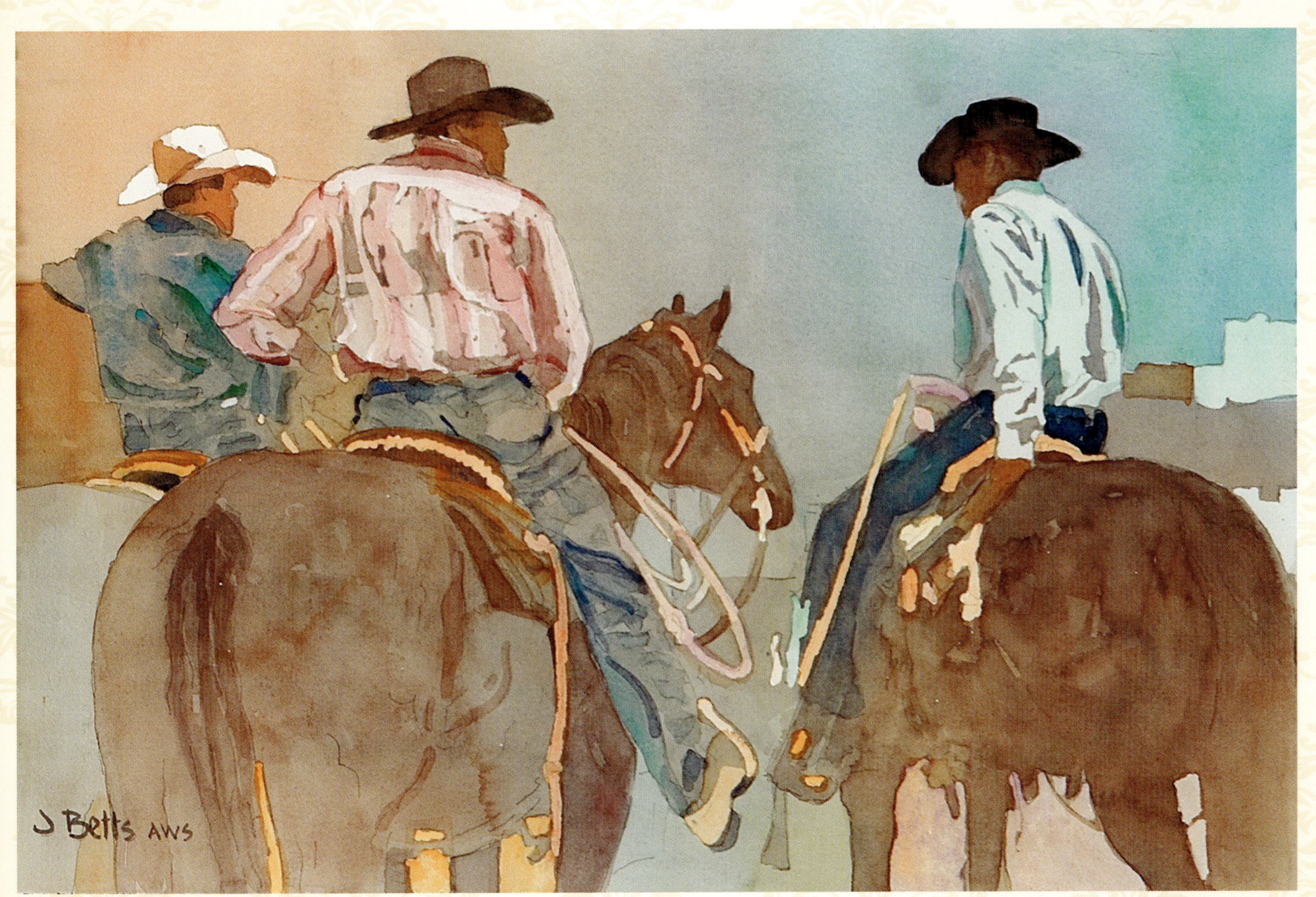

"Ropers' Rest" by Judi Betts

Suzanne Wilson ● ● ●

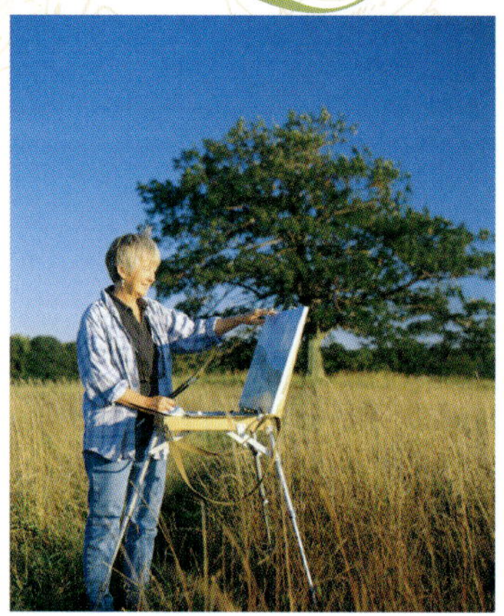

Suzanne Wilson at work

After I no longer worked *at* the Leech Studio, I honored the commitments I had made to carry out traveling workshops already planned, by working from my home. One of those commitments was with Suzanne Wilson of Glen Arbor, Michigan. Suzanne had come in the Studio one day presenting an idea of exchanging instructors from the Leech Studio with instructors from the art colony of her home town. While the idea of exchanging instructors never materialized, Suzanne did teach in Sarasota and originated an innovative idea of watercolor workshops that became known as "On the Trail of Winslow Homer."

Suzanne and her husband, architect Don Wilson, had stopped at Homosassa Springs as they drove south in Florida. Knowing that this was one of the sites painted by Winslow Homer, the famous American turn-of-the-century watercolorist, Suzanne became enthusiastic about taking a group there to paint. As Suzanne and Don and I had dinner that night at a restaurant on South Tamiami Trail the idea grew in our minds, and later became an actuality, as "On the Trail of Winslow Homer" workshop trips. Between 1989 and 1992, there were five of them: to Old Homosassa; the Abaco Islands in the Bahamas; an old estate in Bermuda; Homer's own studio at Prout's Neck, Maine; and Cullercoats, on the Northumbria coast of England. The first two of the Winslow Homer trips were part of the Leech Studio program. The last three were part of a series of workshops I originated and carried out on my own. In addition to the "Homer" trips, Suzanne led workshops for me to Patagonia, in the high plains of southern Arizona. Alice Boudreau, one of the students there who is now an active artist in Sarasota, spontaneously sent me an image for my collection, which I consider the essence of "buffalo."

The trips with Suzanne Wilson attracted a devoted following as we worked in the attractive locations that Winslow Homer had chosen. Kathy Tuttle, who took all of them, wrote me recently from her home in Vermont, "Suzanne sat me down the first day in Old Homosassa and gently steered me on as I struggled. . . I appreciated the fact she led us but didn't demand. . .The trips, so carefully researched by you to pick spots so relevant, and so different, were a joy."

Suzanne Wilson's charismatic personality, contagious laugh, and creative devotion to the arts made her a natural leader. After she passed on in 2004, Jacob Wheeler, editor of the Glen Arbor Sun,

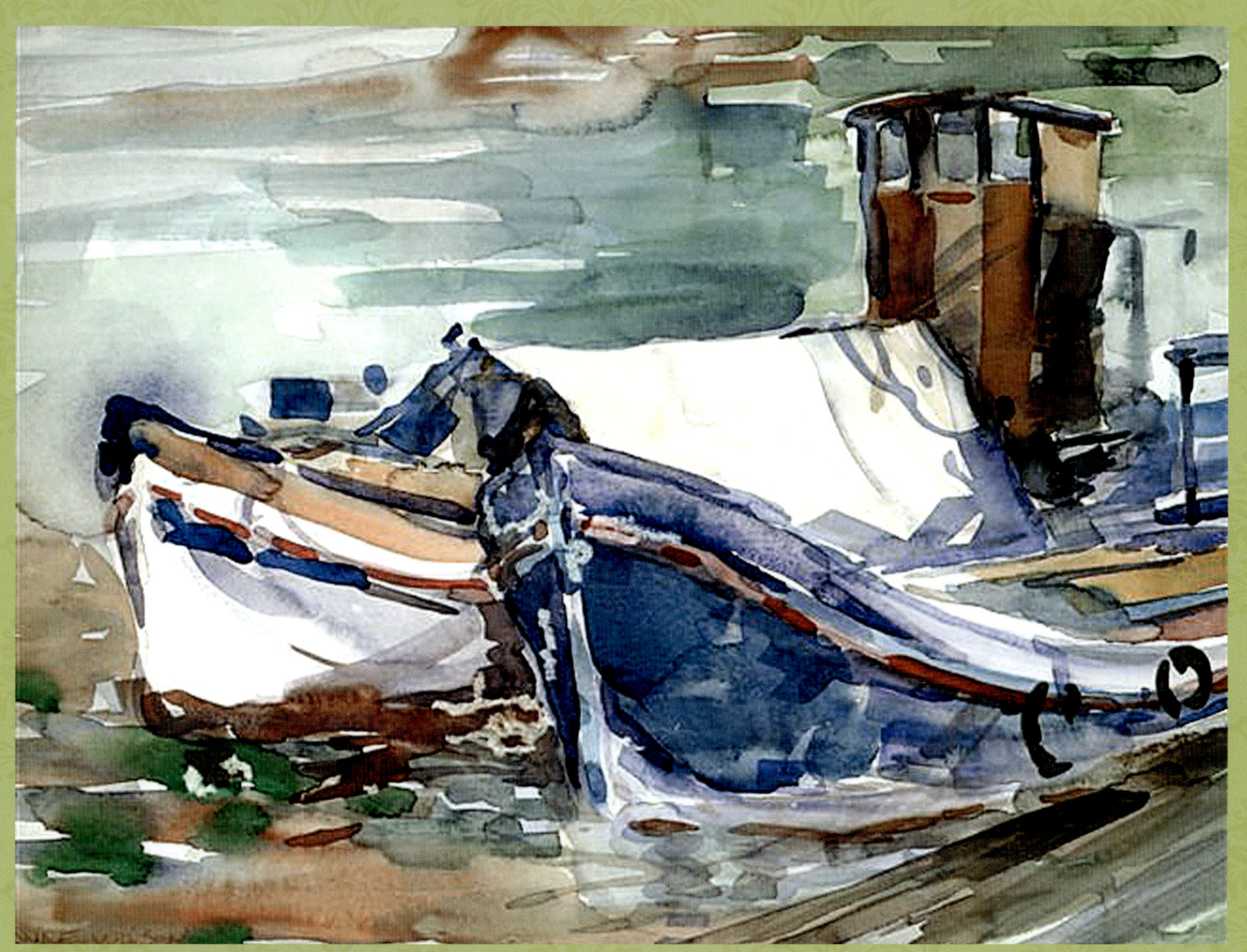

"Puerto de Fruitas, Argentina" by Suzanne Wilson

called her a "visionary and pioneer," the "heart and soul" of the Glen Arbor artist community. Her friend and associate, Midge Obata, called her the "guiding inspiration of the Glen Arbor Art Association," encompassing her love of music as well as of the visual arts.

I followed Suzanne to Michigan to spend summers in Glen Arbor, using it as a base from which to plan and conduct workshops. One winter while I was in Florida, Don Wilson designed a delightful studio home for me which the Wilsons had built in the woods behind their own house, just a few blocks from Lake Street Studios, owned and operated by Suzanne and her partner, Ananda Bricker.

My next adventure in Michigan was to buy a small building across from Lake Street Studios. The concrete block building was not a thing of joy but the large old trees on the back of the property were. I enhanced the building by painting the trim a rich turquoise, and filling the matching window boxes with purple petunias. I brought paintings and family things from Sarasota and opened "Katherine's World, Art and Antiques." That first spring my Miller cousins came to Glen Arbor for a family reunion. I fed approximately a dozen people by heating frozen macaroni and cheese in a microwave.

In a year or two I had a small addition put on the back of the building so I could live there and be in the center of town. Don Wilson took over the little studio house in the woods to use as his Architect's Office.

Artists with whom I had worked in Sarasota came to Michigan to teach: Maxine Masterfield, Beth Arthur, Frank Webb, and Bruce and Fox McGrew. When I needed to travel, Shirley Hummel came from Florida to care for the shop; or when I needed to get away for a short time, Judy McLaughlin brought her spinning wheel and demonstrated her craftsmanship.

After I closed "Katherine's World, Art and Antiques" in 1995, the property was purchased by Bob Sutherland to expand a growing business which he had started next door. Now it is part of his complex called "The Cherry Republic," a thriving enterprise creatively promoting the fruit for which that part of the Lower Peninsula of Michigan is noted. He, too, is devoted to protecting the stand of large trees which I cherished.

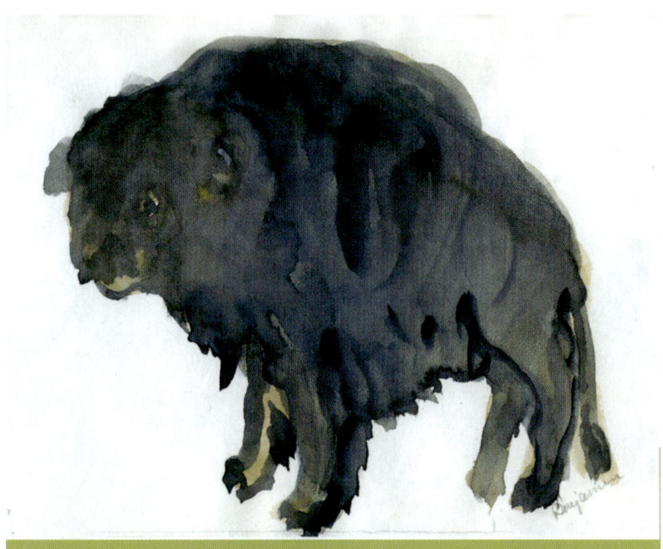

"Buffalo with my left hand" by Alice Boudreau

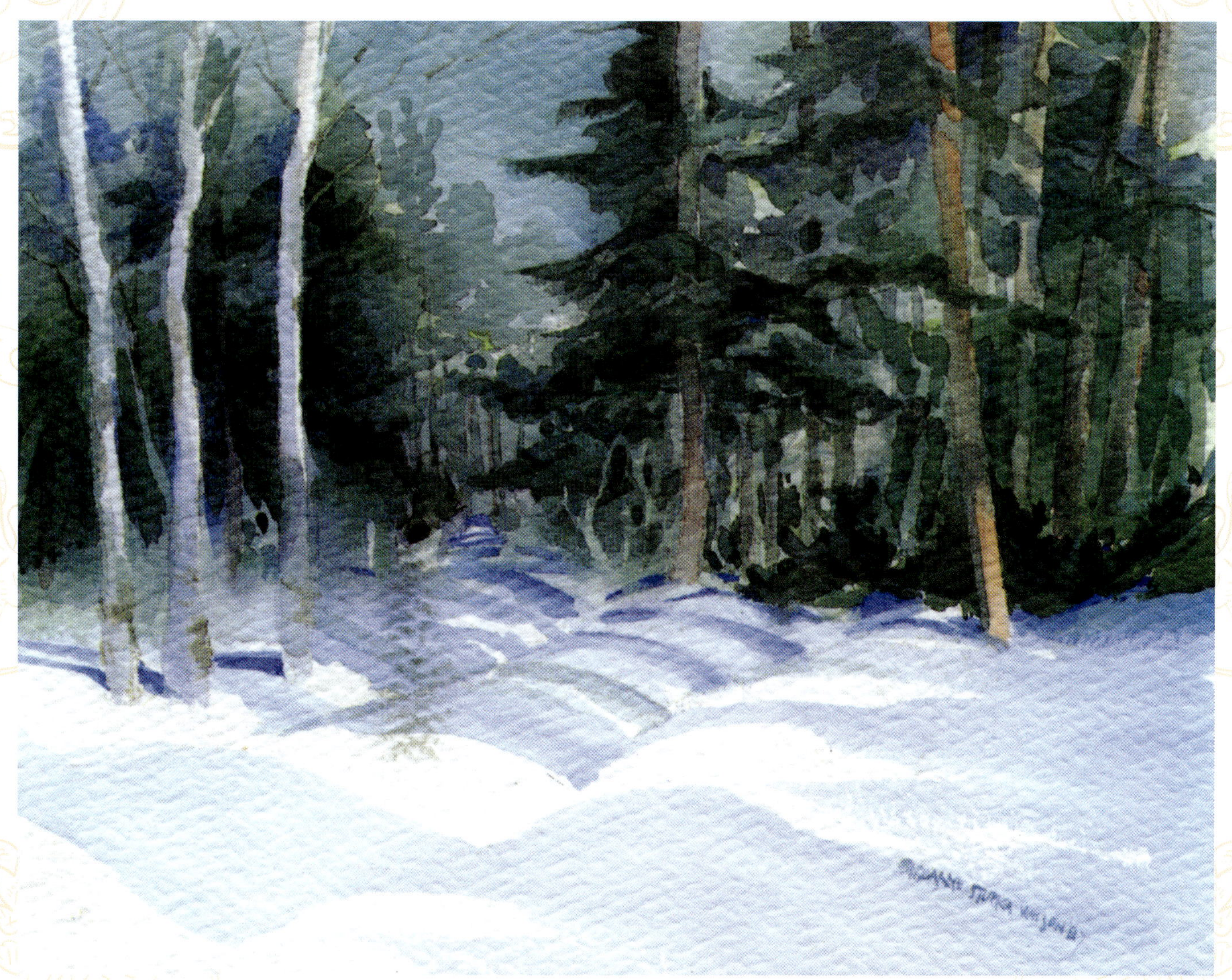

"Winter in Michigan" by Suzanne Wilson

Frank *Webb* in Montana ● ● ●

I grew to know Frank Webb, and his wife, Barbara, when he was a popular teacher at the Leech Studio workshops in Sarasota. Later, when I was sponsoring workshops on my own, I was pleased that he could fit three sessions for me into his busy schedule between 1994 and 1997, one in Michigan and two in Montana.

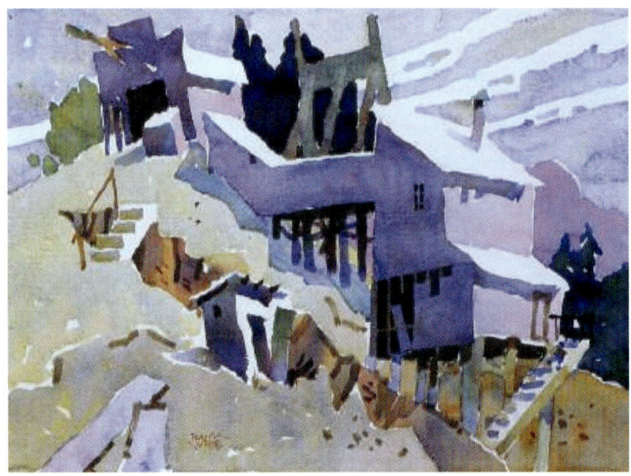

"Gold Mine in the Sky" by Frank Webb

The first of the Frank Webb workshops I sponsored in Montana was held from July 25 through 28, 1994, at KwaTagNuk, at the southern tip of Flathead Lake, just outside of Polson. This beautiful waterfront resort was developed by the Confederated Salis and Kootenai Tribes of the Flathead Nation, and operated by Best Western Inns. The site, in the broad Flathead Valley surrounded by mountains, was perfect for a watercolor workshop.

Frank Webb, A.W.S., D.F., N.W.S., of Pittsburgh, Pennsylvania, has been self employed as an artist since 1958. He has taught hundreds of painting seminars, worldwide and in all of the 50 states. A Dolphin Fellow of the American Watercolor Society, he has served numerous times on the jury of selection and of awards. North Light has published three of his books, *Watercolor Energies, Webb on Watercolors, and Strengthen Your Paintings with Dynamic Composition.*

Marj and Nils Johnson, from Sarasota, were part of the group at Flathead. Marj, an accomplished painter, and her husband Nils, were devoted followers of Frank Webb, and Barbara Nechis, and others of the watercolor instructors, and followed them to interesting workshop locations. At the end of the Flathead classes, Frank flew on to other commitments and Marj and Nils stayed to see a little more of Montana with me as I drove to Bozeman. At Bozeman, my niece, Kathy Lollar, joined me and she and I went on to spend a week in the Yellowstone area. Yellowstone Park, although I have visited it or traveled through it countless times, never ceases to fascinate me. Its vast wildness, its thermal features, its animals, and waterfalls, and big old log Lodge, always offer something new, and exciting.

After Kathy and I returned to Bozeman, she went home, and I flew to Denver on my way to Steamboat Springs, Colorado, where I sponsored an August 8 to 12 workshop with Judi Betts at the Sky Valley Lodge. I also sponsored workshops with Judi in the Gallatin Valley of Montana and in Hawaii. The story of the latter one appears elsewhere in this book.

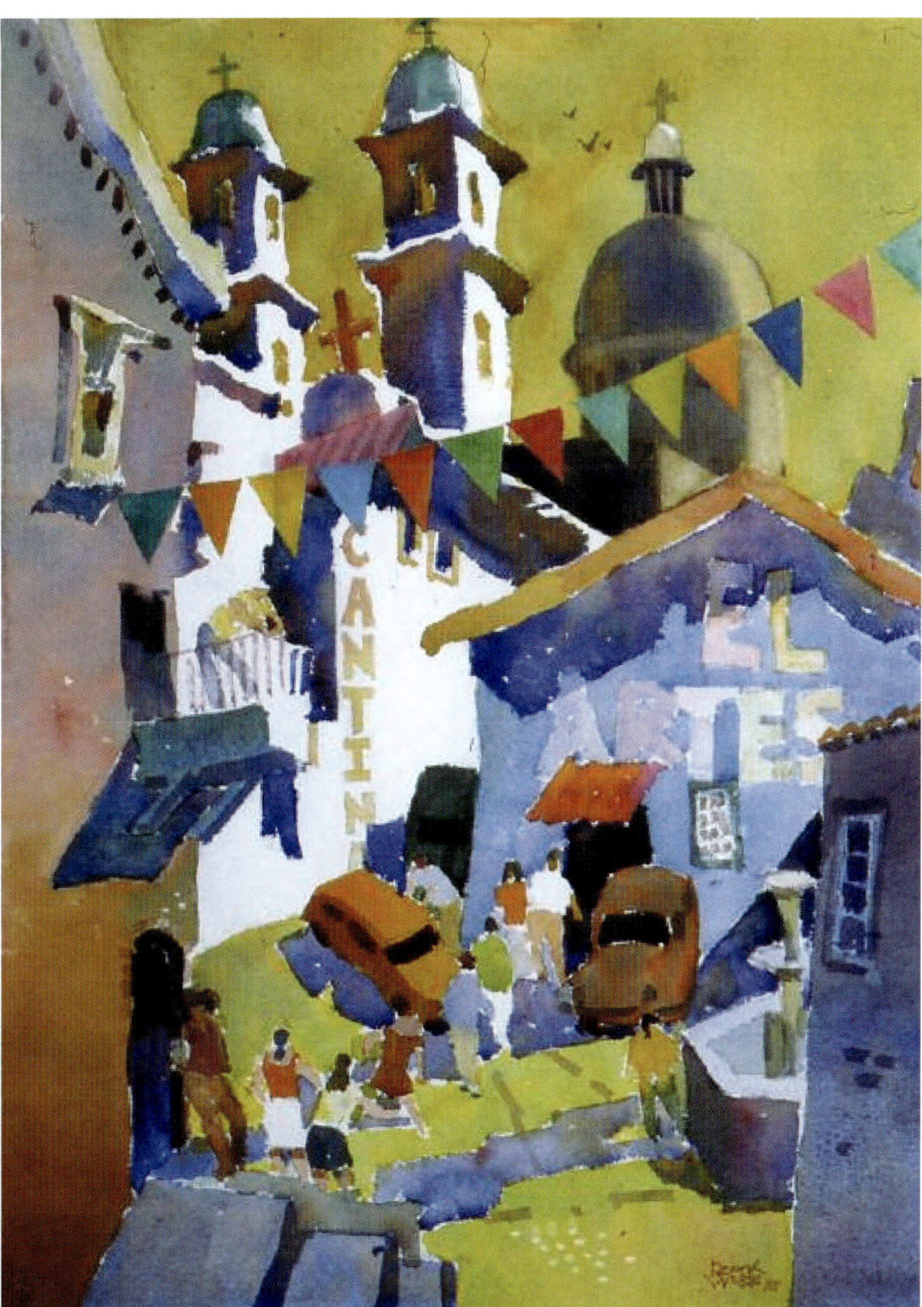

"Taxco" by Frank Webb

Robert S i s s o n ● ● ●

In April of 1990 a fine new announcement appeared: "Katherine L. Rowland of Sarasota, Coordinator—Traveling, and On-Location Workshops in Photography, Art, and Nature."

Printed on card stock of shades of soft pink, it listed five workshops for 1990-91 and four more in the planning, under the logo which Elden had designed and cut for his Rowland Traveling Exhibitions Service. An adaptation of the Rowland family crest, its lion with sword design seemed appropriate for my new venture.

Proudly, at the top of the list was "Welcome to the Small World of Bob Sisson, Advanced Macro Nature Photography Workshops." It goes on to say "Bob, former chief of the Natural Sciences Division for National Geographic, brings his 48 years of expertise in the natural sciences to you in six 5-day workshops at his studio in Englewood, Florida."

Robert Sisson had been one of my heroes ever since my brother Bob first subscribed to *National Geographic Magazine* for me as my Christmas present in 1940. I was fascinated by the new worlds the stories of nature and science and art and history the magazine opened up for me and kept every issue for fifty years. I first met Robert Sisson in Seattle, Washington, in the late 1970s. Pat Matthews had arranged a Friends' Members

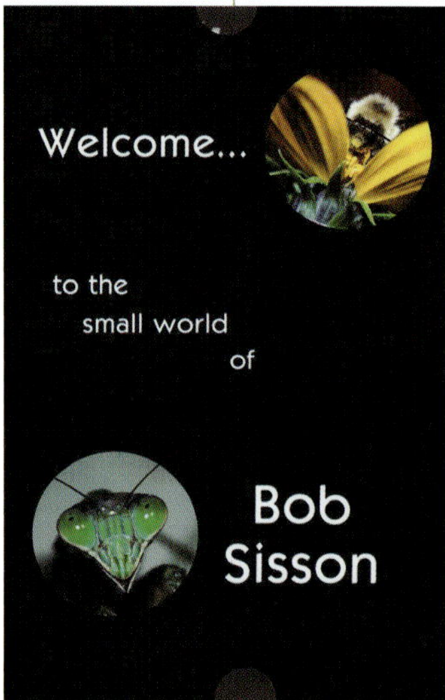

trip to the Northwest, with an option to Alaska. She was leaving the group in Seattle, and I was to go on with them to Alaska. Before she left us at Seattle she asked Elden and me to come for a drink to meet my hero, who happened to be passing through on his way to an assignment. Bob had lived in Washington, D.C., but after his wife died, had come to see friends in Sarasota and met Pat. Pat had also lost her partner, Dr. Lamar Matthews, a few years before. Pat and Bob were married and built their a home and studio on the bay in Englewood, south of Sarasota.

Thus began my association with Bob Sisson. He was a pioneer in the world of close-up photography, long before developments in technical equipment made present-day results possible. In the announcement, Bob said, "Macro/Nature photography is not a mystical science, it is an intimate look at the world around us. . . Learn the technique of using nature's light correctly and learn to THINK before exposing film."

Later, when Bob was trying to complete his set of copies of the scores of issues of the *Geographic* which had carried his articles, I was glad that I was able to glean some missing copies from my 50-year collection to give to him.

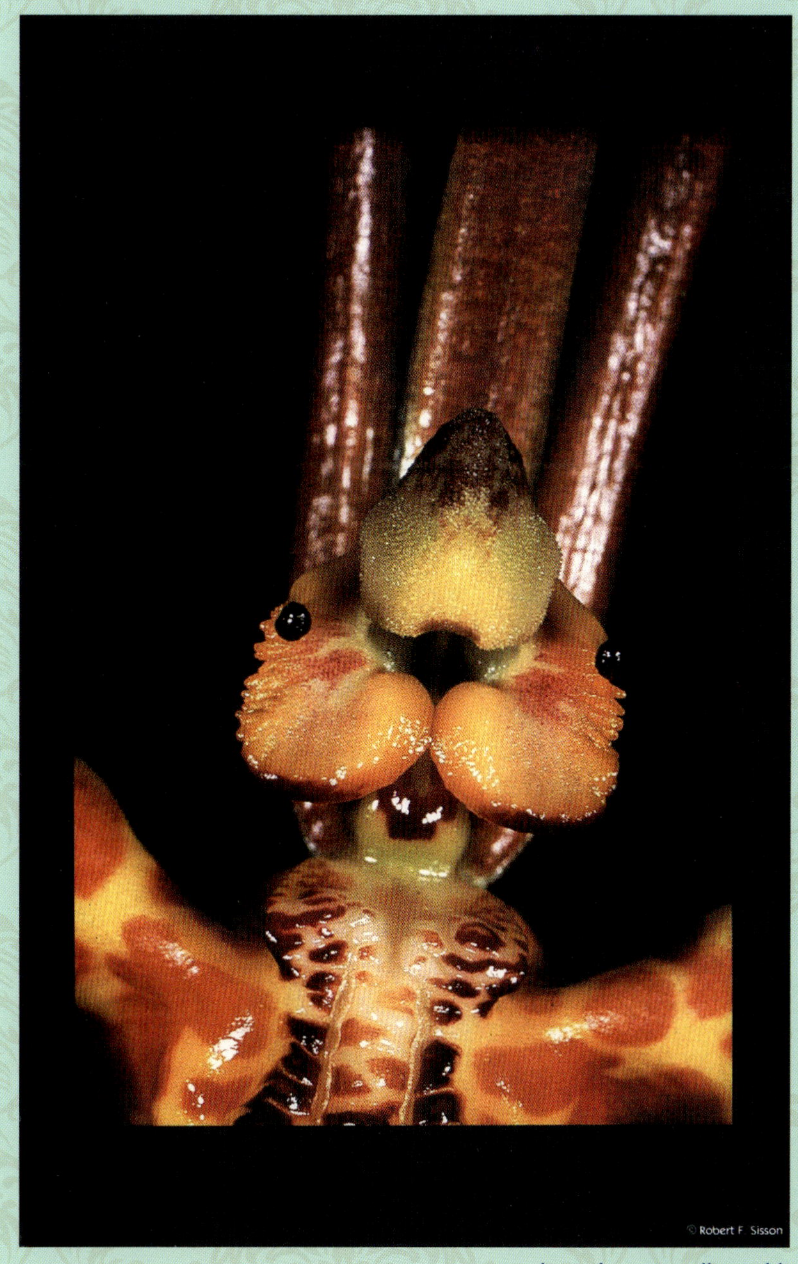

Brochure for a Small World

I first met Bruce and Fox McGrew on a Christmas trip to Tucson, Arizona. Peg O'Flyn, an artist friend from Sarasota, had gone with me to join my brother Bob, and his family, for The Holidays. When Peg and I went to the Tucson Art Museum we saw an exhibition that really excited us: powerful large watercolor paintings by Bruce McGrew and compelling clay sculptures by Fox McGrew. At that time I was always looking for instructors for the Watercolor Workshops at the Leech Studio and Peg, who was a sculpture student, thought it would be great to have an exciting teacher in her field, too. We knew we wanted these people to come to Sarasota!

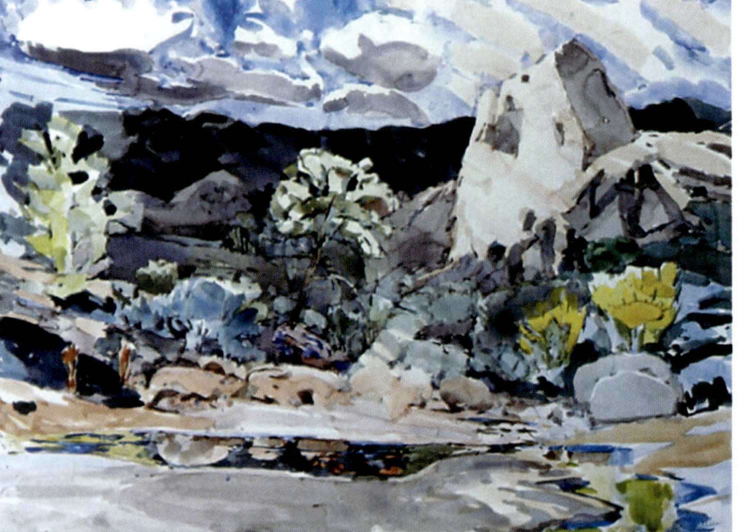
"Catalina State Park" by Bruce McGrew

We got the Museum to give us the McGrews' address and drove twenty miles or so north out into the country to the little town of Oracle in the high desert at the foothills of the Catalina Mountains. We found them at Rancho Linda Vista, where their home and studios were part of an artists' community founded in 1967 by a group of families largely affiliated with the University of Arizona. Bruce and Fox were gracious to their drop-in guests, Peg and me, and before we left we had agreed I would contact them about coming to Sarasota.

They came to Florida and Bruce taught a workshop at the Leech Studio but since it did not have facilities for clay sculpture, Fox taught at the Art League of Manatee County in Bradenton. While I was still at the Leech Studio, Bruce was the painting instructor, with Margarette Mead, as photography instructor, on a 1985 Two Arts trip to Hawaii. Bruce was a logical choice, because he had once been artist-in-residence at Haleakala National Park on Maui. Fox (also Joy Fox), a gifted naturalist especially knowledgeable about birds, was always an asset, enhancing our understanding and enjoyment of whatever environment we happened to be in. I had an amazing small plane trip while making plans for this Hawaii workshop. I had flown from Florida to the main airport on Maui and arranged to fly from there to check the Hana Inn, high on the mountain. The pilot of the small plane knew that I was exploring for a group so flew low over the gorgeous shoreline of the island. And when we landed at the little Hana airport, I was met by a big Hawaiian man who put a lei around my neck and kissed me on both cheeks and escorted me to the inn in their big old red limousine. The whole Hana experience was outstanding. Reached only by flying, or a narrow, winding two-lane road, Hana's special flavor has been maintained. Not far beyond Hana is the home to which Charles Lindbergh retired, a quiet, peaceful spot where he is buried.

Both Bruce and Fox were highly trained and successful in their chosen careers. Both exhibited widely, and won many prizes. Bruce, who had been born in Wichita, Kansas, and received a BFA from Wichita State, came to Tucson in 1964 to earn his MA. Two years later he started to teach and was a professor of Art at the University of Arizona for 33 years, until his death in 1999. Fox studied at institutions in California, Minnesota, and Kansas and received her BA from the University at Tucson. Of her sculpture she says, "A constant source of inspiration for my work has been the desert: its geology, plant and animal forms and the art of its early peoples."

The McGrews came to Michigan to teach workshops for me at Glen Arbor in 1993. In 1995 they were the instructors on what I have considered the climax of the workshops I sponsored under my logo of Katherine's World: Scotland—Highlands,

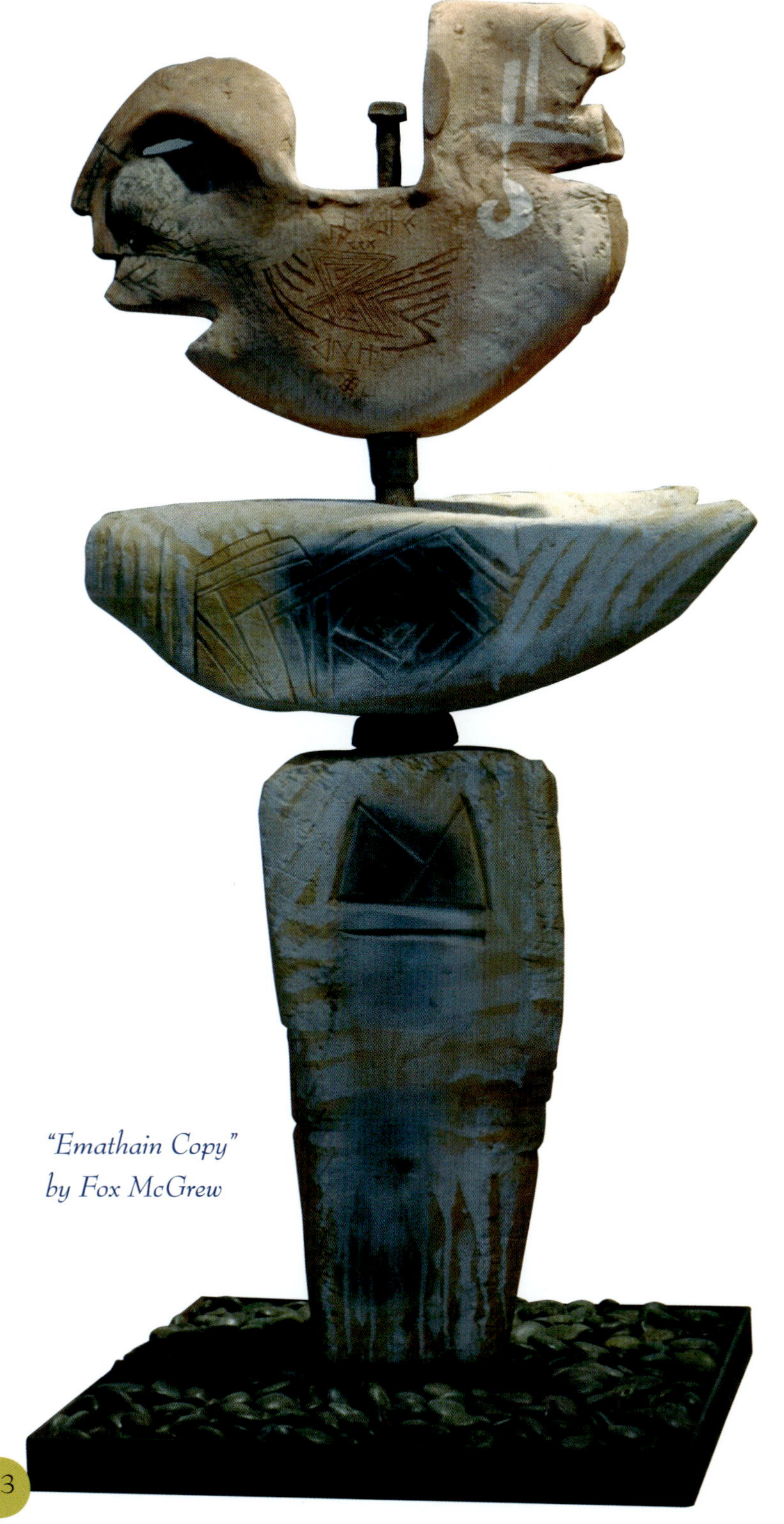

"Emathain Copy"
by Fox McGrew

Islands, Glasgow & Edinburgh! In previous years, I had taken birding trips to England and Wales and Scotland sponsored by professional trip organizers. Always interested in birds, I loved the glimpse these trips gave me of the natural world of the British Isles. And, also, they served as exploratory trips for possible future painting and photography workshops. A couple of these birding jaunts were organized by Caledonian Wildlife Tours of Inverness, Scotland. I also went with them to Iceland, but a workshop did not grow out of that exploration.

So, when I began to make plans for the trip to Scotland I contacted Sinclair Dunnett, founder and proprietor of Caledonian Wildlife Tours, outlining what I would like. We set up the itinerary by correspondence. In those days before e-mail, it required patience and commitment to excellence—and we were successful. The prospectus I had printed said, "Enjoy a leisurely experience in Scotland, staying three or four days at each location (Glasgow, Oban, Isles of Mull & Iona, Kyle of Lochaish & Isle of Sky, Inverewe, Edinburgh), offering adequate time for sketching and painting, photography, visiting local artists' studios, museums, galleries and archaeological sites."

For some of us, the memories of the beautiful, dramatic Scotland Highlands were enhanced because in the long June evenings Sinclair would take any of us who wanted to go with him in the little bus as he further explored the area. Since it was a custom trip, he had not done that particular route before, and he wanted to familiarize himself with details so he could add it to his offerings. After we returned to the United States, I received a card from Bruce saying, "I think it was our best trip." Thrilling to me to have such high praise, because the McGrews were world travelers and had been to Scotland twice before. That was my last foreign trip.

In February of 1997, I received a card from the McGrews suggesting we do another trip together, perhaps in May to Oaxaca, Mexico? Bruce often painted in Mexico, knew it well, even had a bed and breakfast to suggest as a possibility for the group. Oaxaca had been one of my favorite places when I went on many tours of Mexico with the Friends' members groups. However, by that time I was losing my contacts in the world of workshops, my mailing lists were out of date, and at 79 years of age I felt ready to turn to other adventures. I remain in contact with Fox, who recently sent me the list of month-long events celebrating the 40th Anniversary of Rancho Linda Vista. Her daughter, Shelley, who works in choreography and the performing arts, and other younger-generation residents, have secured a not-for-profit status for the Rancho with websites rancholindavista.org and rlvoracleart.org. Shelley has gathered a selection of stream of consciousness quotes from her father's notebooks, including: "Watercolor: transparent sheets of light, veils of color, sense of touch, lift off, the joy of making marks."

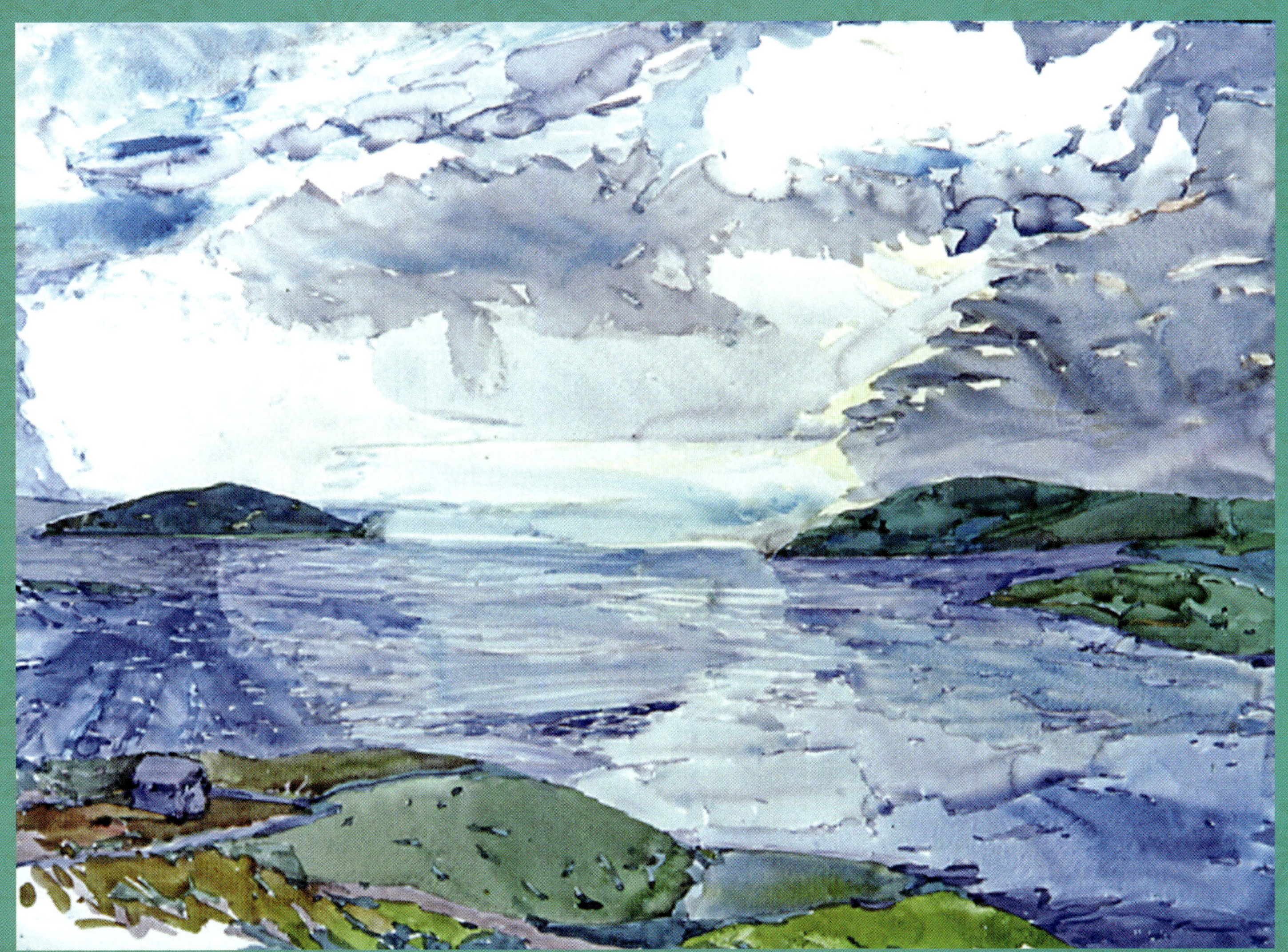

"Scotland" by Bruce McGrew

Poetry and Flowers

Several new elements entered my world with my return in 1999 to where my roots are—Warren County, Ohio. First, there were flowers: The apartment into which I moved at 4001 Bluebird Court at Otterbein Retirement Community, four miles west of Lebanon, was surrounded by bountiful beds of blooming plants, legacy from a former resident who had been a master gardener. Having spent most of my adult life in Florida, I was unfamiliar with those so I dove in enthusiastically to try to learn their names and how to care for them. Second: suddenly, I began to write poetry, and continued to do so for a few years. Then, as mysteriously as I had started, I stopped! And third: I discovered the joy and ease of traveling by train! All the while, studying family history and doing research about the Last Fifty Years of the Shakers, who had in 1805 originated the site on which Otterbein-Lebanon is located. Selections have been taken from my poems to tell the story of the decade since that year of 1999 when my life took off in new directions.

PURPLE IRIS, PINK PEONIES . . . AND MEMORIES

These mornings in late May I awaken early, grateful daylight has preceded me
In these lengthening days of late spring.
Eagerly I pull aside the night-drawn draperies to see what's new
In my north-facing flower beds, treasured legacy from an earlier resident

This morning—three iris, sentinels standing tall, as if at attention
Brilliant purple in the low cross-light from the east
Next to them, lush green low-lying bush, laden down
With shaggy blossom heads, still wet from last night's rain

Pink Peonies
Full-blown blossoms, bursting buds, even those past their prime
Still beautiful, petals edged in contrasting warm beige
Like a Japanese artist's carefully thought-out color scheme

And with the peonies comes a flood of memories of my childhood days
When my mother and my aunts
Thought peonies the very best flowers to
Take to the cemetery on Decoration Day

Early in the morning while the dew was still on the shaggy bushes
They would cut the freshest blossoms, divide them into bouquets
For family plots, being sure there were enough to decorate
The grave of every treasured departed relative

They'd fill quart canning jars with water for every one
Most popular, their oldest Mason jars whose hand-blown green bubbled glass
Would obscure the bright perfection
Of their carefully-preserved tomatoes, peaches and pears

Little did they anticipate that I, among others, would all these years later
Cherish those very old Mason jars as collectors' items,
Every irregularly-shaped bubble adding to their desirability
To be exhibited atop the tall bookshelf in a place of honor

Sometimes, in an unusually warm spring, when flowers were ahead of the season
They would cut huge masses of the fragrant blossoms and store them
In the cool, moist cellar, alongside round gallon pans of fresh milk, crusts of
Rich cream rising to the top ready for home-made ice cream for the holiday picnic

How I loved to be sent down to the cellar to bring up a jar of fruit, to go outside
Through the summer kitchen, to tug open the slanting double wooden doors
And at the bottom of the short flight of steep cement steps
To be enfolded by the pervasive scent and sight of all those peonies

On the holiday, even before time for the annual parade
They converged on Lebanon Cemetery from farms on different sides of town
Mother, and I, in the big old Overland touring car, Aunt Nell in new Model T Ford
Accompanied by Uncle Earl, because she did not drive

There to be greeted by other similarly-prepared ladies
And to chat with them about children, and church suppers, and gardens, and weather
Perhaps not to see each other for another year
But bonded by proximity of family plots in the big tree-shaded burial ground

In this year 2000, sight of pink peonies inspires me and cousin Nancy
Although it is not yet what we now call Memorial Day
To take MY Peonies to Lebanon Cemetery, to honor mothers and aunts,
Along with all the earlier generations which they had so faithfully remembered

Otterbein-Lebanon
May 24, 2000

ICE CRYSTALS IN THE SKY

This morning , as I greeted the dawn from my solarium windows
I happened to see brilliant, dazzling colors
Where no such colors ought to be
Not the sun, rising some twenty degrees north,

Not a rainbow in the brightening blue sky
But spectrum colors in a loosely-defined ball
Shifting, evolving , as I watched
Suddenly, I knew, ice crystals in the sky!

It lasted for a long, long time, as nature's bestowals go,
And then, man's touch, long, sharp contrails crossing in the shape of a star!
Were others watching, enjoying, marveling, or only I,
Unaccustomed as I am to winter's changing face?

At last it faded, almost reluctantly it seemed,
Leaving striations of cloud and azure sky, and calm stability
Of puffed-up mourning doves perched, sleeping perhaps,
Intuitively-placed, like Oriental ornaments in a shapely, unleafed tree

Leaving with me, a treasured memory
To add to a life-time collection of heaven's spectacular displays
Light effects so desired by photographer's eye, but none to excel
This morning's unexpected view, of luminous ice crystals in the sky

December 8, 1999
Otterbein-Lebanon

THE PEONIES ARE BLOOMING!

In a class I have been attending
I have been given homework—to write a poem about a tree
In structured line, structured verse, based on four lines by
Robert Frost, an unimaginable stretch for me!

Instead, even though I love trees,
I have a need to write a poem about peonies
To celebrate nature's never-ending gifts of color and growth
And—perhaps—to assert my carefully-treasured independence?

And so, as soon as I arise on a drippy, misty morning
I inch my way around space-consuming van,
Past ever-reproachful garage clutter
To go out the back door to find the morning's miracle

The peonies have begun to bloom!
Some full-blown, some half unfurled, some tightly wound
All covered in droplets of mist and rain, a symphony of pink and red and white,
Thrusting forth from their nurturing foliage of varying shades of green

I cut two of the fragrant beauties and take them in to my breakfast table
Where I ponder memories of childhood Memorial Day trips
With my mother and my aunts to place blossom-filled Mason jars
Alongside mossy family markers on shady burial plots

And memories, too, of a shadowy person known as " Doc," who called them "pineys,"
As he always had from his early childhood days in the hill country of Kantuck—
Doc—beloved hired man, whom I early-on adopted as a
Make-believe grandfather, because I had none of my own.

And I puzzle to try to understand the urgent need I feel these days
To protect my independence, my own creativity—
Why not respond to the request of a teacher who is opening up to me
A richness of American culture of which I had been totally uninformed?

Why not try to write a poem about a tree?

Trees, peonies, dedicated teachers, distinguished poets, and me
All a part of the great marvelously-structured
Infinite Scheme of Things we call Life,
Needing to be celebrated, needing to be pondered upon, needing to be understood

In honor of all of the above, even Robert Frost—I'll try

May 14, 2004
Lebanon, Ohio

Family History ● ● ●

Learning the stories of my ancestors (Jameson-Lollar on my father's side, and Evans-Miller on my mother's side) was a fun and productive activity after I took an apartment at Otterbein-Lebanon in 1999. There was much to be found at the Warren Historical and Genealogical Societies since numerous lines on both sides of the family had come to the Area Between the Miami Rivers even before the state of Ohio was formed in 1803. And the fun was enhanced by sharing the search with others along the way:

Nancy Miller Myerholtz, my first cousin once-removed, and I, took trips to Pennsylvania and Missouri, following our common Evans ancestors. Her husband, Dave Myerholtz, did the charming drawings of the Lollar and Miller homesteads which appear in this book. Ruth Stevens entered my life because we were both researching the same Charles McCristy, who had married Phoebe Dunham Lollar, widow of David, my first Lollar ancestor. Ruth has remained a close friend and helper and still aids and abets me in many ventures.

When I became interested in posting information on websites, Tim Fauley came from Wilmington to set up katherinelollarrowland.com on which we put "The Lollars and the Land," the story I wrote about that line from 1767 to present. Arne Trelvik, Warren County Webmaster of OhGenWeb graciously posted material about the Jameson line, and also opened a web page called "Union Village and the Shakers of Warren County, Ohio." It is pleasant to know that there have been 12,049 visitors to my Shaker site since September 4, 2004.

DAVID'S LAND

On a clear, crisp autumn day in the year 2000
I walk upon the very piece of land
Purchased and settled 200 years ago
By David, my great, great, great grandfather,
First Ancestor in the Lollar Line.

From marvelously-kept records in court houses and genealogy libraries
I had long ago learned how David, though born in Maryland in 1767
Married Phoebe Dunham in New Jersey in 1792
And came to the Land Between the Miamis
In wild Ohio Territory a few years after that

I knew that he, in 1797, for $100, purchased a lot in Deerfield ,
First plotted town in the area, and sold it
Two years later for $200—
And then he bought HIS LAND, his one hundred acres on Bee Run,
Before Turtle CreekTownship, or Warren County, or even the state of Ohio existed

Now, in this year 2000, what was for 200 years a farm,
Is being developed, as are so many of its neighbors, into residential plots
And because rudimental streets have been put in for Caltalpa Ridge
I am able to walk on David's land, get to know the nature of it,
See the grove of big trees where, until recently, a venerable house had stood

For the house is gone, but the long entry lane is still here
Narrow, as befits vehicles drawn by horses—or even oxen—
Encompassed on both sides by a double row of large, old trees, leaves just falling,
Rustling under my feet as I try, in vain, to capture on film
My feeling of connectedness with the first David, and his Phoebe

To imagine what it was like for the two of them to arrive,
With a child on the way, having already lost a boy and a girl in New Jersey,
To find shelter, to start to clear the land, less than half of the 100 acres
Level, suitable for farming, the rest beautiful steep hills,
Cut by a deep ravine, even now heavily wooded

We can feel sure they were not alone, for the name of Phoebe's brother,
Joseph Dunham, appears prominently in records of those years,
His farmlands were not far away—and it was Joseph who became
Joint guardian with Phoebe of David and Phoebe's children, only a few years later—
For David Lollar died only seven years after he bought His Land

Why he died, or who his parents were, where he is buried,
I do not yet know in spite of much, much searching hither and yon,
But I do know who his descendants were, the Lollar Line he started
Many of whom stayed in his part of Ohio for almost two hundred years
Although I am the only one of them I can find here in this year 2000

It all began with George Washington, who acquired huge tracts of land
Between the Miami Rivers, well before the Revolutionary War,
Portions were offered by land developers, Symmes and Gano of New Jersey—
David, along with countless others, accepted the challenge,
Made the long journey West, to settle, to make friends, to build a family

And now I am able, because of yet another developer, to stroll and think,
All by myself on a sunny Sunday morning on Catalpa Ridge,
To pick up bits of fossil rock, and sculptural chips from a recently-cut
Old, old tree, which surely could have been here
When David , first of the Lollar line, walked as I am now, on HIS LAND!

Sarasota, Florida
December 30, 2000

KATHERINES FOUR . . . AND MORE!

The Jameson Line

In our family—four generations of Katherines
Only I, the second in time
Have known all the four
Only I, now, in Ohio—this place called home

When I was a little girl
Growing up in the country
A sought-after treat was to stay overnight
With Father's mother, Grandma Kittie

In town
Where there was a secret, sweetpea-covered walk
Leading to forbidden places—
Much-used railroad track, steep banks of Turtle Creek!

Grown up, I moved away, came back to be married
And Grandma Kittie, guest at my wedding
Just two days later—left us
Treasured memory!

Years went by
And brought another Katherine—
Niece, child of brother Bob
Called Kathy, she travels the world all unafraid

And in time—one more Katherine
Kathy's daughter, Kittie,
Like the first of the four,
A teacher, following *her* star to far-away Japan

That's the FOUR
And, all unsuspected, there had been MORE
Seven more
Each a delight when met through yellowed pages

From the Old Country, through Bermuda and Barbados
The lines came to Rhode Island
Katherine, daughter-in-law of Henry Bull, in 1685
By Royal Decree made Governor of the colony

Brandreth, Rodman, Greene, Brown, Jameson, Koogle,
Katherines all
Founding members of Quaker church
New York's Dutchess County, Nine Partners Meeting

From Lake Champlain, the journey Westward to Ohio
Going on two hundred years ago
Through it all
Strong sense of family, love of land, and devotion to church

But—in the end—a mystery—
How could it be—that from this devout Quaker stock
There came so many generations of good Ohio Presbyterians
And not even *one* Ohio Friend?

Lebanon, Ohio
November 4, 1999

CEMETERIES—*MY* CEMETERIES!

To some folks, the very word Cemetery
Has connotations of sadness, a scary place
But to me, it brings memories of ancestors and friends
Respectfully put to rest when their tasks were done

Parks, carefully searched for hints of history—
Is three-times-great grandfather David in that spacious
Steep-hilled burial ground at Deerfield?
Or perhaps at Bethany, where widow Phoebe helped found the church?

Or perhaps, earlier—grandfather Caleb in Champlain country, New York
He sold the land, for cemetery and church (Meeting House long since gone)
This one enclosed with sagging, rusting wire strands,
The more to say—"It's old!"

Older still, in Dutchess County, completely unkempt plots
Could Grandfather's marker (another Caleb) be under that lilac bush
Or there, where the stone wall has crumbled inward on itself?
Not vandalized, just OLD.

There's a movement afoot now to RESTORE the old cemeteries,
To clean the lichens from the headstones, set them in neat array
I'm of two minds—Yes, nice to be able to read inscriptions
"Here lies grandfather, parent, child"

Stones decorated with lambs and scrolls and weeping willows
Appealing in their glimpse into caring minds
Would I love them just as much if they were
All bleached white, stark, robbed of the years' encrustations?

I think of more recent markers—Grandfather whose stone
Has been encompassed, engulfed, by huge tree—maple, I think
I say not a word—sure that Grandpa Bruce would not want
To sacrifice such a noble tree

Another, a precious well-remembered friend and mentor
Who lies atop a high, high hill in the Montana he loved so much
Only his artist's signature inscribed in natural boulder
To show how much those who loved him cared, understood

I think of many, many cemeteries visited,
Thrill of finding Mother's grandfather's stone—
We had not even known he came to this country over a century ago
From his native Germany to make a home, change his name

I think, most recently of all, of husband's neat marble marker
Set in the modern way—buried flush with the ground
In semi-tropic site, so far from his Appalachian roots—
But seeming right, somehow: another there, waiting for me

Lebanon, Ohio 11-11-1999

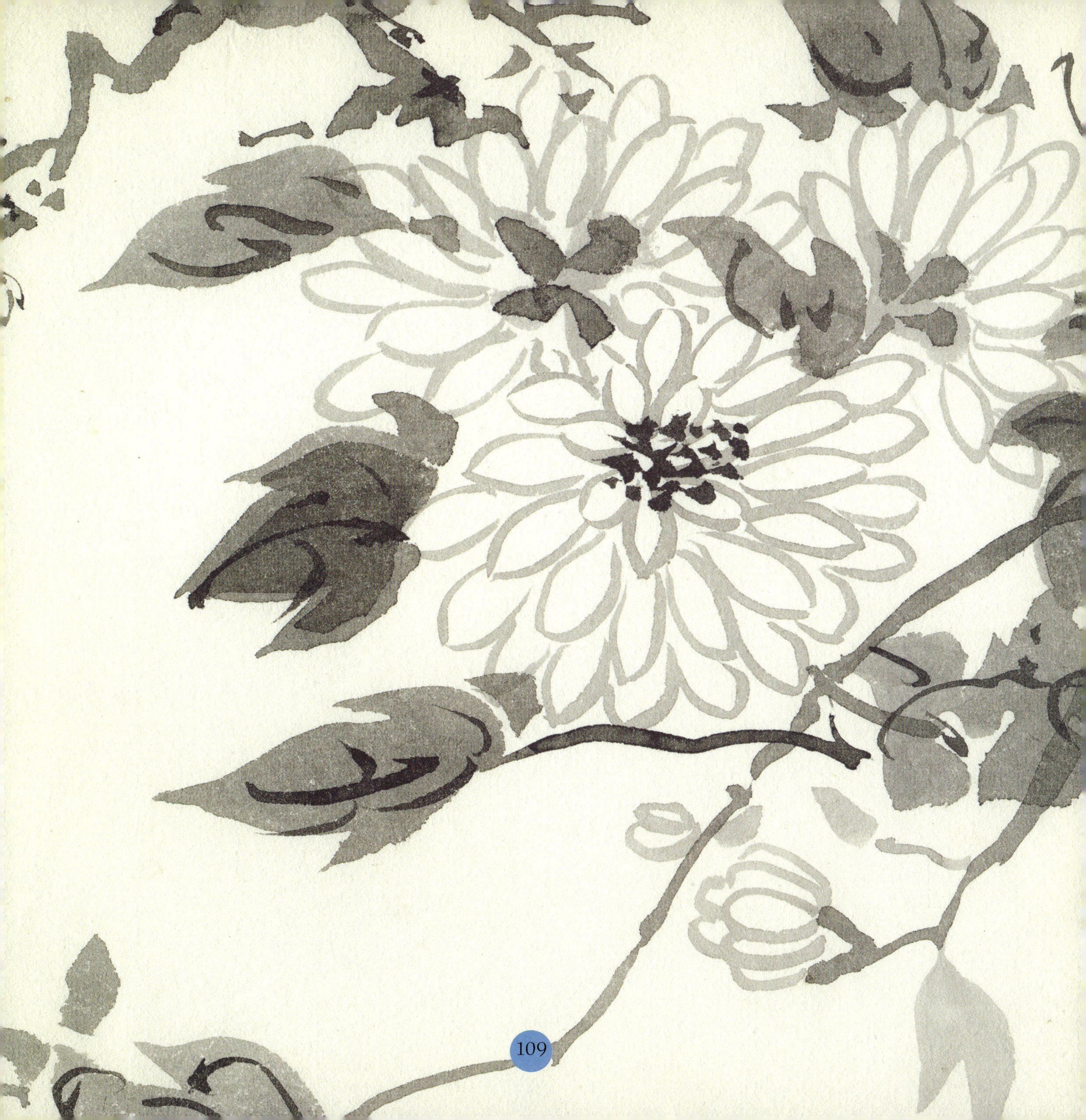

Travel by Train ● ● ●

In 1999 I became so enthralled with travel by train that I took not one, but TWO, rail trips across the country that year. In September of 1998 I had flown to Bozeman for a two-week visit with Jayre Leech in Montana. I had rented a car and driven on westward over Lolo Pass for my 80th Birthday Celebration and Miller Family Reunion at Skamania Lodge, a very nice resort overlooking the Columbia River Valley, 45 miles upstream from Portland, Oregon. It was all lovely, but driving back to Bozeman and flying back to Cincinnati made me think I needed a less strenuous way to travel. The next summer I graduated to trains!

In mid-summer of 1999, on Canada's excellent rail lines, I fulfilled a long-held dream of seeing the Queen Charlotte Islands, off the Pacific coast of British Columbia. I took VIA CANADIAN from Toronto to Jasper, Alberta, and transferred to VIA SKEENA to Prince Rupert, farthest north of the Canadian ports, just south of Alaska. A seaplane then took me out to the Queen Charlottes for a three day stay at the bright little town of Massett. There I was fortunate to see a performance by Haida children of their native dances. And as the climax of it all, a flight by helicopter equipped with floats to Skedans, a remote, uninhabited island where the remnants of ancient totem poles, now eroded and covered with vines, still stood as they had been since they were carved and installed generations earlier. The quiet, and untouched historic quality of the island, with only the helicopter pilot to give me a little history and keep me from getting lost, was, indeed, the fulfillment of a dream!

In contrast, my second train trip of 1999 had a touch of the surreal of modern day culture. As the century, and the millennium, drew to a close, a near-hysteria arose in print and internet media questioning whether computers would be able to make the turn from one century to another, conjecturing all kinds of chaos that might result. However, I went ahead with plans to spend Christmas with family in the West. I took AMTRAK to Vancouver, Washington, to join my niece, Kathy, and drive down with her to central California where my grandnephew, Brian Schwarz, had recently built a house in the foothills. After a happy Christmas, which included a day trip to Yosemite National Park, I boarded the CALIFORNIA CORRIDOR SAN JOAQUINS at Sacramento, changed to the SUNSET LIMITED at Los Angeles, which took me all the way across the South to Orlando, Florida. Amtrak provided a bus to Sarasota, where I arrived to peace and quiet and an easy taxi ride home in the middle of the night. Happily, the doomsday forecasters had all been wrong!

On August 30, 2001, I took AMTRAK out to visit Jayre Leech in Montana. I got off the train at the flag stop at Essex, near Glacier Park, and stayed overnight at the delightful Izaak Walton Lodge before renting a car to drive south across the state to the Madison Valley. At the end of my delightful two weeks with Jayre, she and I planned to go to Bozeman to have lunch with Kay and Ray Campeau before I drove on to Essex to meet the train east, on which I had a reservation for a handicapped room. But then, we saw the second plane hit the Trade Center Tower in New York City! Jayre did not go to Bozeman but I followed through with my plan, supremely grateful to have a quiet, comfortable way home to Ohio in spite of all of the confusion and lack of transportation that followed that terrible September 11th!

SPRING 1999

Semi-tropical winter comes to gentle close—
In one day, Wright Brothers' miracle takes me to
Jayre's new log home

MONTANA'S WONDERS!

Madison River, Valley, Mountains
Spread in one magnificent panorama
From picture windows and wrap-around deck

I meet the animals
I had learned about in marvelously descriptive e-mails
Well-trained Horses, Dog, Cockatiel, House cat, Barn cats
All carefully-named and treasured

And wild creatures—seen and remembered—
Black-capped finches, magpies, eagles,
Antelope, black bear, deer, elk,
Two wide-antlered moose in a forest pond looking at us

Exciting journeys into the high mountains
Secure with four-wheel drive.
Another day, over the Varney Bridge
Through vast Valley ranchlands 'til we come to Yellowstone

The town still, in late March,
Buried to the eves in winter's accumulated snow.
Drive north through the Gallatin
Soft new snow clinging to every pine and guard rail

A fairyland! All the way to Bozeman
To visit saddlery shops
Fragrant with leather smells and
Colorful with blankets for horse and man.

And so, off to flatter lands
To find a new home—and old roots!

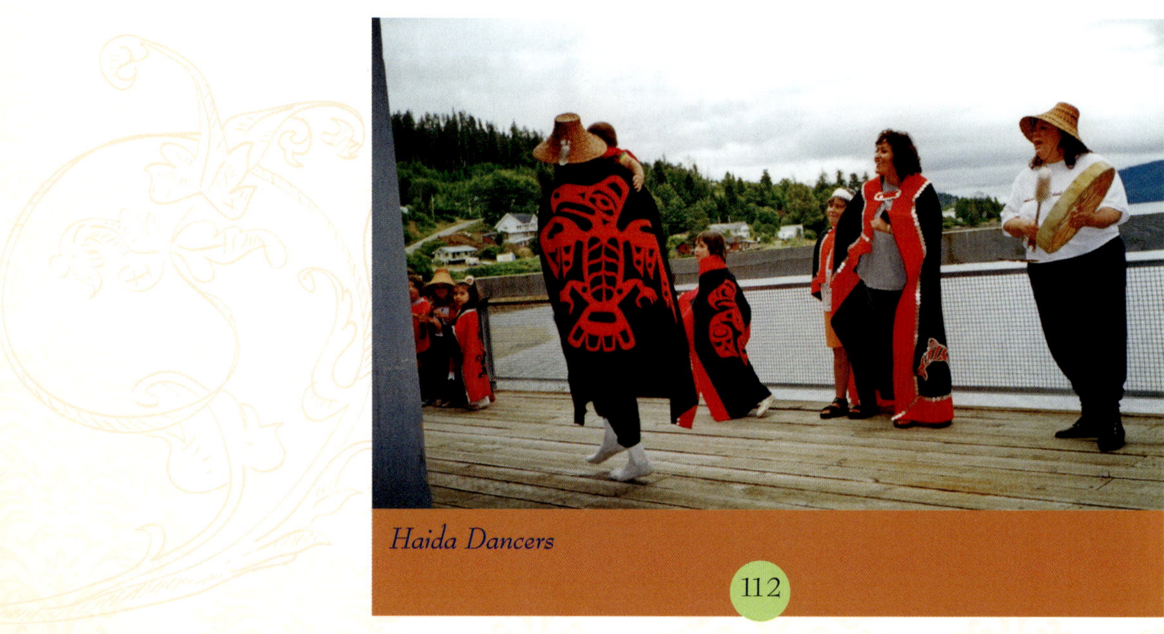

Haida Dancers

TRAIN...NIGHT

Train rushes through the night
Carrying me miles away
From well-loved place
And people for whom I care

"Be sure to come back," they said
But other places called,
Other persons as well loved as they
And so I am traveling now to another home in a warmer clime

Meanwhile I lie in my stateroom
Writing by a tiny lamp
Listening to the sounds of the night
Horns in multiplicity

Our diesel engineer way up ahead
Warning "Here we come"
Doppler effect of others as they approach, recede
Metal wheels on metal track, varying with our speed

And watching myriad of lights reflecting from mirror on the wall
My own special effects show as we flash past
Lonely crossing guards, smallish seaside towns, cities large and intermediate
And stop momentarily to discharge a single passenger into the misty dark

I think how good it is to spend
Some transitory time in reverie
Sorting out memories of the past and
Anticipating, joyfully, the reaching of a familiar place

And events that are sure to come
Fitting climax to my experience, solitary, surreal
Hurtling through space on a transcontinental
Railroad car in the middle of the night

On the Sunset Limited,
North Florida, December 30, 1909

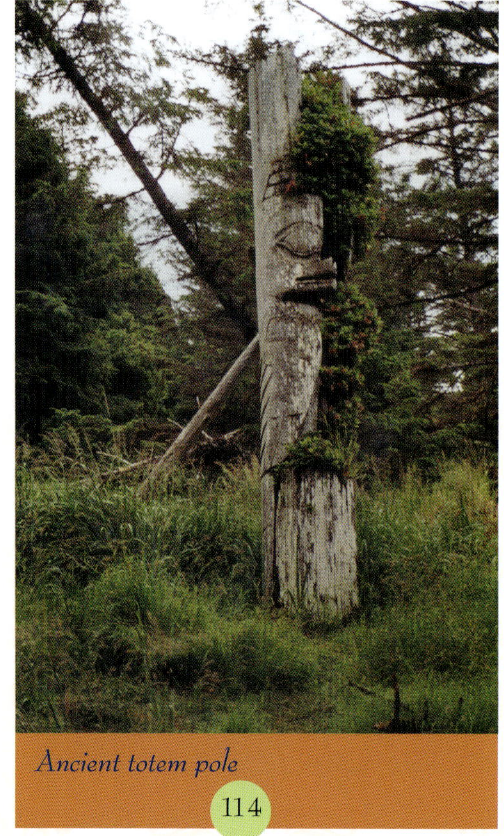

Ancient totem pole

114

CHOCOLATE PUDDING WITH A KNIFE

Luncheon in my room
Sandwich with
Chocolate pudding in a cup

Cutlery elegantly
Wrapped in snow-white linen
But—regrettably, only a knife

Spoon—mistakenly left out
In rush of ending
Transcontinental trip

Not to be deprived
Of a favorite
Treat—chocolate!

In spite of lurching train
I use what's at hand,
And deposit

On sweater nor table nor floor
Not a single drop
Of chocolate pudding from my knife!

On the Sunset Limited
Florida, December 31, 1999

A Painter and His Wife

Publication of *A Painter and His Wife*, a memoir, in 2006, was a thrilling high point in Katherine's World. Over the years, I had kept journals, and itineraries, and newspaper clippings, and even written small essays and articles about the life Elden and I had lived in the art world, but I never really dared to hope that I could "write a book." So, when it came out, the book was the culmination of an unspoken dream, and the beginning of new experiences. It all began when I saw a small book in which an artist's drawings were printed on facing pages with another person's poems, and I was inspired to think that I could do that with my poems and Elden's paintings.

I gathered up my courage, and a sampling of my poems and other writings, along with reproductions of a few paintings, and went to Orange Frazer Press in Wilmington, Ohio. The charming publisher, Marcy Hawley, said, Yes, they could do a book under their logo! Thus began a delightful year with Marcy's guidance and direction. Ideas grew and changed, resulting in 160 pages, more than fifty color images of Elden's work,

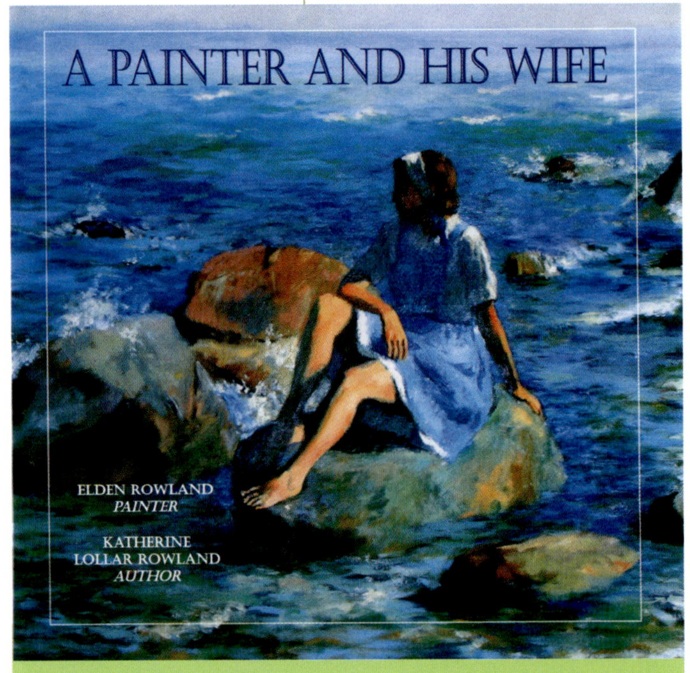

The book

and text, which I wrote to illustrate them. The poems survived as a few pages in the back of the book!

In July of 2006, just a few days after the first thrilling copies of *A Painter and His Wife* arrived in Ohio from the printer in China, my niece Kathy Lollar Divens, and I started on a trip to Cape Cod for book signings at the Cape Cod Art Association and Dennis Library. These came about through a serendipitous e-mail connection with Susan Orr, of Brewster, who had an "Elden Rowland" painting she was trying to identify. Kathy and I spent a couple of weeks enjoying The Cape, eating delicious seafood, and visiting some of the many small independent book stores in the little towns. We found the book sold itself, and none of the stores refused to handle it. The cover, with "Blue Water," one of Elden's Girl-on-the-Beach paintings, and fine design by Orange Frazer, had great appeal.

After returning to Ohio, several signings were held

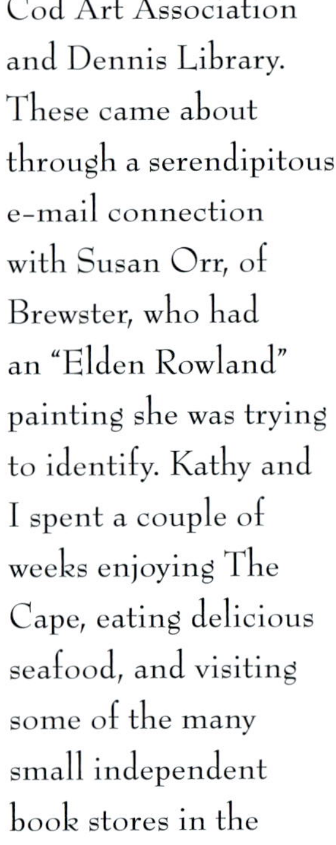

at Otterbein and in Lebanon. And Kathy graciously drove me on other trips: To Sarasota, in spring of 2007, where I did a program at the Selby Library, followed by a luncheon of thirty old friends at the Bijou Café. And, in April of 2008, she met me at the train in Shelby, Montana, to drive me to a book signing at Main Stope Gallery in Butte, in connection with an exhibition Ray Campeau arranged of Elden Rowland and Hilton Leech paintings. While in Montana, Kathy and I had a lovely visit with Jayre Leech at her ranch in the Madison Valley, and then drove out to Kathy's home in Vancouver, Washington, for a reception.

In the summer of 2007, Kathy drove me on a different kind of a trip—a search for the solution to the "Mystery of the Sanskrit Palm Leaf Manuscript," an artifact which Elden left. Preliminary Internet searches led us to Indiana University at Bloomington. Although the gracious ladies there entertained us for lunch but could not read the tightly written characters of the manuscript, Kathy and I enjoyed staying at Nashville, the art colony in nearby Brown County. Not far from Nashville, we found Bean Blossom, where, in 1943, Elden had painted the watercolor which is the first picture reproduced in *A Painter and His Wife*.

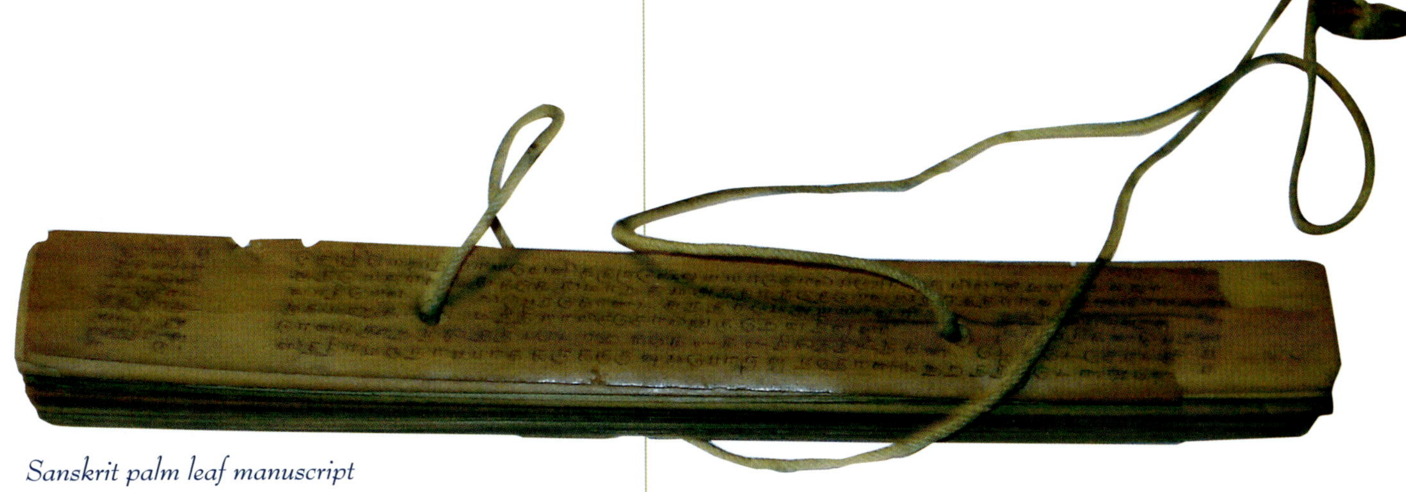

Sanskrit palm leaf manuscript

Ninetieth *Birthday* Celebration ● ● ●

My niece, Kathy Lollar Divens, arranged an amazing Ninetieth Birthday Celebration for me at Otterbein over Labor Day 2008. I wasn't actually to reach ninety until September 24, but taking advantage of the long holiday weekend made it possible to make the event a wonderful Family Reunion and gathering of friends, with people coming from California, Washington State, Colorado, Michigan, Indiana, Connecticut, North Carolina, and various points all over Ohio.

Saturday was a full day. Donna Coleman, an Otterbein staff member, invited us to her lovely home in Landon for breakfast; at Fort Ancient Historic Monument, near Oregonia, we were greeted by Jack Blosser, Site Manager, and then had lunch under the big trees in the picnic grounds; and finally, dinner at the historic Golden Lamb, a not-to-be-missed part of anyone's visit to Lebanon.

Activities on Sunday, August 31, at the Phillippi Room in the Campus Center began with breakfast, went through buffet lunch, and afternoon cutting of the birthday cake. Geneaolgy records, photographs and treasured mementos were on display, perused by family and visitors alike. Kathy had made big charts of the Evans/Miller line, from which we are descended on my mother's side. On my father's side, there are just seven of that blood line living, and we were ALL present!—Katherine Lollar Rowland (age 90), Katherine Lollar Divens, Katherine Punteney, James Punteney, Brian

Schwarz, Kevin Schwarz, and Alexander Liu Schwarz (age one year, four months). Happily, spouses were present, too: Hongfei (Jessica) Liu Schwarz, and Don Divens.

Early Monday, people began to scatter, but my friend Patty Hodgins, whom I have known since she was four years old, was able to stay and have lunch with me at my apartment before leaving for her home in Denver. She had much to tell me about her work as a geriatric social worker with people of low vision. Only she could get every one of them to go horse back riding!

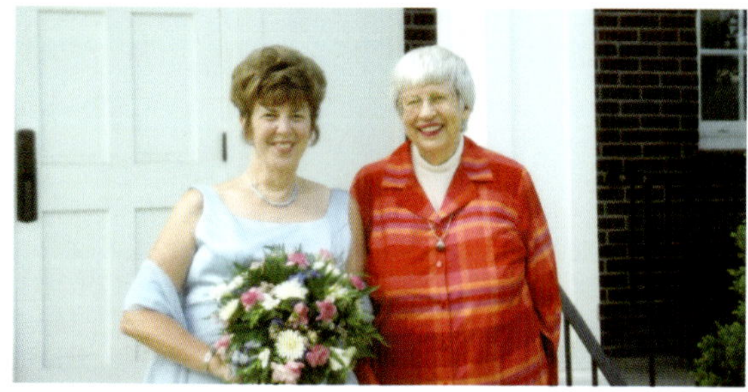

Katherine and Kathy at Kathy's wedding to Don Divens

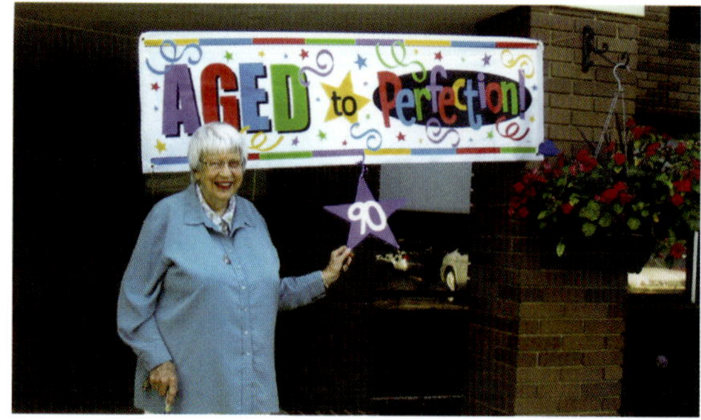

Aged to perfection

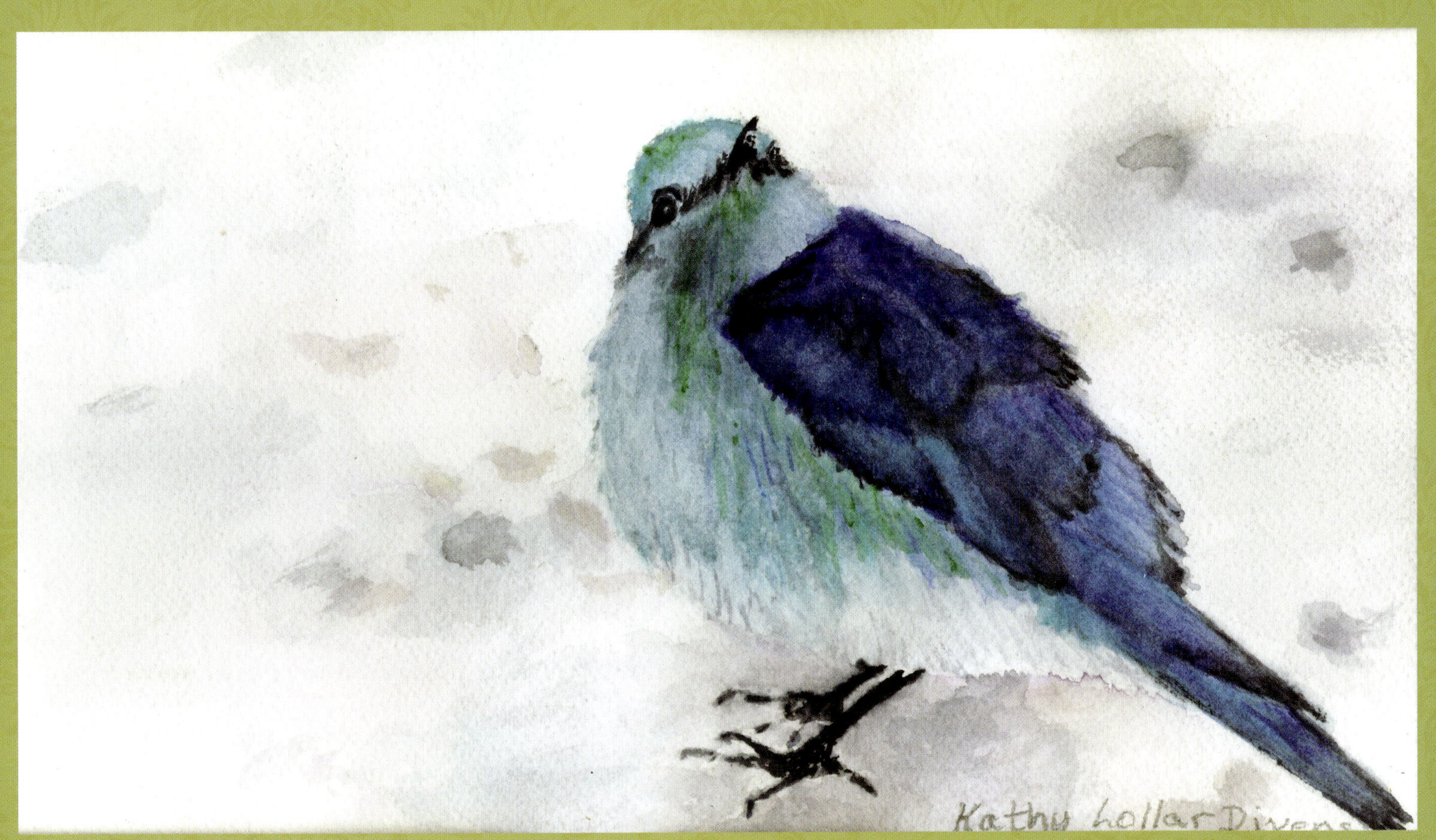

"Mountain Bluebird in the Snow" by Kathy Lollar Divens

What's Next ● ● ●

As September turns into October, 2008, and I prepare to send text and images to Orange Frazer Press, Publishers, in Wilmington, Ohio, I have the expectation it will be returned to me in May of next year as a book —*Katherine's World*. My experience with Orange Frazer two years ago when *A Painter and His Wife* came out was so good I feel privileged to work with them again and expand the scope of the story of my life. As I prepared copy for the first book I wanted to include work by many artists who had been important to me and Elden, but had room only for his paintings. Now, in celebrating my own life, I am celebrating the lives of other artists—more than thirty of them. Being in contact with these artists, or their heirs, has been a joy.

In the meantime, I am packing to move into a larger home at Otterbein-Lebanon Retirement Community, on a thousand-acre-plus farm in Warren County, Ohio. After ten years of happy living in Bluebird Court, on November 6 I will move to what is called a "ranch home," the first one on the left in Daybreak Drive. There I'll have more space.

More space—to organize research material I have already gathered on various subjects, in particular, "The Last Fifty Years of the Shakers at Union Village," and "The Jamesons on The Ridge," not necessarily in that order. Websites are already opened on both of these subjects, waiting for more postings while I worked on two books about my own life. I need to complete the story of the Lollar farm after it came to my brother Bob (Robert Miller Lollar), and me, the story of how Bob was always there for me when the Rowlands came through Ohio on our travels; how he gained his PhD in Chemical Engineering at the age of 25, and went on for a career at the Leather Research Laboratory at the University of Cincinnati and was Professor Emeritus at his alma mater when he died. I need to tell the story of how the Lollar Home Place became the beautifully-cared-for home of Robert and Rosie McClung and how the Roosa place was acquired by Fujitech, a Japanese firm making elevators and escalators, who built a test tower visible for miles around. And, while more-qualified persons are writing about The Shakers, I want to tell some human interest stories about the English Shire draft horses and the doll the Shakers made for the blind girl. And when all that's done, to sort and file all the countless papers that have been pulled out and disorganized in the search for material for the books.

More space—so I can corral all of the above into one big "office" and have the luxury of a spare bedroom in which I hope to entertain family and friends from far and wide.

More space—to store my E-Z-GO golf cart (better known as the "Blue Beastie") for quick runs around Otterbein Campus and possible "antless" picnics in the grove of black walnut trees.

But—before winter sets in—select a place in which the redbud tree, kindly provided by Otterbein resident

Park Gast, will be planted by the Otterbein Grounds crew; get tulip bulbs put in along the front walk; and last, but not least, have "Bugle" and "Coy," my two big crane sculptures from Thailand put in place at my front door, just down from the corner of Sunset and Daybreak Drives. Meanwhile . . .

THE WILD GEESE FLY

Today, as I sit engrossed in keyboard chores
I hear a tantalizing sound, a distant call
Well-remembered from my childhood in this place—
The call of the migratory wild geese!

Hastily I go out my front door and
stand a few moments
Waiting, as the sound approaches
And there they are!—Just overhead
Dozens, hundreds even, all in orderly file

All headed south, roughly southeast, all in formation
Following the leader at the head of each
feathered wedge
But still in graceful, undulating, fluidity
Sound fading, as they disappear

Yet, individual voices, one or two, perhaps conversing
As to why they had been late, not with the main group?
And four or five, way over there, not lost, just
Responding to a different drummer, doing
their own thing?

Thrilling against autumn sky, broken clouds
and a bit of blue, just enough
To "Make a Dutchman a pair of breeches,"
as my old Cape Cod friend would say,
Powerful, downstroking wings—but stumpy tails,
Not like the sandhill cranes I went to Indiana to see

As my gaze returns to earth, I chance to glimpse,
A friendly wave from neighbor in Bluebird Court
And think how blessed I am to have come
back to where my roots are,
To find new friends, new interests, to enrich
my memories of a life well-spent!

Lebanon, Ohio
December 4, 1999

Katherine's Photographs

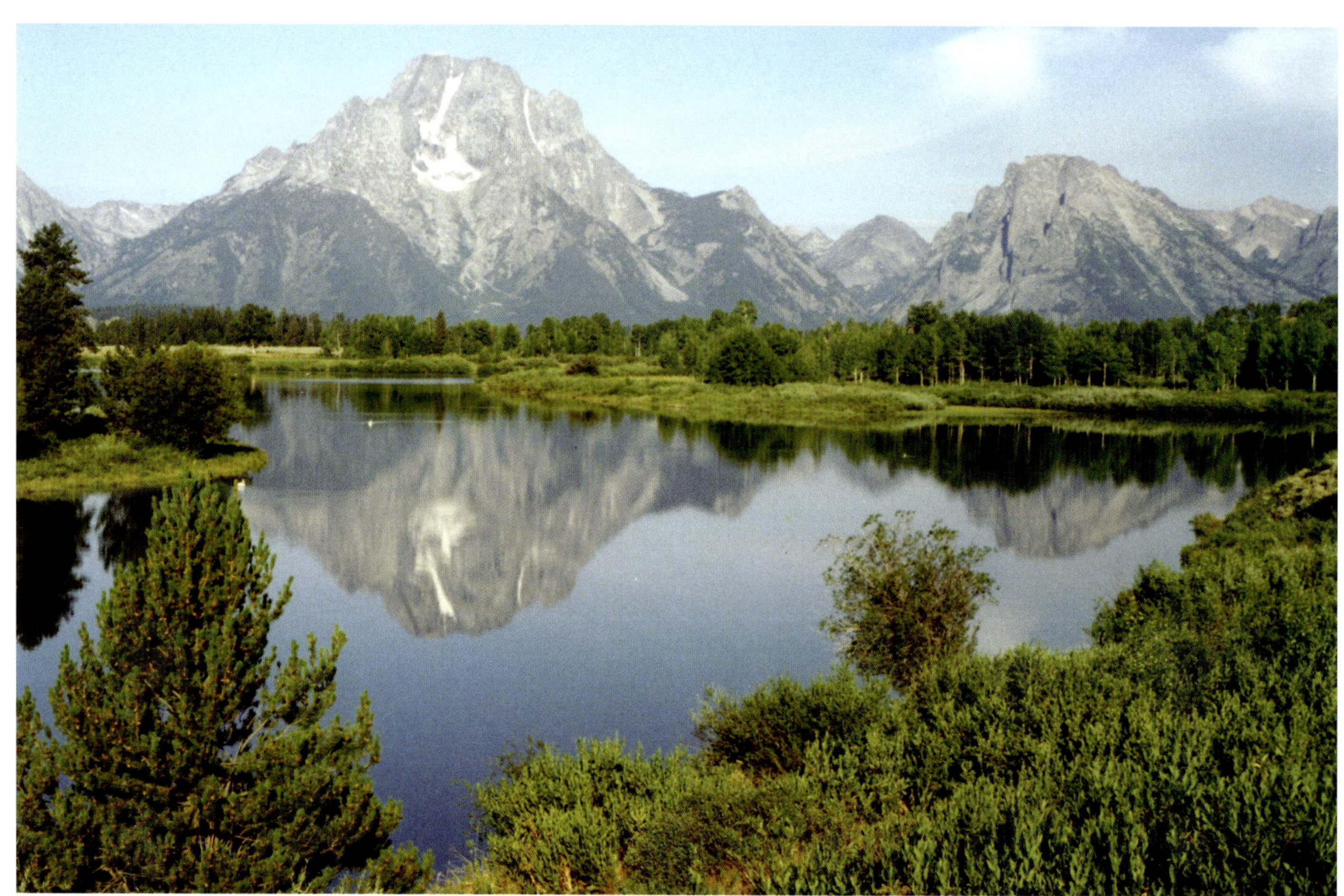

Ox Bow Lake and Tetons

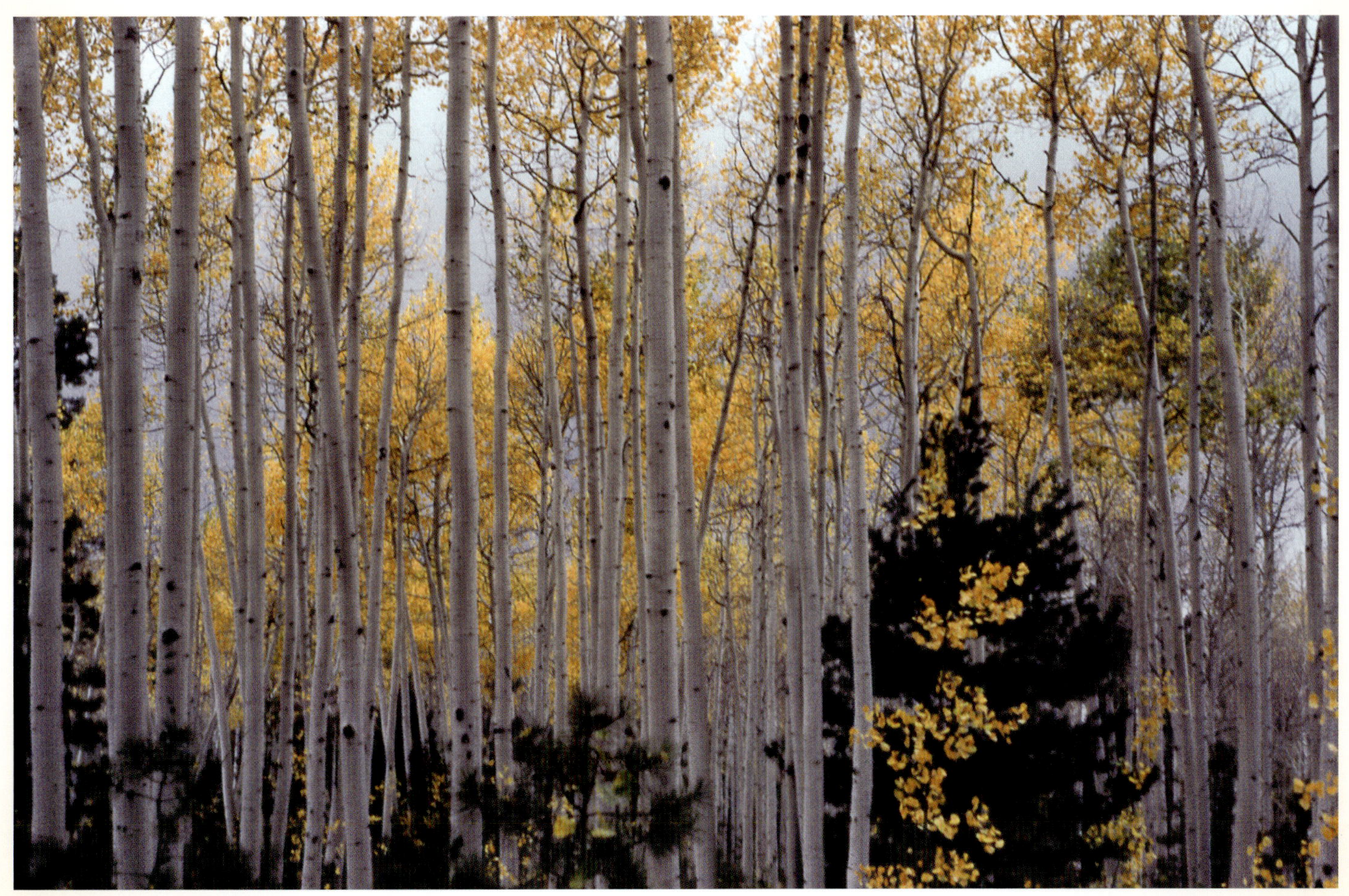

Aspen in the Fall

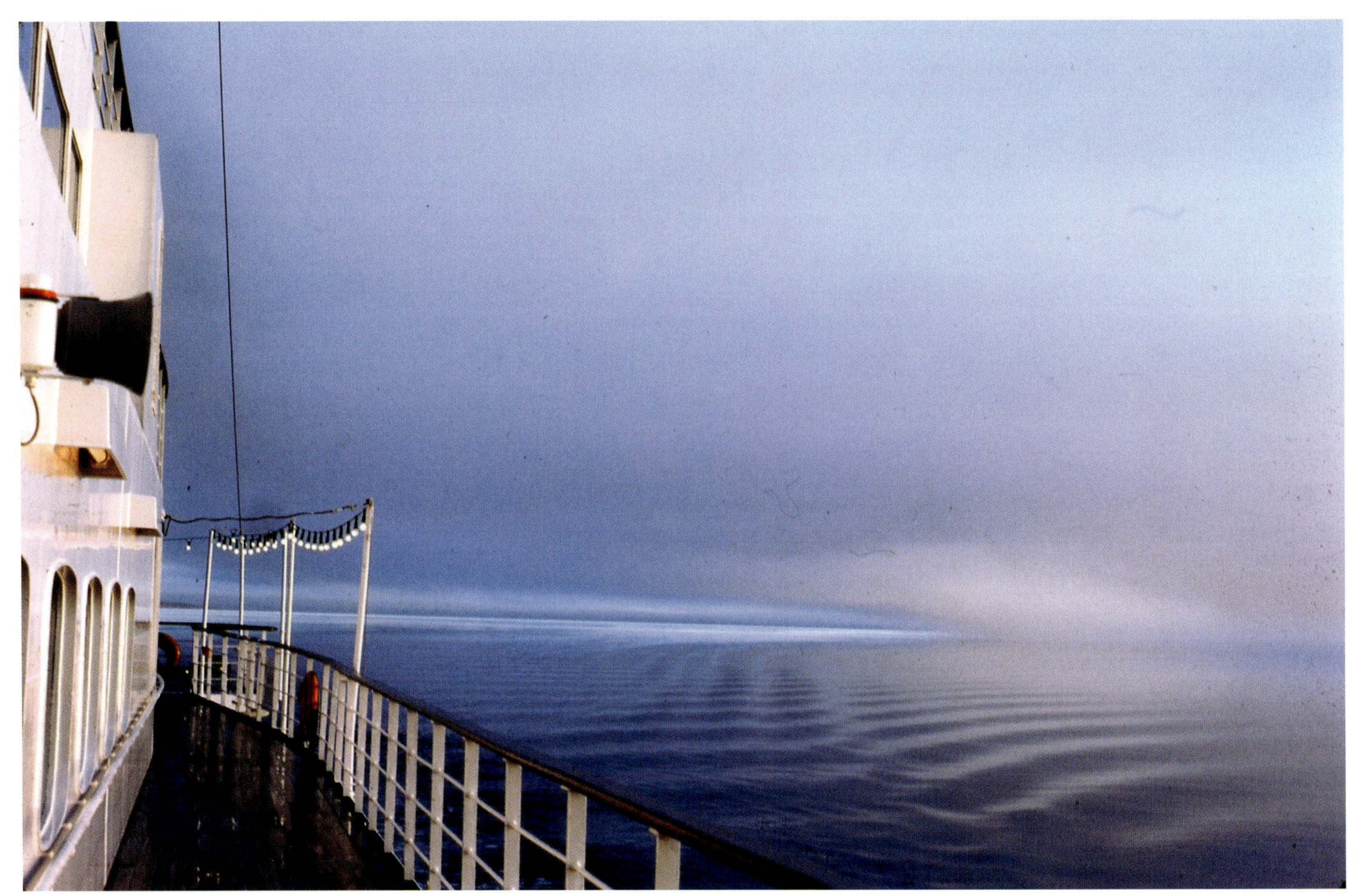

Alaska Ship at Dawn

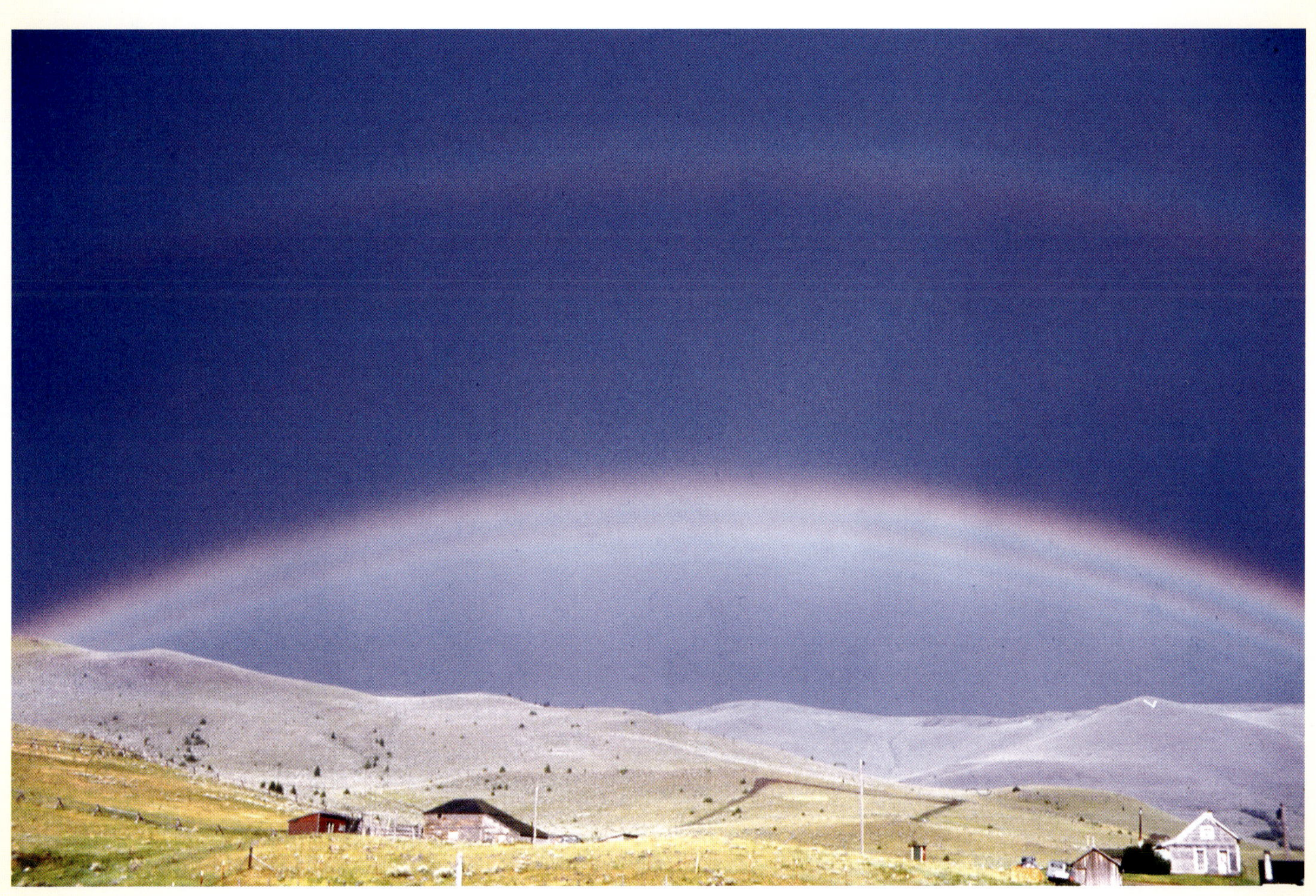

Double Rainbow over Virginia City Hills

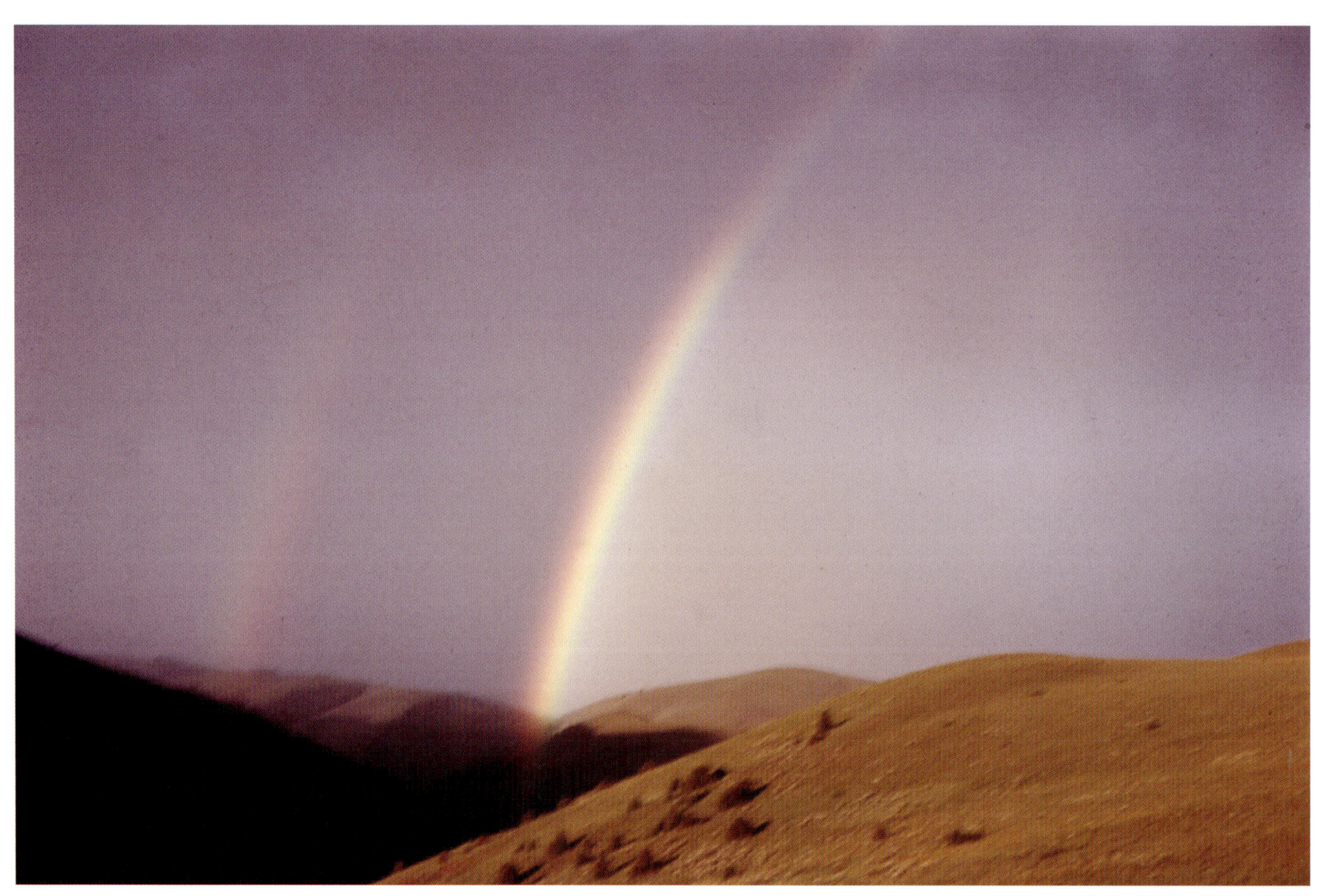

Rainbow over Alder Gulch

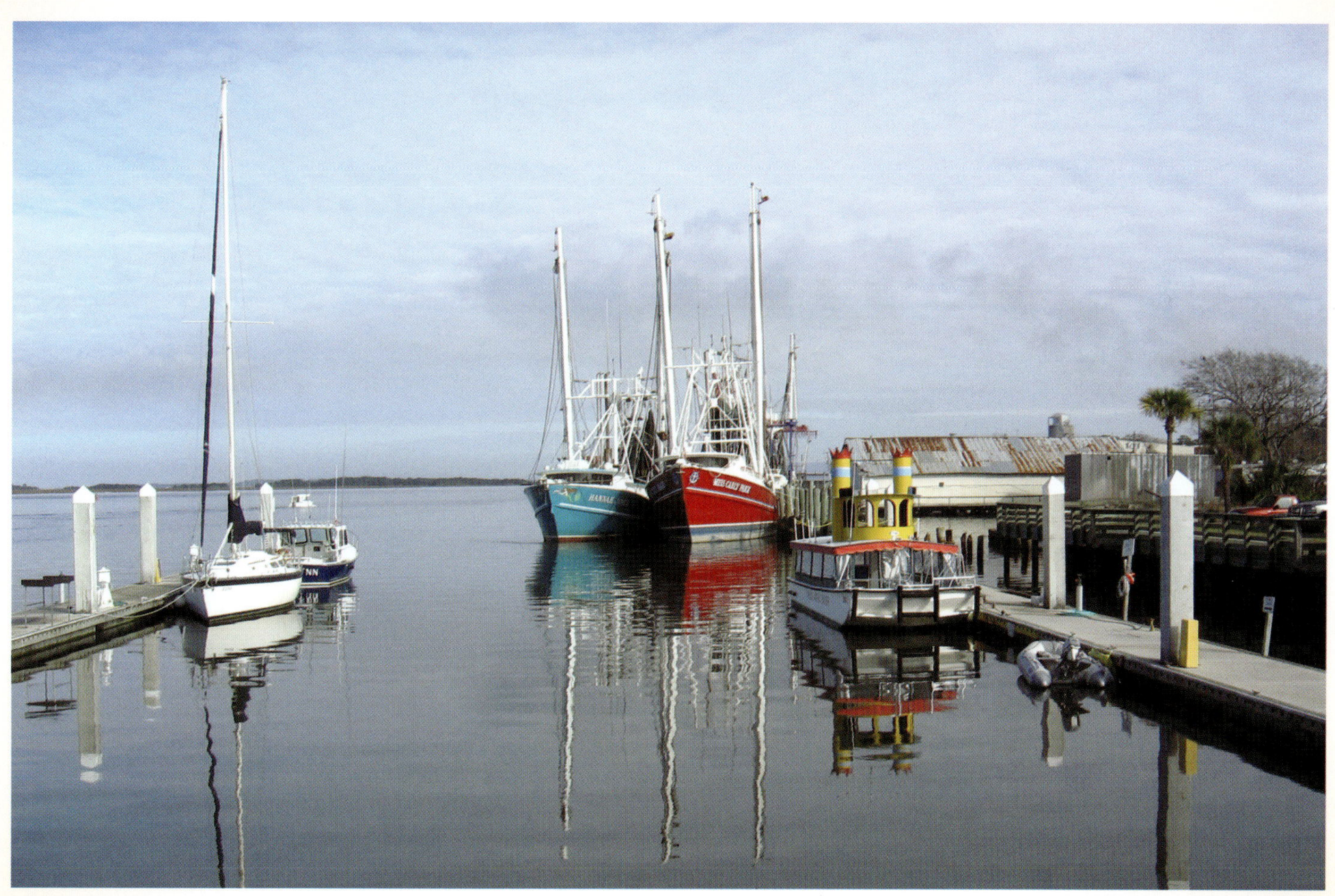

Boats at Fernandina

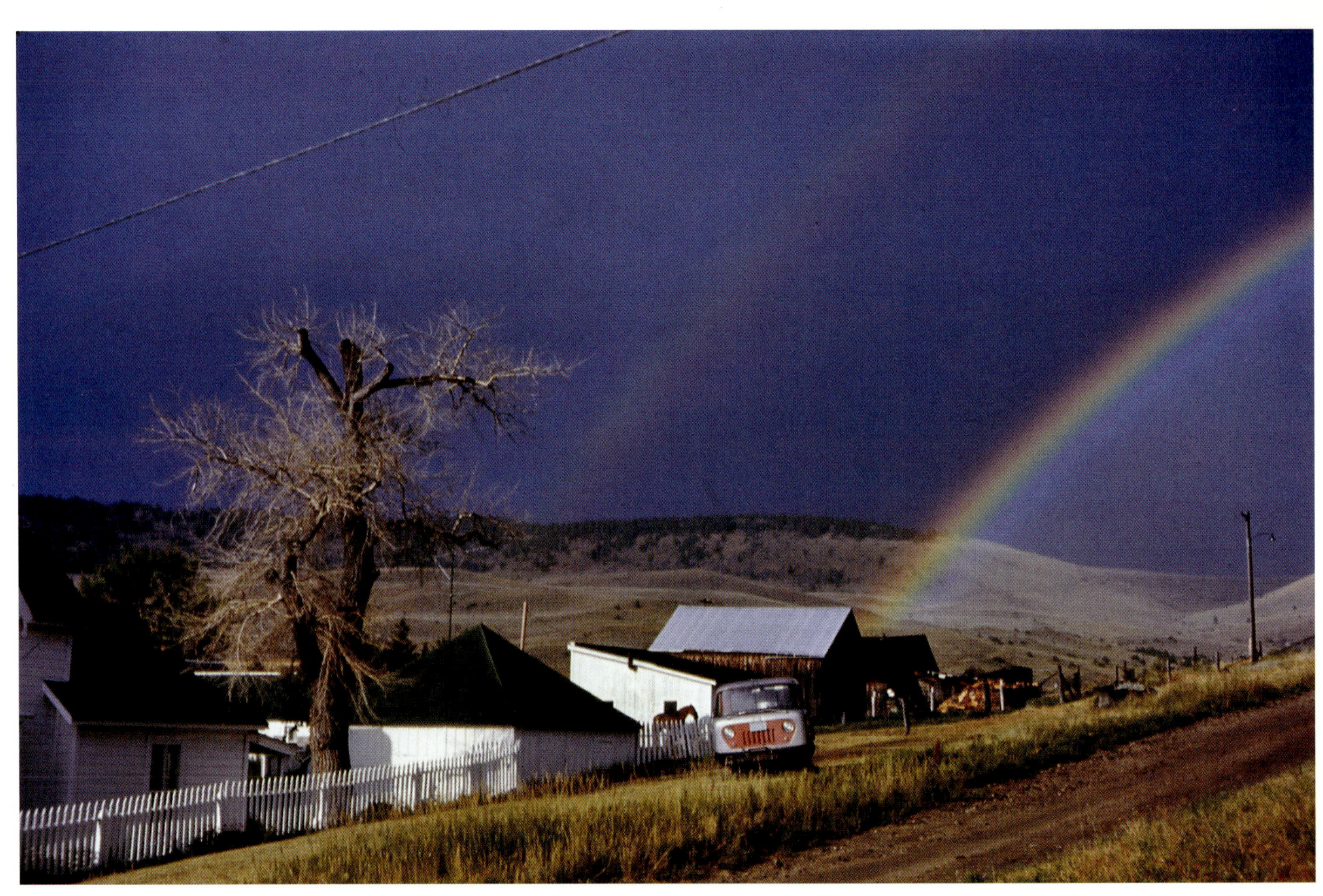

Rainbow over Virginia City

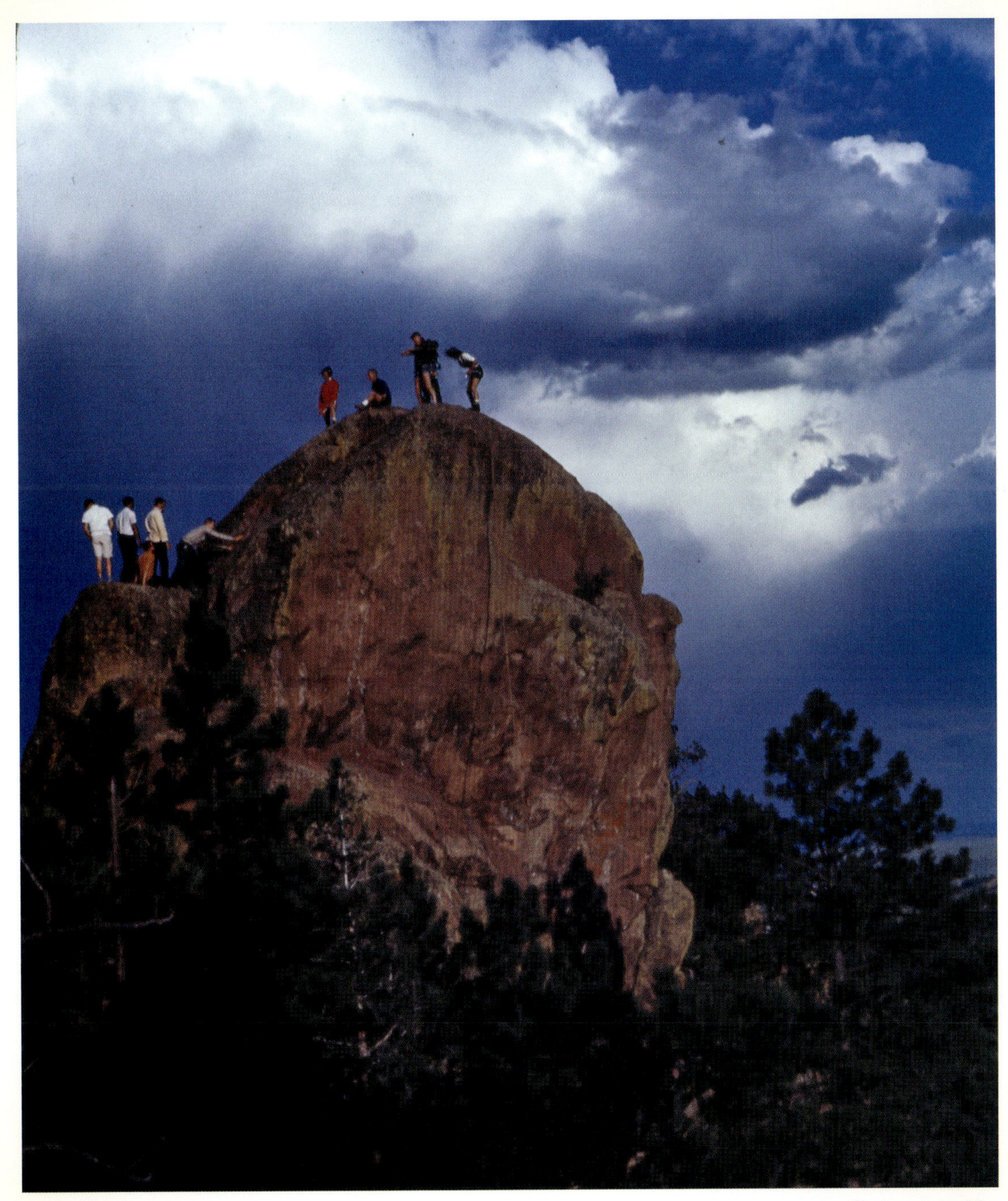

Rappelling at Boulder

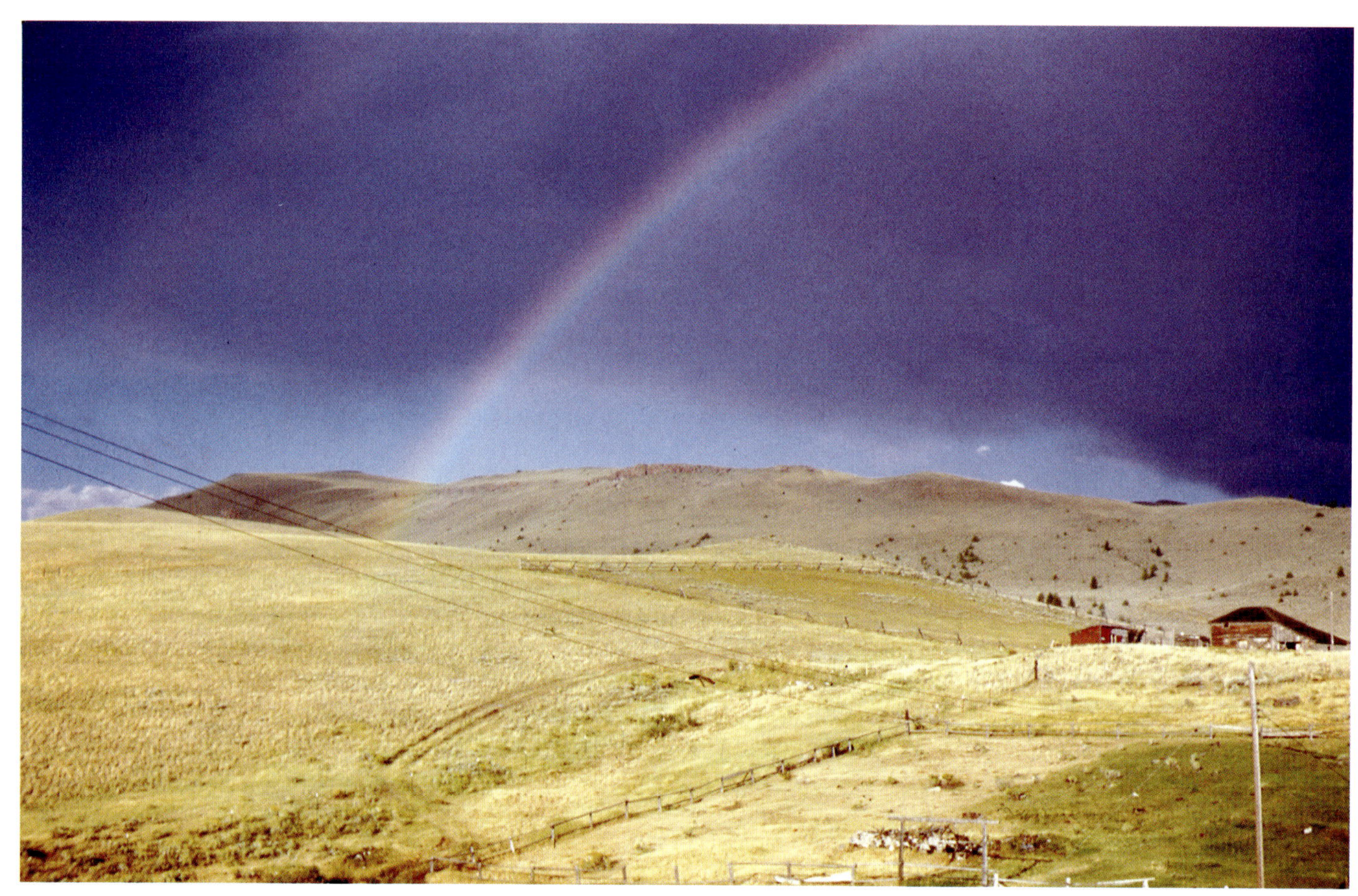

Rainbow Virginia City East

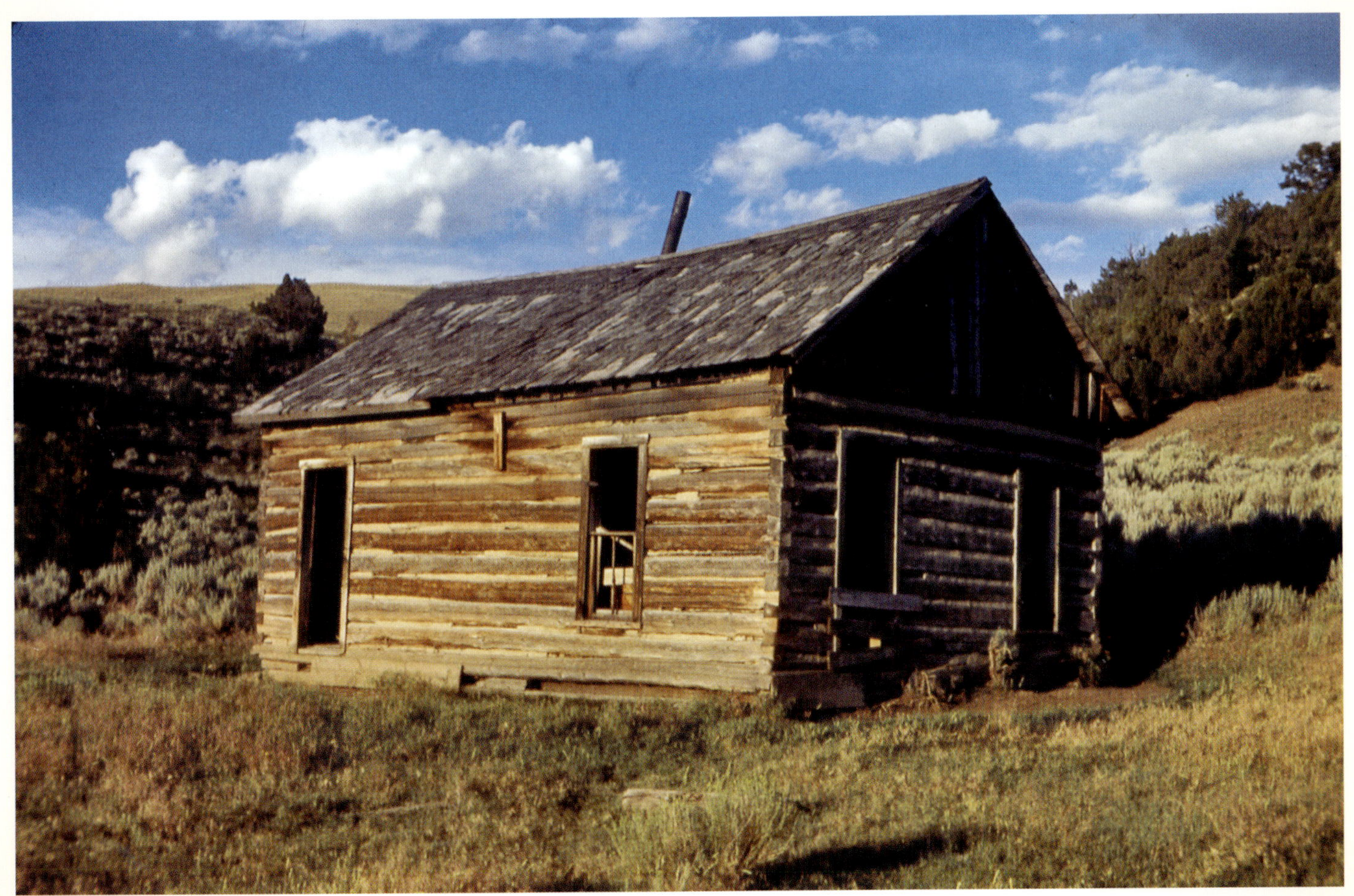

Cabin in Williams Gulch

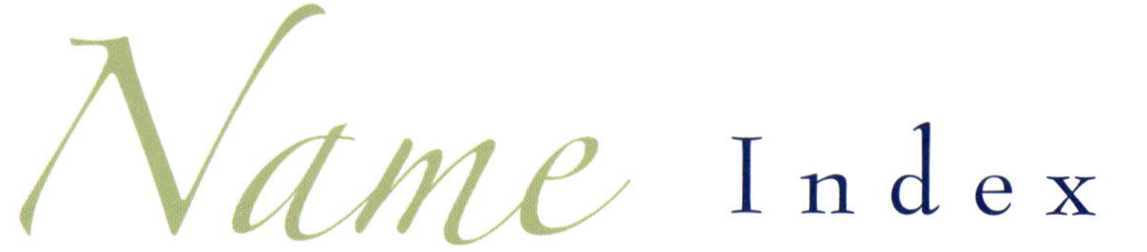

Name Index